How to Launch Your

WINE CAREER

Liz Thach, Ph.D.
Brian D'Emilio

Foreword by
Michael Mondavi

Other Books by The Wine Appreciation Guild
"The Best Wine Publisher in the US."

Africa Uncorked, John and Erica Platter (ISBN 1-891267-52-3)

Armagnac, Charles Neal (ISBN 1-891267-20-5)

The Bartender's Black Book, 9th ed. Stephen Kittredge Cunningham (ISBN 1-934259-17-9)

Benefits of Moderate Drinking, Gene Ford (ISBN 0-932664-60-1)

Biodynamic Wine Demystified, Nicholas Joly (ISBN 978-1-934259-02-3)

California Brandy Drinks, Malcom R. Hebert (ISBN 0-932664-21-0)

California Wine Drinks, William I. Kaufman (ISBN 0-932664-19-9)

Champagne & Sparkling Wine Guide, Tom Stevenson (ISBN 1-891267-41-8)

The Champagne Cookbook, Malcolm R. Herbert (ISBN 1-891267-70-1)

Cheese, Gabriella Ganugi (ISBN 1-891267-69-8)

Chile the Art of Wine, Sara Matthews (ISBN 1-891267-73-7)

Chilean Wine Heritage, Rodrigo Alvarado (ISBN 1-891267-80-9)

Chow! Venice, Shannon Essa and Ruth Edenbaum (ISBN 1-934259-00-4)

The Commonsense Book of Wine, Leon D. Adams (ISBN 0-932664-76-8)

Concepts in Wine Chemistry, Yair Margalit (ISBN 1-891267-74-4)

Concepts in Wine Technology, Yair Margalit (ISBN 1-891267-51-5)

Desert Island Wine, Miles Lambert-Gocs (ISBN 978-1934259-01-6)

Encyclopedia of American Wine, William I. Kaurman (ISBN 0-932664-39-3)

Epicurean Recipes of California Winemakers, Malcom Hebert (ISBN 0-932664-00-8)

Essential Guide to South African Wine, Elmari Swart (ISBN 062035500x)

Favorite Recipes of California Winemakers, (ISBN 0-932664-03-2)

Fine Wine in Food, Patricia Ballard (ISBN 0-932664-56-3)

Food & Wine Lovers' Guide to Portugal, Metcalfe and McWhirter (ISBN 095-57069-0-4)

The French Paradox, Gene Ford (ISBN 0-932664-81-4)

Ghost Wineries of the Napa Valley, Irene Whitford Haynes (ISBN 0-932664-90-3)

The Global Encyclopedia of Wine, Edited by Peter Forrestal (ISBN 1-891267-38-8)

Good Wine, Bad Language, Great Vineyards: Australia (ISBN 0977514722)

Good Wine, Bad Language, Great Vineyards: New Zealand (ISBN 0977514722)

Grands Crus of Bordeaux, Hans Walraven (ISBN 0-932664-94-6)

Grape Man of Texas, McLeRoy and Renfro (ISBN 1-934259-04-7)

Grappa, Ove Boudin (ISBN 91-633-1351-0)

Greek Salad, Mile Lambert-Gocs (ISBN 1-189267-82-5)

Harry Waugh's Wine Diary, Harry Waugh (ISBN 0-932664-53-9)

How and Why to Build a Wine Cellar, Richard Gold (ISBN 978-1-891267-00-0)

Hungary, David Copp (ISBN 963-86759-6-9)

I Supertuscan, Carlo Gambi (ISBN 88-88482-40-7)

Icon: Art of the Wine Label, Jeffrey Caldewey and Chuck House (ISBN 1-891267-30-2)

Imagery: Art for Wine, Bob Nugent (ISBN 1-891267-30-2)

In Celebration of Wine and Life, Richard R. Lamb and Ernest Mittelberger, (ISBN 0-932664-13-X)

Journey Among the Great Wines of Sicily, Carlo Gambi (ISBN 88-88482-10-5)

Making Sense of Wine Tasting, Alan Young (ISBN 978-1-891267-03-1)

Napa Wine: A History, Charles L. Sullivan (ISBN 1-891267-07-8)

New Adventures in Wine Cookery (ISBN 1-891267-71-X)

The New Italy, Daniele Cernelli and Marco Sabellico (ISBN 1-891267-32-9)

New Wines of Spain, Tony Lord (ISBN 0-932664-59-8)

Northern Wine Works, 2nd ed. Thomas A. Plocher (ISBN 1-934259-18-7)

Olive Oil, Leonardo Romanelli (ISBN 1-891267-55-8)

Oregon Eco-Friendly Wine, Clive Michelsen (ISBN 91-975326-4-9)

Pasta, Fabrizio Ungaro (ISBN 1-891267-56-6)

Piedmont, Carlo Gambi (ISBN 88-88482-43-1)

Pleasures of the Canary Islands, Ann and Larry Walker (ISBN 0-932664-75-X)

Po Folks Favorite Recipes, William I. Kaufman (ISBN 0-932664-50-4)

Pocket Encyclopedia of American Wine, Northwest, William I. Kaufman (ISBN 0-932664-58-X)

Pocket Encyclopedia of California Wine, William I. Kaufman (ISBN 0-932664-42-3)

Portugal's Wines & Wine Makers, New Revised Edition, Richard Mason (ISBN 1-891267-01-9)

Prosciutto, Carla Bardi (ISBN 1-891267-54-X)

Red & White, Max Allen (ISBN 1-891267-37-X)

Rhone Renaissance, Remington Norman (ISBN 0-932664-95-4)

Rich, Rare & Red, Ben Howkins (ISBN 1-891267-63-9)

Rum, Dave Broom (ISBN 1-891267-62-0)

Sauternes, Jeffrey Benson and Alastair McKenzie (ISBN 0-856673-60-9)

The Science of Healthy Drinking, Gene Ford (ISBN 1-891267-47-7)

Secrets of Chilean Cuisine, Robert Marin (956-316-014-2)

Secrets of Patagonian Barbecue, Robert Marin (956-316-015-0)

Secrets of Peruvian Cuisine, Emilio Peschiera (956-8077-71-5)

The Taste of Wine, Emile Peynaud (ISBN 0-932664-64-4)

Tasting & Grading Wine, Clive Michelsen (ISBN 9-197532-60-6)

Terroir, James E. Wilson (ISBN 1-891267-22-1)

Tokaj, David Copp (ISBN 963-87524-3-2)

Understanding Wine Technology, David Bird (ISBN 1-891267-91-4)

The University Wine Course, Marian Baldy (ISBN 0-932664-69-5)

Vine Lines, Wine Cartoons, Judy Valon (ISBN 978-1-891267-93-2)

White Burgundy, Christopher Fielden (ISBN 0-932664-62-8)

The Wine Buyer's Record Book, Ralph Steadman (ISBN 0-932664-98-9)

A Wine Growers' Guide, Philip M. Wagner (ISBN 0-932664-92-X)

Wine Heritage, Dick Rosano (ISBN 1-891267-13-2)

Wine in Everyday Cooking, Patricia Ballard ((ISBN 0-932664-45-8)

Wine, Food & the Good Life, Arlene Mueller and Dorothy Indelicato (ISBN 0-932664-85-0)

Wine Investment for Portfolio Diversification, Mahesh Kumar (ISBN 1-891267-84-1)

Wine Lovers Cookbook, Malcolm R. Herbert (ISBN 0-932664-82-2)

Wine Marketing & Sales, Paul Wagner, Janeen Olsen, Liz Thach (ISBN 978-1-891267-99-X)

Winery Technology & Operations, Yair Margalit (ISBN 0-932664-66-0)

The Wines of Baja California, Ralph Amey (ISBN 1-891267-65-5)

The Wines of France, Clive Coates (ISBN 1-891267-14-0)

Woody's Liquid Kitchen, Hayden Wood (ISBN 0975212397)

World Encyclopedia of Champagne & Sparkling Wine, Tom Stevenson (ISBN 1-891267-61-2)

Zinfandel, Cathleen Francisco (ISBN 1-891267-15-9)

How to Launch Your

WINE CAREER

Liz Thach, Ph.D.
Brian D'Emilio

Foreword by
Michael Mondavi

The Wine Appreciation Guild
San Francisco

How to Launch Your Wine Career

Text Copyright © 2009
Liz Thach, Ph.D., Brian D'Emilio
Published by:
The Wine Appreciation Guild
360 Swift Avenue
South San Francisco, CA 94080
(650) 866-3020
www.wineappreciation.com

Managing Editor: Bryan Imelli
Copy Editor: Erica Bishop
Cartoons: Doug Pike *Gone with the Wine*, 2009
Book Design: Diane Spencer Hume

Library of Congress Cataloging-in-Publication Data

Thach, Liz, 1961-
  How to launch your wine career / Liz Thach and Brian D'Emilio.
    p. cm.
  ISBN 978-1-934259-06-1
  1. Wine industry. 2. Wine and wine making. 3. Vocational guidance. I. D'Emilio, Brian. II. Title.
  HD9370.5.T53 2009
  663'.2068--dc22

                        2008038348

Although all reasonable care has been taken in the preparation of this book, neither the author nor the publisher can accept liability for any consequences arising from the information contained herein, or from use thereof.

ACKNOWLEDGEMENTS

Liz Thach

Special thanks to my husband, Mike and daughter, Zia, for their support and patience during the long hours of typing away on the book. Thanks to my father for his kind suggestions on the book; to my mother for her constant support; and to my mother-in-law, JoAnna, a fellow writer who has always encouraged my efforts. Also, thanks to good friends, Janeen, Lupe, Liz Burch, Iris, Leslie, Paul, Susan, Peter, Gordon, Lois, Peg and Ron for listening to me. I'm incredibly grateful to the tremendous—as usual—support from the wine industry. Not one person turned me down when I requested an interview. They are all so generous with their time to help others and promote wine education. It is truly one of the friendliest industries on earth—and really, just one big family. Finally, special thanks to Sonoma State University for making writing articles and books a fun part of my job.

Brian D'Emilio

Special thanks to Ma, Tina, Nolan, and Mara, for putting up with all the first-time-author blues. Thanks to Kathleen McLeod, Scott Edwards, Tom Baril, Phillipe Thibault, Bob Beck, Sharon Anderson, and the entire Chateau St. Jean Hospitality team; to Diana Gerlach, Sandy Hook, Brenda Wild, Lucinda Wolf, and the Beringer Hospitality team; and to Mora Cronin, Nicole Carter, and finally, Matt Lane. You all taught me generously and patiently about this wonderful industry. I hope I've done justice to what you taught me.

Liz & Brian

We are both very grateful to all of the following wine industry colleagues who so generously shared in their experiences and advice and suffered through our interviews:

Heidi Peterson Barrrett, Paul Bonarrigo, Michael Browne, Jim Caudill, Miryam Chae, Larry Challacombe, John Collins, Chris Crowe, Paul Dolan, Phil Durrett, Curtis Eaton, Stephanie Gallo, Patty Held-Uthlaut, Bruce Herman, Diane Holst, Ray Johnson, Tom Johnson, Mel Knox, Geoff Labitzke, James Laube, Chuck LeFevre, John McGregor, Lucie Morton, Gordon Peacock, Lily Peterson, Virginia Philip, Jim Russell, Renay Santero, Ed Sbragia, Leslie Sbrocco, and Jack Thornton. And very special thanks to Harvey Posert and Michael Mondavi for their encouragement and kind words.

The Publisher

Thanks to Gale Sysock for his professional insight and sound suggestions to make this a very realistic and useful book.

CONTENTS

FOREWORD

Wine careers is certainly a subject I know plenty about, having had several of them during a lifetime in the business. This book should be a perfect introduction for people who are thinking about going into the wine business, as well as a guide for people who are now in the business and want to move up the career ladder.

I always approached the wine industry as fun and entertaining, and this book does a solid and entertaining job of laying that out. (Stephanie Gallo, who is interviewed in chapter 5, probably had more difficulty getting into the wine business than I did!) It demonstrates that the wine industry is made up of so many factors, from its history and tradition, through agriculture in the vineyards and science in the laboratories and the wineries, to the vital work of marketing the product.

This follows my precept of "take the mystery out of wine, but keep the magic." And central to the whole enterprise is the fact that it is a business and needs finance, administration, human resource development, and every other aspect and job function of any successful enterprise.

The Robert Mondavi Winery was often called "The University of Wine" because we believed so strongly in education, and I have continued in that dedication with Folio Fine Wine Partners.

I wish all the readers of the book great careers in the wine industry. It can be very challenging, but it is a lot of fun as well.

—Michael Mondavi
Founder
Folio Fine Wine Partners
www.foliowinestudio.com

Introduction to Wine Careers:

Authors' Perspectives & Key Considerations

I think we can skip the résumé.

Chapter 1

BRIAN D'EMILIO

I have a wickedly cool job. Part of that is loving what I do. I head up Training and Organizational Development for the Americas region of a major global wine company. It is an awesome job. Just as important is the industry I work in.

You see, I'm one of those incredibly lucky people who get to say, "I work in the wine business." Believe me, when people start the "so what do you do" conversation, that's a line guaranteed to make you the most interesting person at the dinner table, on an airplane, or in a bar. Everyone, and I mean *everyone,* wants to hear about how cool it is to work in wine.

My heritage is French and Italian. I grew up with the repurposed Philly Cream Cheese glass container, half full of whatever wine was being poured for dinner, and thought of it as a perfectly normal part of a meal. I can't tell you what my first wine was, but I can tell you wine was part of my upbringing. I did not know much about it then, but I liked it.

Wine continued to be a passion through college (I was probably one of the only college students who had cases of wine stashed in his closet). After college, I moved to the San Francisco Bay Area, and heading to the local supermarket for the first time was quite a wine experience. I was amazed at the selection available. I can even remember my first visit to Napa Valley, taking the tours at Mondavi and Beringer. Northern California seemed like an oasis of great wine—and man, was I thirsty! Wine became a staple for me. I couldn't imagine a special meal, a social occasion with friends, or a grocery bill without it!

I have now worked in the wine business for more than seven years. I've learned more than I ever could have anticipated about wine, and I have met amazing people filled with extraordinary knowledge, passion, and commitment to this industry. Their passion is only surpassed by their generosity in sharing their knowledge, experience, and advice with wine novices like you and I.

And yes, even after seven years, I am **still** a novice and loving the apprenticeship.

I was flattered when Liz asked me to help write a book to give people like you sound advice on how to break into the industry I love. Before moving into training and development, I spent several years in human resources—which also meant spending a lot of time reviewing resumes and interviewing people just like you!

The advice I will give you is based on that "expertise." I won't claim to be an authority on **every** avenue into this business, but by following the example of the folks who've been so gracious in teaching me about the wine business, I am happy to share my insights, and the insights of friends and industry contacts about what other people just like you have done to successfully make a move into wine.

LIZ THACH

Like Brian, I wasn't born into the wine industry. Though fifth generation Californians, my parents left the state when I was three years old and we lived in South Dakota, Idaho and New Mexico. These were great states in which to grow up (and now they all have wineries too!), but my family did not have wine on the table every night with dinner. Therefore, I didn't taste wine until returning to California for college. On my 21st birthday, my best friend drove me from Belmont to the Napa Valley, where I fell madly in love with wine.

It is hard to explain why some people are smitten by the "wine bug," but as you read the stories in this book you will see this same theme over and over again. A certain event, person, or place brings wine into your life and all of a sudden, you have a new passion.

And it is a great passion to have. It is so much fun to study, taste, and talk about wine to like-minded souls. So that is what I did. Since that first visit to Napa, I have spent the rest of my career researching wine. I subscribed to wine magazines and read them religiously; I received wine books for Christmas and other occasions; and I joined wine tasting groups. Once married, I got my husband hooked on wine—and every year we visit one or more wine regions for vacation. That is why I can say I have visited every major wine region in the world except for South Africa—which I will do someday!

Unlike Brian, however, I wasn't lucky enough to get recruited into wine early in my career. Instead, I worked for fifteen fascinating years in corporate America and learned a lot! I wouldn't trade those years with Texas Instruments, Compaq Computer, Amoco, or US West because they launched my career in Human Resources and helped me get my Ph.D. Though I was located in Texas and Colorado, I had the opportunity to travel all over the world with these companies, and discovered that many top executives like wine too!

Eventually, the day came where I saw my dream job ad posted on the Internet: "Seeking a professor with a Ph.D. in Human Resources, industry experience, and interest in wine to work in Sonoma County, California." There it was—my dream job! I applied, and eight years later I'm still enjoying every day as a management and wine business professor at Sonoma State University. I teach in both the B.S. and MBA wine programs at SSU, as well as WSET courses with Copia in Napa. As a full-time professor, I also write many wine articles and have published three wine books to date. I even planted a hobby vineyard and have won medals on my home-made wine in local fairs. Best of all, I get to travel to the wine regions of the world and meet many wonderful people—and it is all part of my job as a wine educator.

Wine is a charmed industry, but it does have it downsides. It is important, if you are considering launching your wine career, to know all sides of the glass. Like a lovely shimmering Riesling, the wine industry is filled with many facets of light and covered in layers of flavors—some are more fruity while others are more minerally. Through these pages, you will learn about the advantages and challenges of working in the industry, and can make a final decision of where you want to be. So fill a glass with your favorite wine, sit down, relax, and read on.

IMPORTANT CAREER CONSIDERATIONS

There are five things you need to consider before starting your wine industry job search:

- Location, Location, Location
- Would You Like That Small, Medium, or Large?
- Who You Know Matters
- A Word About Social Responsibility
- What You Really Need To Know About Wine

LOCATION, LOCATION, LOCATION

When you start thinking about wine country, most of you will first think of California, yet there are now more than 6000 wineries in all fifty states. Though 90% of wine is produced in California, there are more wineries outside of California than within. The growth rate of wineries has been phenomenal—more than 102% since the 1990's. So there are many locations from which to choose.

However, Northern California is one of the most *expensive* places to live in the US. In December 2007, CNNMoney.com listed the median home price in the San Francisco-Oakland-Fremont area as $825,400. For perspective, the median home price of a single family dwelling nationally was $220,800. Living closer to wine country will reduce the price tag to a median of $589,165 in Napa and $533,779 in Santa Rosa.

The bottom line for most job seekers is simple: you will live in a fabulous place, but you will also pay handsomely for the privilege.

A less obvious insight is that wine is typically not a "pay leader." Don't expect to receive a salary increase that compensates for the difference in cost of living. Good wine companies are competitive within the industry and the Bay Area from a salary standpoint. If you've got $250,000 worth of house in the middle of the country however, you're in for quite a shock when you see what that same equity buys you in this extremely costly part of the West Coast. Only the largest employers offer cost of living stipends as part of a relocation package, and normally only for senior level positions. Even these stipends are temporary, usually lasting for no longer than three years.

Relocation is typically based on geography and resources. Most wine companies will only pay relocation costs for senior level roles (e.g., Director-level or higher) and for hard-to-find, technically-specialized roles. Relocation may also be paid for mid- to senior-level Sales professionals. If you're interested in working in California, your resume will be doing battle with a large, talented, local labor market, of whom more than a few are also interested in working in wine. This is not to say that out-of-geography candidates do not get looked at and hired—they do. However, serious candidates need to consider spending some time—or possibly moving—to the wine region of their choosing.

Another factor for the potential job seeker is the geography of Northern California. Many folks who aren't from the area have hopes of living in San Francisco and working in Napa or Sonoma—thinking that they'll have at most a twenty or twenty-five minute commute. Imagine their chagrin when their first inkling that their California dream might not work out as planned is their first two-hour drive during rush hour from the San Francisco Airport to a winery for their in-person interviews.

While living in San Francisco or the trendier parts of the East Bay is very possible, your commute will be a bit longer than many hopeful candidates imagine. Average commutes from the northern part of San Francisco to south Napa average 50 minutes to an hour—barring accidents. East Bay suburbs like Walnut Creek and Pleasant Hill, or north of Oakland on the Interstate 80 corridor in places like Berkeley and Albany are somewhat closer—roughly 35–45 minutes to southern Napa. Santa Rosa, located in Sonoma County, can be reached in about an hour and 15 minutes from the northern parts of San Francisco, and an hour and a half from the East Bay suburbs. St. Helena can be reached in about an hour and a half from both.

The bad news is the relative distances, and the number of two-lane roads you will need to take to get to your destination. The good news is that by Bay Area standards, the commute times and conditions are reasonable. A rule of thumb is that going north is much, *much* better than going south, all things being equal. Public transit is unfortunately not a viable option for most commuters. The BART system, efficiently provides transportation between locations in the East Bay and San Francisco, does not extend up to Napa or Sonoma.

For folks seeking the total wine country experience, it is possible to live and work in wine country. Napa, a city of 81,000 people, offers a small city feel with plenty of great restaurants and wine bars, yet it has a relatively sleepy nightlife by San Francisco standards. Santa Rosa, located in the center of Sonoma, is a medium-sized city of 149,000 people. It provides a bedroom community feel and has its share of fine dining.

There are plenty of smaller areas to consider as well. Many wine country commuters hail from northern San Francisco, the East Bay suburbs along the Highway 24 or Interstate 80 corridors, Santa Rosa and the town of Sonoma.

Before considering relocating to the Bay Area, it is important that you do your research. You should also spend the money and time necessary to visit your prospective location. A week spent in Northern California that includes driving between San Francisco, the East Bay, Napa and Sonoma especially during peak commute times, will be invaluable. If you are a prospective home buyer, it is important to understand the various housing markets and neighborhoods, and to remember that there are no "undiscovered" areas within reasonable commuting distance of wine country.

Using books and the Internet to research the region can be useful as well. Friends or contacts who know or live in the area can provide a realistic picture of what areas and driving times are actually like.

Above all, visit some wineries, eat at some great restaurants, spend some time outdoors, and talk to some locals. That, more than anything else, will help you decide if Northern California is the place for you.

There are of course other places in the US to work in wine. These include California's Central Coast, Oregon, Washington, New York's Long Island, Finger Lakes regions, Texas Hill Country, and many others. Keep in mind that there is now at least one winery in each of the fifty states—and new ones being established every year.

Though these regions are outside of Northern California, the location factors previously mentioned still apply. Factors to consider include:

- Cost of living
- Availability of your target communities
- Climate
- Commute distances and times from your target communities to the various wineries (online maps are helpful in determin-

ing distances, but talking to someone local who really knows what the traffic is like is your best bet in determining commute times.

- The number and size of wineries in the area (which is important if you think you will ever need to change jobs, as this is your pool of potential employers).

With the exception of Long Island, most of these areas are more rural, agricultural communities. Though California's Central Coast will be less expensive than the North Coast, nowhere in California is inexpensive.

You may have better luck in the growing wine regions of Washington, Oregon, and New York's Finger Lakes. Cost of living on average will be less than California, but more so than other parts of the country. The wineries in all three locations are producing some outstanding wines. They also offer beautiful scenery and are great for people seeking outdoor lifestyles.

WOULD YOU LIKE THAT SMALL, MEDIUM OR LARGE?

It would be impossible, or at least impossibly arrogant, to suggest that we can give you foolproof tips on how to get a job in any winery or wine company. The industries are too diverse for that.

The simplest way to understand the various companies is to segment them into three categories of wineries and wine companies: **Small**, **Medium**, and **Large**.

Small refers to low case production, typically sole-proprietorship wineries, with case volumes below 25,000 annually. Many of these wineries are family-owned. They tend to have less than 100 employees, and most have far, far fewer. Examples of these include Sbragia Winery, La Sirena Winery, and Kosta Browne Winery. Many of these wineries sell their wines through their tasting rooms, direct sales via wine clubs, or through relationships with local retailers and restaurateurs.

Small wineries are often romanticized and become many a wine career seeker's idea of the perfect job. They are envisioned as a series of small buildings clustered in a valley, surrounded by vines—the kind of place where you can be doing pump overs in the morning; tastings for customers at a small bar in the middle of the cellar in the afternoon; and writing back-label copy for the winery's next release in the evening.

However, smaller wineries are like most small businesses across the country. They are entrepreneurial start-ups, driven by the energy and enthusiasm of their owners. They are generally the least bureaucratic places in the wine business.

People working at small wineries have more opportunities to try their hands at a number of different job duties and tasks, whether that be pruning, picking, crushing, pumping over, or bottling. They may even participate in the marketing and selling of the wines themselves. The hours are variable, and depend simply on what needs to be done.

Many of the formal job roles described in this book do not exist in pure form within small wineries. Employees tend to wear two or three hats. This makes for a truly broad experience within the wine business.

If the benefit of a small winery experience is the lack of bureaucracy, and the opportunity to try your hand at a variety of things, a potential downside is that it is often difficult to achieve significant job growth within a small winery. The reason is simple—there are just so many jobs, and only so much sophistication that these wineries needs.. As with many family-owned businesses, there is a limit as to how far a non-family member can go with the business.

Locating positions within small wineries takes a bit more initiative than sending out a few resumes or calling a favorite headhunter. Many small wineries don't employ Human Resources professionals or use staffing agencies to fill their openings. You may see ads in local newspapers such as the *Napa Register* and the *Santa Rosa Press Democrat*. Other possibilities include browsing online listings at Winejobs.com.

Small wineries will find help through networking. I've had a few friends offered jobs working harvest for small wineries simply by striking up a conversation at the tasting room bar with their friendly host (who on a couple of occasions turned out to be the owner/winemaker himself). Others meet owners/proprietors socially—for example, at industry events—and find that a casual conversation can segue into a job interview.

Don't expect any small winery to be interested in paying relocation—or to be that interested in out of state candidates. A local address, and lots of hands-on networking, is your best bet to crack this part of the wine business.

Suffice it to say, if the ambition is to have the true small winery experience, the best bet is to be open to doing pretty much anything (especially working harvest) to get your foot in the door, and using your networking skills to progress from there. While perhaps not the place to build an executive-level resume, a small winery is a perfect place to launch your wine career and to experience the industry to its fullest.

Medium is the broadest category among these classifications, and easily has the most variation within its ranks. It refers to wineries with production levels in the tens of thousands, or approximately 25,000 to 500,000 cases annually. Ownership trends to be private, though there are publicly-owned wineries of this size. Such organizations include Stag's Leap Wine Cellars, Chateau Montelena, and Ridge Vineyards.

Medium-sized wineries often pursue dual routes to market, selling both through a direct sales channel, and through distributors. They may employ anywhere from 100 to 1,000 people.

In these wineries, you will find recognizable jobs and functions, though some may be combined, for example, Sales and Marketing or Finance and Human Resources (HR). Medium-sized wineries will typically have limited numbers of roles in administrative professions like Finance, Information Technology, HR, and even Marketing. Those opportunities are typically mid-level, and are generalist in nature. The majority of roles and opportunities for progression will be in Winemaking and Winery Operations, Sales, and Direct Sales.

Medium-sized wineries may use a variety of methods to find talent. These include the traditional and non-traditional, such as web advertising, employment agencies, employee referrals, and networking at wine events.

Large refers to the biggest producers of wine. At least 500,000 or more cases are produced annually, with many producing millions of cases of wine each year. They include organizations like E&J Gallo, Constellation Wines, The Wine Group, Foster's Wine Estates, Trinchero Estates, and Jackson Family Wines. These organizations are some of the largest producers of wine in the world.

Large wine companies produce, market, and sell a significant percentage of the wines available in supermarkets or on liquor store shelves. They run the spectrum between public and private ownership—Constellation and Foster's being good examples of the former, Gallo and Jackson Family Wines of the latter. They typically employ large numbers of people, well in excess of 1,000 people in the US.

Large wine companies often behave similarly to medium-sized corporations. They will have recognizable departments and jobs in Sales, Marketing, Finance, Information Technology, Procurement and Logistics, and Human Resources. Career progression within these departments is often possible, though the availability of entry-level positions varies as many of these organizations are not prefer to hire experienced professionals. Specialized roles common in large companies may exist at large wine companies.

Many of these companies are looking outside of wine, and even outside of beverage alcohol for professionals. For the past decade, large wine companies have increasingly focused on acquiring talent from other industries, notably consumer packaged goods, to bring some of the knowledge and experience from those industries to bear in wine. In Northern California, there is also pull on the Financial and Information Technology talent available in the Bay Area, particularly in San Francisco and Silicon Valley.

The openness to non-industry experienced talent varies based on both the organization, and the job function in question. As a general rule, wine companies are more open to out-of-industry talent in functions like Marketing, Finance, Information Technology, Human Resources, and the non-winemaking aspects of Winery Operations.

For obvious reasons, winemaking talent comes almost exclusively from within the industry. There is also a strong preference for sales professionals with existing knowledge of the industry and who have relationships with key distributors.

For individuals currently working in the corporate world, large wine companies will seem most familiar, and be most comparable in terms of environment, job responsibilities, salary and benefits packages, and career opportunities with other industries.

They are also most likely to use traditional recruitment methods, including newspaper ads, online job postings, career fairs and networking forums. They may also participate in college recruitment programs or partner with contingency and retained recruitment firms. Networking is still a key method of finding talent, and in functions like winemaking and sales, industry experience and reputation are still critical to success in securing a role.

WHO YOU KNOW MATTERS

Wine is an ***extremely*** networked industry.

Some jobs, like sales, are almost impossible to crack without aggressive networking (unless you're related by blood or marriage to the winery's owner).

Networking is your best bet in obtaining a job at a small winery. In medium to large wineries, you may be able to get your foot in the door through traditional means, but networking is your surest bet for landing a phone call or an interview, or putting your candidacy over the top in a two-horse race. There is a similarly small network of contingency and retained search firms that specialize in wine and alcohol beverage.

Keep in mind that wine is no different from other industries: the best jobs are often never advertised, and are only found through networking.

There are a number of great books on the topic of networking. The last chapter, Chapter 12 "Creating Your Action Plan," provides a list of resources that target specific associations and events and can aid in developing a networking strategy.

A WORD ABOUT SOCIAL RESPONSIBILITY

One of the great things about working in the wine industry is that you get to taste a lot of great wine. In fact, some people outside of the industry mistakenly believe that insiders get to drink wine frequently on the job. This is not true, and in fact most wine companies frown strongly upon this, and some even have policies prohibiting it. This is because the wine industry is very serious about social responsibility, which includes promoting responsible drinking, giving back to the community, treating employees with respect and dignity, and embracing environmental stewardship.

Therefore, if you obtain a job in a tasting room, you will most likely be trained to "spit" rather than "swallow" wine on the job. Indeed, you can usually tell if someone is a wine industry professional by the fact that they do spit. This is because they need to remain clear-headed to perform their jobs. Indeed, winemakers—who must taste fermenting wine to track its progress—always spit, and then often choose to drink beer after work, rather than wine!

Many members of the wine industry have also adopted voluntary codes of ethics. One example is the Code of Sustainable Winegrowing, which provides guidance on how to implement environmental and socially responsible practices. Another example is the Code of Advertising Standards published by the Wine Institute, which prohibits members from advertising wine on college campuses and using ad models under twenty-five years of age.

All of these efforts are to protect wine's image as a drink of moderation that enhances food and connects people. The wine industry doesn't want wine to be perceived as a provider of party beverages. Therefore, as you consider launching your career in wine, it is important to understand this mindset. You may also want to practice spitting!

WHAT YOU *REALLY* NEED TO KNOW ABOUT WINE

What you need to know about wine varies by job. To put your mind at rest, there are only a few professions within the wine industry where significant wine knowledge is required. For many jobs, the only requirement is that candidates demonstrate their interest and ability to learn about the business aspect of wine. Having a passion for and an interest in wine itself will virtually always be a positive in the eyes of an interviewer.

Winemakers especially need to know a lot about wine. Educational requirements for winemakers will be discussed further in later chapters.

Sales professionals typically need some knowledge in wine, and to have worked in the industry. The knowledge requirements for entry-level sales positions are moderate. Ideally, this includes some knowledge of basic viticulture, including key varietals; flavor profiles; major growing regions and appellations; and key competitors in the industry and their products.

For other professions, knowledge of wine is a plus, but is not required. Examples of such professions are: Marketing, including Direct Marketing; Public Relations; Hospitality; and Winery Operations. All of these roles will require developing a knowledge base of the wine industry and some depth of knowledge of wine itself, similar to that of sales professionals. Said knowledge should be acquired within the first six to twelve months on the job in order to perform the roles in these functions effectively.

For roles in administrative functions such as Finance, HR, and Information Technology, you do not necessarily need to know anything about wine. Employees in these roles, however, should be willing to and interested in learning about the industry. A passion and interest in wine may very well help to advance a job seeker's candidacy.

For people looking to learn about wine, and the business of wine, there are a number of books, forums, and associations available. For more information on educational requirements for Winemakers, see Chapter 3 "Becoming a Winemaker."

ARE YOU READY FOR A WINE CAREER?
A BRIEF QUIZ...

The following short quiz is provided to help you determine your readiness for a career in wine. Answer honestly, and your readiness will be revealed.

Questions:

1) Is food, or wine and food, one of your hobbies?
2) Have you visited the wine region you want to work in?
3) If yes, was your visit for a week or more?
4) Have you talked to family members, friends, or networking contacts who work in wine about how to go about finding a job in the industry?
5) Have you taken any wine appreciation classes or seminars in the last five years?
6) Are you a current member of any wine associations like Wine-Brats?
7) Do you read wine industry business publications and web-sites?
8) Do you read the wine columns of newspapers, subscribe to *Wine Spectator*, *Wine Advocate*, *Food & Wine*, or similar magazines?
9) Are you a member of any wine clubs?
10) Do you know what California grape varietal is thought to be genetically identical to the European varietal Primitivo?

If you answered yes to...

Questions 1–3: You should read this book from cover to cover. Your wine career action plan will be long, but worthwhile.

Questions 4–6: You are definitely interested in wine. The next step is for you to translate that interest into a few tangible steps to move your job search forward.

Questions 7–8: You are seriously into wine. Read this book for the industry insider knowledge. Drink some Primitivo while reading.

Questions 9–10: You are a total wine geek. The authors may even know you.

Now that you're armed with some basic knowledge about the industry, it's time to take a deeper look at the global wine business. Good basic knowledge of the industry will help you regardless of your ultimate career path. So read on!

Overview of the Global Wine Market & Key Issues

Stop at Earth to pick up wine?
You know all they carry is domestics.

Chapter 2

If you want to launch your wine career, you will be much more successful if you first gather some background information on the global wine market and key issues surrounding wine businesses. In this way, you will be better prepared for job interviews, as well as providing yourself with a more solid foundation for any wine business you may want to start yourself.

With this in mind, this chapter is intended to be a crash course on the wine industry and covers the following five topics: 1) a short history of wine; 2) the major wine countries; 3) the wine industry value chain; 4) major global wine companies and multiple smaller players; and 5) financial and competitive issues.

A SHORT HISTORY OF WINE

The latest carbon-dating technology suggests that the first wine made from cultivated grapes was most likely produced around 6000 B.C. in the Caucasus Mountains of South-Central Asia in the present day country of Georgia, north of the Caspian Sea. There is other evidence of grapes being grown and processed for wine around the same time period in Turkey, Armenia, Iraq and China. Regardless of its actual birthplace, wine has been around for thousands of years, and has been used not only as a beverage but also for medicinal purpose in many cultures.

It is surmised that the custom of making and drinking wine spread from Central Asia west towards modern day Israel and Egypt. Some of the earliest wine labels, dating from 3000 B.C., have been found in Egypt on clay amphorae. From Egypt, winemaking jumped to the islands of the Mediterranean before moving to Greece and then Italy. In these two countries wine became so popular that the wine gods Dionysus (Greek) and Bacchus (Roman) became part of the cultures and were celebrated in religious ceremonies and festivals.

Though the Roman Empire has been given the most credit for establishing vast vineyards and wineries in France, Germany and even parts of England, it was the ancient Phoenicians who actually first brought wine to southern France and parts of Spain, Portugal and North Africa as early as 600 B.C. It was the Romans, however, who made wine an everyday drink by making sure that each soldier had his daily ration, and encouraging citizens to add wine to water to kill bacteria and make the water safer to drink. It was also the Romans who helped to establish some of the great vineyards of France and Germany by setting up trade systems along major rivers, beginning in the south of France as early as 125 B.C. Later, the Catholic Church encouraged vineyard development with some monasteries, such as the famous Citeaux Abbey of Burgundy established in 1098 A.D., becoming centers of excellence in viticulture and winemaking.

From Europe, wine spread to the New World via the explorers, with the Spanish establishing some of the oldest vineyards in Chile and Argentina in the 1500's. As they moved towards North America, vineyards were planted in Mexico, New Mexico and Texas as early as the 1600's. The Spanish entered California in the early 1700's where the grapevines they planted as part of the mission system thrived in the sunny dry climate. Soon other European settlers from Italy, France, and Germany arrived and planted vines not only in California, but many other parts of the United States and Canada.

Wine spread to other parts of the globe in a similar fashion. The Dutch took vines to South Africa in the late 1600's, and the British established some of the first vineyards in Australia in the early 1700's and New Zealand in the 1800's. Figure 1 illustrates how wine has expanded around the globe.

Figure 1: Movement of Wine from Central Asia to Europe and Beyond

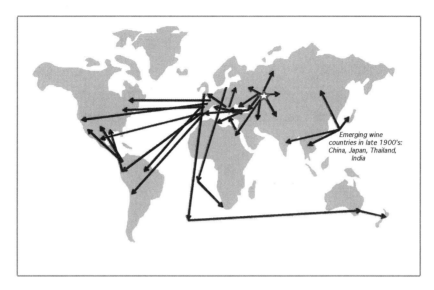

Today, wine is grown in more than seventy countries around the world, with new countries adding vineyards each year. Some of the more recent newcomers include Thailand and India. Other countries, such as China, Russia and Japan, have also increased their vineyard holdings greatly in the past decade.

THE MAJOR WINE COUNTRIES

Though wine is produced in many locations, almost 50% of production currently comes from France, Italy and Spain. According to the Organization International Vin (OIV, 2008), the organization which tracks grape statistics around the world, there were 270.9 million hectoliters of wine produced globally in 2007, with 131 million hectoliters produced by the top three countries (see Figure 2). The US comes in at fourth place with 20 million hl. It is also important to note that 35 million hl was used for other purposes than wine, such as vinegar, brandy, or conversion to fuel for vehicles.

Figure 2: Top 12 Wine Producing Countries
(Source: OIV, 2007 Data)

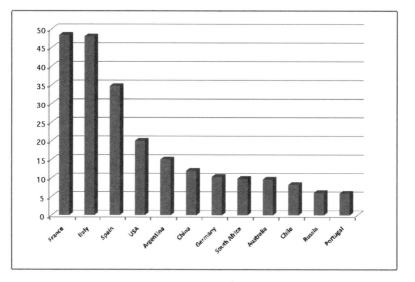

France, Italy and Spain have held the top places for wine production for many years and are expected to continue to do so for a while to come. However, with newly emerging wine nations, such as China and Russia, the balance of supply is starting to shift. Indeed Europe has decreased total production by 10% since 1990.

Wine consumption is also changing. The largest wine consuming nation is still France, but Italy fell to third place when the US moved into second position at the end of 2007. Wine consumption is increasing in countries such as the US, China, and India, but is decreasing in France and Italy. Interestingly, the US is still far behind from a per capita consumption basis, with Luxemberg and France taking first and second place, respectively.

The data changes when examining import and export numbers. The largest wine importing nations are Germany, the UK, and the US, respectively. The largest exporting nations are logically the largest producers (Italy, France and Spain), but Australia joins in at fourth place exporting more than 50% of its production and Chile takes fifth place exporting more than 80% of the wine it produces, but from a smaller production base.

IMPLICATIONS FOR YOUR WINE CAREER

So what does this tell you about the world of wine and your career future? There are several important implications:

- ***Learn About Wines From Around the World:*** Europe is still predominant in wine production and therefore it is useful to know about European wines. At the same time, the data illustrate that the world of wine is shifting with new players emerging on the scene, and therefore it is prudent to stay up to date on what is happening in other wine countries.

- ***Recognize Shifting Supply and Demand of Wine:*** The data also suggests shifts in supply and demand. Indeed wine has historically moving from surplus to shortage positions every eight to ten years. This is due to many factors, including over-planting when prices are high, weather and vintage issues, fluctuating currencies, changing regulations, economic and political shifts, and changes in consumer preference for different types of wine. Indeed the reason that so many hectoliters of European wine were converted to fuel for vehicles is because of an excess supply situation.

- ***Understand the Impact of Mother Nature:*** As you begin your career in wine it is important to recognize the power of nature and its impact on global wine production. Wine is an agricultural product and therefore, is subject to the whims of Mother Nature, which can impact supply and price. For example, in recent years a drought in Australia has reduced their crop size and forced them to raise wine prices. Floods and extreme rain in Italy hurt the Pinot Grigio crop, which reduced their supply, but other countries, such as Hungary, rushed into fill the gap. Therefore the global picture of wine is always changing, which makes working in the wine industry quite exciting.

- ***Recognize the Relationship of Climate to Quality:*** Finally, there is a reason that certain regions of the world have become so famous for high-quality wine, such as Bordeaux, Burgundy, Tuscany, Napa, Rioja, Margaret River, and the Mosel. This is because the climate and soil are ideal for producing great wine. Though the weather may change each year, the fact that these regions are located in cooler or more moderate climates allows them to ripen their grapes to achieve a balance of fruit, acid, and tannins. This translates into great wine. New winemaking technology also assists in creating good wine, but without perfectly ripened grapes, even technology cannot help. This is why global warming is of such a concern to the wine industry, because some classic regions may become too warm to produce high-quality grapes, whereas cooler regions, such as the UK and Tasmania, may begin to offer different types of wines.

THE WINE INDUSTRY VALUE CHAIN

Like other industries, the wine industry has its own value chain. A wine company may choose to operate in only one part of the value chain, such as grape growing, or it may choose to operate in all segments of the chain. Figure 3 illustrates a simplified depiction of the wine industry value chain. Understanding how the value chain works will help you determine in which part of the industry you would like to launch your wine career.

Figure 3: Wine Industry Value Chain

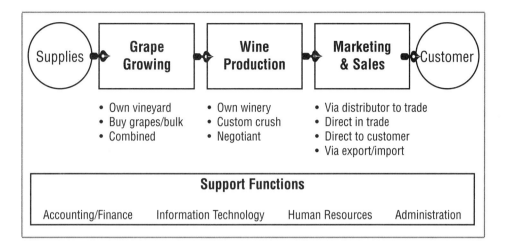

Supplies: In order for any industry to operate effectively, they need to purchase supplies, such as raw materials, equipment, services, and labor. In the wine industry common supplies are rootstock, tractors, barrels, tanks, pumps, corks, bottles, software, building materials, storage facilities, shipping services, and labor contractors. Though not typically part of the "actual value chain," a company may choose to integrate backwards and manufacture some of its own supplies. For example, some large wineries, such as Brown-Foreman and Château Margaux, have their own cooperage, or barrel making facility. Working in the supply side of the wine industry can be very rewarding, and this is covered in more detail in Chapter 11 "Working for a Wine Supplier."

Grape Growing: Since the main product within a bottle of wine is grapes, this is obviously a very important part of the value chain. Being a grape grower and selling your crop to wineries is a very viable business, especially if you own a vineyard in a highly desirable appellation, such as in parts of the Napa Valley, Champagne, Burgundy, or

Barossa. This is because high-quality grape growing land is limited, so you can receive more money for your crop. At the same time, a winery may choose to not only buy grapes but also have their own vineyards. A winery that only produces wine from its own vineyards is said to be "estate operated."

Raw grapes and bulk wine are also traded and sold over the Internet and at auctions. For grape growers who do not have a contract to sell their grapes to a winery, this is another method to make money—however, it can be highly speculative, because in surplus years there may be fewer buyers and very low prices. It is generally recommended that if you are going to grow wine grapes, that you should secure long-term contracts with several wineries in advance. Wineries that sell bulk wine usually do so because they have too much wine, or because the quality is not high enough for their brand. Bulk wine brokerage houses such as www.turrentinebrokerage.com buy and sell wine from around the world on the Internet.

Wine Production: Many people outside the wine industry assume that you need to own a winery in order to produce wine. This is not true. You can also outsource the wine production part of the value chain to a "custom crush" facility that will perform the winemaking part of the job. You provide oversight and money, but other people do the work. This is a good option for a new winery that doesn't have the funding to buy all of the equipment to build a new winery. (In general, a small 10,000 case winery costs around $8 million to buy all of the tanks, facilities, and permits to begin production). Several now famous wineries, such as Peter Michael and Kosta-Brown, have used this method to start their businesses.

On the other hand, it is beneficial to be able to produce wine in your own winemaking facility. In this way you have greater control over quality and cost efficiencies. Most large wine corporations have multiple facilities for this reason. For example, Gallo makes its popular-priced wines at its very large winery in Livingston, California, but makes its higher-priced premium wines at its Gallo of Sonoma facilities outside of Healdsburg.

Another aspect of wine production is being a **negotiant**. This is someone who purchases grapes or bulk wine and produces wine under their own label. Examples include Mouton-Cadet in Bordeaux and Sebastiani & Sons in the US (with their very famous line of brands, including Smoking Loon). In France, some negotiants also purchase labeled wine from small wineries and sell it for them. Likewise, some supermarkets, restaurants, and large retailers such as Costco, contract with wineries to produce a **private label** brand for their establishments.

Overall wine production is the "heart" of the wine industry value chain. It calls for highly skilled and dedicated winemakers and cellar support. It is for this reason that hiring a talented winemaker is so important. Some wineries will also hire **consulting winemakers**, or flying winemakers, from other parts of the world to work in partnership with their in-house winemaking staff in order to enhance and maintain quality.

Marketing & Sales: Marketing and sales is one of the most complicated segments of the value chain because wine is sold differently in different parts of the world. This is because being an alcoholic product, there are regulations about how wine can be produced, marketed and sold. For example, in some countries, such as Sweden and Canada, wine is sold only through government agencies. In the US, wine is regulated by each state, with very different laws, taxes, and fees. For instance, in California, wineries can sell direct to stores and restaurants, but in many other states they cannot do so. In Utah, wine is sold only through approved state stores, and there are counties in Texas which do not allow any alcohol sales. Other countries, such as the UK, Australia, and France have much more open marketing and sales systems for wine.

Because of this wine marketing and sales practices are very different by country. However, wine is generally sold via four channels. The first is through a distributor who purchases the wine from a winery and resells it to trade establishments such as restaurant and stores. The distributor provides a useful service in storing and transporting the wine, as well as assistance with marketing and sales. This is described in detail in Chapter 7 "Wine Marketing & Sales with a Distributor."

Wineries can also sell their wine directly to the trade in certain countries and states. However, this usually requires that they contract with transportation and in some cases warehousing companies to deliver the wine. This is described in more detail in Chapter 5 "Wine Marketing, Sales & Public Relations for a Winery."

Many small wineries choose to sell directly to the end-consumer where this is allowed. In this case, customers come to their tasting room to buy the wine, or they may also be able to purchase it by joining the winery mailing list, wine club, attending special events, or buying online. This is described in more detail in Chapter 6 "Direct-to-Consumer Sales at a Winery."

Finally, wine can be marketed and sold as an imported product. Many wine enthusiasts around the world enjoy trying wine from different countries. Therefore, large wine companies, distributors, and importers will purchase wine from other countries and import it for sale. This is described in more detail in Chapters 5 and 7.

It should be noted that though wine is sold from the winery via the four major channels, the large majority of wine is then sold to the end-customer through trade retailers in on- and off-premise establishments. On-premise sales are those in which the wine is consumed "on the premise," such as restaurants, wine bars, and hotels. Off-premise sales are those in which the wine is purchased and consumed "off the premise," such as from a grocery store, wine shop, or other retail outlets. This is described in more detail in Chapter 8 "Wine Marketing & Sales with a Retailer."

Customers: There are different categories of wine consumers, ranging from avid enthusiasts and collectors to the casual consumer. As mentioned previously, wine consumption rates differ by country based on cultural and religious practices. For example, the per capita consumption rate in France is fifty-five liters per person, whereas it is only eleven liters per person in the US. Some consumers drink wine once a day with a meal, whereas others only drink wine on special occasions. Wine market researchers have developed different segmentation systems for wine consumers which vary by country. One segmentation system developed by Constellation Brands classifies US consumers into six categories (see Figure 4).

Figure 4: US Wine Consumer Segmentation
(Source: Project Genome 2006, Constellation Brands)

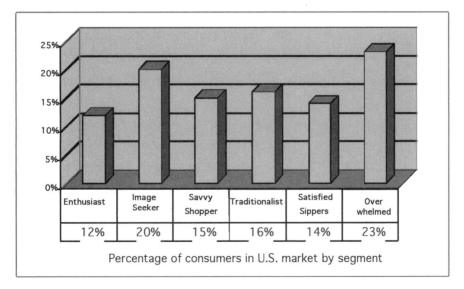

Enthusiast	Image Seeker	Savvy Shopper	Traditionalist	Satisfied Sippers	Over whelmed
12%	20%	15%	16%	14%	23%

Percentage of consumers in U.S. market by segment

31

Customers also prefer different types of wine, depending on their country of origin. For example, in France, Italy and Germany, most consumers buy wine based on region such as buying a Bordeaux, Chianti or Mosel. Whereas in New World countries, most consumer purchase wine based on varietal, such as Chardonnay or Cabernet Sauvignon. Wine preferences change based on trends and time of year. For instance, merlot used to be more popular in the US than it is today, and sales of rosés will often increase with warm summer weather. Research shows that other buying cues such as price, medals, and occasion also impact wine choice. Savvy wine companies make sure to conduct consumer research in the markets in which they operate so that they can target consumer segments with their preferred type of wine.

Support Functions: The final aspect of the wine industry value chain are the support functions for a wine business. These include finance/accounting, human resources, technology, and all of the administrative functions including support personnel, legal, corporate, facilities management, etc. Depending on the size and type of wine business, some of these functions may be outsourced and purchased on an as needed basis from consultants and other service providers. However, most large wine companies have departments staffed with full-time people for these important functions.

MAJOR GLOBAL WINE COMPANIES

There are thousands of wineries around the world—and even more vineyards. Because of this the global wine industry is considered to be one of the most highly fragmented industries in the world, especially when you realize that each winery often produces several different wine labels. The only other industry to come close to the large number of offerings is considered to be the music industry where each artist produces many different songs. Unlike other beverage industries where a few large companies dominate market share, for example, according to *Beverage Digest* (2007) Coca-Cola holds approximately 40% of the soft drinks market—the largest wine player only holds approximately 2% of the market. Figure 5 illustrates the ten largest wine companies based on millions of cases produced.

Figure 5: The Major Wine Players by 2006 Case Production
(Source: Rabobank International 2007)

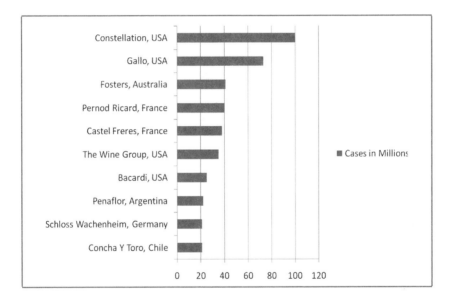

It is important to note that many of the large wine companies also sell beer and spirits as well as wine. This is because of fluctuations in demand and varying margins in these three categories. In some years, wine provides better returns than beer, but in other years beer and spirits out-perform the wine category. Therefore having a diversified portfolio makes more sense for large publicly traded firms. Indeed, some such as Brown-Foreman and LVMW (not listed in Figure 5) also sell other products such as luggage, dishes, and perfume.

Even though these large wine corporations may not command a big market share globally, within their own countries they generally tower over the small and medium-sized wineries. For example, in the US, the three largest wine companies produce more than 60% of the wine. A small winery, in comparison, produces less than 10,000 cases according to the definition of the *Family Wineries Association*, and often only sells locally or within a small region. More than 50% of the wineries in the US fit the small winery definition. Medium-sized wineries have been variously described as producing from 50,000 to 500,000 cases depending on the definition applied. Their market is much more competitive because they usually lack the economies of scale of the large corporations, but must sell larger volumes on a national or international basis in order to turn a profit.

The number of wineries by country also ranges widely. Table 1 shows the number of commercial wineries in several different countries based on information from *Harper's Country Reports 2007* and *Wine Business Monthly*. It is important to recognize that many of these wineries are small family enterprises that only sell locally.

Table 1: *Example of Number of Commercial Wineries by Country* (Source: *Harper's Country Directory 2007 & Wine Business Monthly*)

Country	# of Commercial Wineries
France	112,500
US	6,000+
Spain	4,400+
Italy	4,000+
Australia	2,000+
China	500+
Argentina	830
Chile	250
UK	100

Because of the large number of wineries and vineyards around the world, as well as the range of sizes, the industry is quite competitive. In some years this can be aggravated by large crops of varying quality levels. Therefore, there are multiple markets ranging from local niche to large international brands, as well as price points starting at less than $2 per bottle and reaching to over $2000 per bottle. This type of diversity makes the wine industry an exciting one in which to work. It also gives rise to many philosophical discussions about the purpose and process of making wine.

FINANCIAL AND COMPETITIVE ISSUES

After reviewing the statistics on the global wine industry a common question often arises: "Is the wine industry a profitable one?" The answer to this question is obviously "yes," or there wouldn't be so many players involved. However, in reviewing the financial history of the industry—especially the publicly traded companies—it is obvious that the wine industry is not as profitable as some fast paced industries, such as high tech or biotech, but many say that part of the dividend of working in wine is the "culture of the industry." As one wine marketing manager for a small winery in Napa reported:

> "I realize I don't make as much money working for small winery in Napa as I would working for a large company in San Francisco. However, I do get to drive to work through the vineyards; pass beautiful wineries; enjoy long lunches with fine wine, food and clever companions; and travel frequently to the wine regions of the world. Because of this, I consider myself quite fortunate."

According to Lewis Perdue, author of *The Wrath of Grapes*, a 10% return on equity (ROE) is the average for most publicly traded wine companies. Furthermore, most have not fared that well in the stock market, because issues such as vintage variation and fluctuating production due to changing weather cannot always be forecast. Therefore these companies are sometimes hard-pressed to meet the analyst's numbers. Indeed shareholders have often received the highest returns when a winery is sold. Because of this, the merger, acquisition, and divestiture activity in publicly traded wine companies is quite high.

Salaries in the wine industry are often not as high as other industries. Generally, the well-known branded companies pay at least market rate, and sometimes a bit higher. Salaries are fair, but small family-owned businesses usually cannot compete with the fancy benefits offered by larger companies in other industries, such as stock options, profit sharing, and generous health benefits. The benefits instead are more intrinsic, such as working close to nature and near people who are passionate about wine.

Despite all of this, most industry insiders say they "relish" working in wine because the people attracted to wine are enjoyable to work with. Most are passionate about food and wine, have a love for the land, and enjoy the good conversation and collegiality that wine often brings to a setting. Robert Mondavi aptly referred to this as "the good life." In addition, the wine industry is never boring. There is always a new product being launched, a new vintage to discuss, and a variety of issues to be considered. Following is a list of the current and future "hot" issues that are impacting the financial and competitive landscape of the wine industry:

- ***Global Warming:*** Rising temperatures, as well as unusual weather patterns such as floods and droughts, will have both positive and negative impacts on grape growing and wine production. New methods, varietals, rootstocks, winemaking techniques, and locations will be sought in an attempt to address global warming impacts on grapes and wine production.

- **Rising Energy Costs:** Like many other industries, the wine industry is and will continue to be impacted by the rising cost of fuel to transport wine, as well as energy cost to cultivate crops and produce wine. New solutions will be sought and developed to combat this issue.

- **Continued Strong Global Competition:** With ongoing fluctuations in global wine supplies, changing currencies, newly emerging wine nations, and economic ups and downs, competition will continue to be turbulent.

- **Ongoing Market for Value, Mid-Price and Luxury Wines:** History has shown that there is always a market for a variety of wine price points. Though the market had been moving up towards mid-priced premium wines, economic downturns often send people to lower priced wines. The good news is that recessions usually don't mean people buy less wine, but will purchase less expensive wines. On the flipside, the wealthy will always have an appetite for the luxury priced rare bottles.

- **Continued Focus on Efficiency:** Most successful wine businesses will continue to drive unnecessary costs out of the system in order to stay competitive.

- **Ongoing Consolidation:** Ongoing consolidation in all parts of the value chain is expected to continue, including vineyards, wineries, suppliers, distributors, and retailers.

- **Growth of New Wineries:** With the ongoing consolidation, it is expected that new wineries will still continue to come onboard, especially in emerging wine nations such as China and India.

- *Lifestyle and Hobby Wineries:* More "lifestyle wineries," or those started by retired executives from other industries more as a lifestyle than a profit generator, as well as hobby or home winemakers, are expected to increase with a rising interest in wine globally.

- *More Innovative & Environmentally Friendly Wine Packaging:* Already, consumers are being offered wine selections in tetra-packs and plastic bottles, as well as cans and glass stoppers. This type of innovation is expected to continue to grow—especially with attempts to reduce the carbon footprint of wine.

- *Introduction of New Grape Varietals:* Innovation will also be seen in the current and continued introduction of new grape varietals to the market. Italy is leading the way by reviving ancient and almost extinct grape varietals, such as Fiano, and bringing them back into the international arena.

- *Sustainable, Organic and Biodynamic Winemaking:* Some wineries are adopting new work processes such as sustainable, organic or biodynamic farming and winemaking to reduce negative environmental impacts and improve product quality.

- *Fair-trade Wine:* Programs that enhance worker health, safety and fair treatment in viticulture and winemaking are being adopted by more wineries in countries such as Chile, South Africa and the US.

- *Responsible Drinking & Health:* Many wine companies are ramping up programs to promote responsible drinking and decrease social problems such as "binge drinking." At the same time, the health benefits of wine are receiving broader coverage in many markets, though not all countries (such as the US) will allow wine and health advertising.

- ***Increased Quality, Traceability & Ingredient Focus:*** The wine industry is already quite quality conscious and most countries have mandatory regulations regarding ingredients and traceability. However, it is expected that the focus on this area will increase with continued pressure for the wine industry to include ingredient and even nutritional and calorie information on labels.
- ***Growing Wine Tourism:*** There is a heightened interest in wine around the world, and with it comes a desire to travel to different wine regions of the globe. Wine tourism, coupled with eco-tourism, culinary tourism, and agritourism, is predicted to increase.

THE IMPORTANCE OF STAYING UP-TO-DATE FOR YOUR WINE CAREER

Whether you are just starting your new wine career or trying to break into the business, it is important to stay up-to-date with what is happening in the industry. This chapter has provided you with a high-level overview of the global wine industry, but it is up to you to stay current. In addition to reading your favorite wine journals such as *Decanter, Wine Spectator, Wine & Spirits, Wine Enthusiast* and many others, consider the following sources to help you stay ahead of the curve.

USEFUL RESOURCES ON GLOBAL WINE STATISTICS

- ***ENews Monitor: General Wine News:*** Free subscription of top global wine news of the day. Contact: editor@bensonmarketing.com

- ***Harper's Wine & Spirits Directory:*** *See* Country Report section, subscription based
- ***Shanken's Impact Database Review and Forecast:*** Fee based annual report
- ***Wine: A Global Business*** (2008): Textbook edited by Liz Thach and Tim Matz

Websites

- **www.awbm.com.au:** Australia wine business magazine
- **www.oiv.int:** *See statistics section*
- **www.winebiz.com.au:** *See statistics section*
- **www.winebusiness.com:** US wine business magazine
- **www.wineinstitute.org:** *See statistics section*
- **www.winemarketcouncil.com:** *See research reports*
- **www.WinesandVines.com:** Online edition of ***Wines and Vines*** magazine
- **www.vwm-online.com:** Online edition of ***Vineyard & Winery Management*** magazine

Becoming a Winemaker

Who's the new guy?

Chapter 3

So you think you may want to be a winemaker? This is understandable, because becoming a famous winemaker can be akin to being a glamorous movie star or a revered quarterback. It can bring wine groupies and celebrity interviews. However that is not the reason most people become winemakers. They do so because they have a passion to make an incredible wine. Something deep within them is stirred to harness the bounty of Mother Nature's grapes and marry it to the science of chemistry and the art of blending. Through this process they are crafting a new life, as the yeasts consume grape sugars and convert them to alcohol, creating the beverage we call wine.

But it is not all fun and romance. Winemaking is long hours in a cold cellar; lots of study and analyzing lab results; and having to taste fermenting wine at eight in the morning. In a small winery, it can also mean cleaning out barrels and tanks, and even sweeping the floor.

Yet the end result can be magical. A well-crafted wine can bring delight to the consumer, rave reviews from the critics, and some well deserved press and revenue to the winemaker and winery. It can mean elegant wine dinners in fancy restaurants where you describe your work of art and autograph wine bottles. It can even mean an invitation for your wine to appear on the White House menu for a famous delegate.

So how do you become a winemaker? Is it necessary to spend years at a university, or can you learn on your own? This chapter describes the job of a winemaker, and how it differs in small, medium, and large companies. It also explains how to gain the necessary skills and education to land a job as a winemaker, as well as the career ladder of winemakers from assistant, head, and consulting winemaker. Most importantly it includes tips on how to get started, helpful resources, job hunting strategies, and advice from winemakers. Finally, this chapter ends with descriptions of other jobs in the wine cellar such as enologist, cellar master and cellar worker.

JOB DESCRIPTION FOR A WINEMAKER

A winemaker is someone who is engaged in the profession of making wine. This generally includes knowledge of the full process of wine-making, extending from the vineyard to delivering the final product to the customer. Specific responsibilities include:

- Work in partnership with the vineyard manager and other employees engaged in vineyard activities to monitor the growth process of the grapes and ensure their quality.
- Determine the best time to harvest the grapes based on lab analyses and taste profiles of the grapes.
- Assist in identification, purchase, and oversight of necessary winery equipment, including tanks, barrels, chemicals and all other necessary winery supplies.
- Oversee the crush and pressing process.
- Plan, implement and monitor settling and fermentation processes.
- Oversee the filtering, racking, testing, and aging process of the wines.
- Actively participate in the tasting process to insure the wines achieve flavor profiles which meet marketing needs.
- Plan and oversee the bottling process.
- Provide advice and recommendations for warehousing control and shipping.
- Implement and monitor the quality control system for the winery.
- Manage the winery documentation system, including inventory control, daily activities, testing, quality control, and other necessary activities.

- Responsible for understanding and complying with federal/ state regulatory guidelines, as well as company policies regarding environmental, safety, and social responsibility.
- Be available to assist the marketing department by hosting wine dinners, conducting interviews/presentations, facilitating tastings, and other needed marketing, sales, and public relations functions.
- Serve as a member of winery taskforces, as needed.

If the winemaker is working in a large winery, he/she may also have supervisory and/or managerial responsibilities. These could include:

- Develop and implement work plan for cellar workers, including daily tasks, quality goals, and required documentation.
- Communicate work responsibilities to employees, ensuring their understanding and compliance.
- Create motivational and safe working environment for winery employees.
- Oversee necessary training and performance management of employees.
- Provide guidance, instructions, and mentoring to assistant winemakers and enologists.

EDUCATION AND SKILLS REQUIREMENTS

In general, in order to obtain a position as an entry-level winemaker, you must be able to verify that you are able to perform the essential duties described earlier. In order to do this, most wineries require a **Bachelor's degree** from a four-year college in enology, fermentation science, food science, or a related field such as viticulture, chemistry, or biology. Five of the most well-known American universities for offering these types of degrees are:

- UC Davis, California
- CSU-Fresno, California
- Cornell University, New York
- Oregon State University, Oregon
- Texas A&M University, Texas

There are also excellent university programs outside of the US, especially in France, Australia, Italy, Spain, and other large wine-producing nations.

If you already hold a Bachelor's degree, but in a non-related subject, there are smaller wineries that may be willing to accept this degree, as long as you have obtained an **Associate's degree or Certificate** in enology, winemaking, fermentation sciences, or a related field. Many community colleges, as well as major universities, offer these types of programs. Some examples are:

- Napa Valley College, California
- Santa Rosa Community College, Sonoma County, California
- Washington State University, Washington
- UC Davis Certificate Program in Winemaking for Distance Learners, California

Finally, even with a college degree, most entry-level winemaking positions also require **prior work experience** in a winery. It is for this reason that many of the better known university programs also include a requirement to complete a six-month internship at a winery. In this way, graduates will have experienced harvest, crush, and all of the follow-up work in the cellar. They also have the benefit of being mentored by an experienced winemaker or winemaking team. Many students will try to complete at least two internships—one in their native country, as well as one working abroad. When hiring, many wineries are impressed to see candidates who have worked harvest not only in the US, but in Bordeaux, Burgundy, the Barossa or Hunter Valley of Australia, and/or the Mosel-Sahr-Ruwer region of Germany.

Even if you are not attending a university program, it is still possible to volunteer or apply for positions working harvest and crush to gain the necessary experience. There are a few well-known winemakers who do not have a college degree, yet have still managed to obtain the necessary skills by attending classes at a community college and obtaining work experience in a small winery. If this is the route you plan to take, you may not be eligible to apply to work in a large, international winery, but you will still most likely be able to obtain a position in a smaller winery—just as long as you demonstrate the passion and skills for making wine. When it comes down to it, much of it depends on how well your wine tastes!

Overall, the **major skills** required of a winemaker are as follows:

- Viticulture knowledge and experience.
- Winemaking knowledge and experience.
- Knowledge of fermentation science, biology, and chemistry.
- A strong working knowledge of all winemaking equipment, cellar processes, testing, and procedures.
- Ability to effectively communicate with others.
- Ability to perform and interpret mathematical calculations and chemical equations.
- Basic computer skills.
- Knowledge of quality control systems and documentation.

- Ability to taste, analyze, and blend wine to achieve market/ customer specifications.
- Knowledge of how to manage others in the cellar.

THE WINEMAKER CAREER LADDER

The four most common career levels of a winemaker are illustrated in Figure 1. The entry-level job title is usually assistant winemaker. In a large winery, there may be many assistant winemakers, whereas in small- to medium-sized wineries, there may be only one or two positions. In general, the assistant winemaker position is held from two to six years, depending on the skills and experience level of the incumbent. In many wineries, it is necessary to wait for the position of winemaker (sometimes referred to as head winemaker) to open up before being promoted from the assistant position. It is for this reason that the position of assistant winemaker usually has a high turnover rate within the wine industry. It is sometimes necessary to move to a new winery in order to achieve the head winemaker position.

Figure 1: The Winemaking Career Ladder

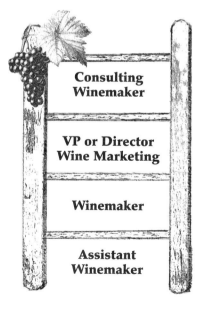

The head winemaker position is one of prestige, and in a medium- to large-sized winery, it usually takes years of experience to achieve. Once people achieve this position, they may remain here the rest of their career and enjoy the opportunity of producing and comparing wines from different vintages. The position of winemaker is actually one in which you generally become more skilled and valuable based on the number of vintages you have completed. This is because a winemaker is always learning and perfecting his or her craft. It is fascinating to be able to go back and taste vintages from ten to twenty years in the past and see how they have aged and changed. The magical quality of wine is often witnessed in these older bottles, as wine takes on new characters and nuances throughout the years.

Some head winemakers, however, enjoy the challenge of moving to a new winery so that they can learn new operating methods or produce wine in a different appellation. In large international wineries, there is usually the opportunity to move into executive winemaking positions, such as director or VP of winemaking. These are usually more strategic in nature and require that the executive winemaker oversee a staff of other winemakers. This type of job usually involves more long-term planning, analysis of consumer trends, and new product development based on trends. This type of position requires more leadership skills and involves less hands-on winemaking.

A fourth level of the winemaking career ladder is that of consulting winemaker. In general, this requires at least ten years previous experience making wine. Usually consulting winemakers have achieved positive reputations by making high-scoring wines. This track record makes them appealing to start-up and lifestyle wineries which need to hire expertise in this area. Consulting winemakers often are in charge of winemaking programs at five to ten different wineries, and find themselves very busy during harvest. Some will work in both hemispheres. For example, they may oversee harvest and crush at

five wineries in Napa, and then fly down to South Africa, Australia, Chile, or Argentina, to oversee harvest and crush at wineries in the Southern Hemisphere.

OTHER IMPORTANT JOBS IN THE WINE CELLAR

If you're not interested in climbing the winemaker career ladder, there are other interesting jobs in the winery cellar which may appeal to you. Following are brief descriptions and job requirement for five other positions in the cellar:

Figure 2: The Wine Cellar Career Ladder

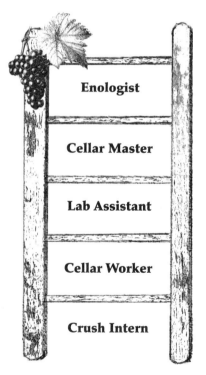

Enologist: In some wineries the term "enologist" is synonymous with "winemaker," though most wineries identify the enologist as someone who primarily performs the chemical analysis on wines.

This includes alcohol levels, acid, pH, SO2, VA, RS, ML, conductivity, acetic acid testing and other necessary tests. The enologist may also assist the winemaker in general winemaking duties, and may be called upon to train other cellar workers or lab assistants. A position as an enologist generally requires a Bachelors degree in chemistry, winemaking, fermentation science or related field.

Lab Assistant: Assists enologist and/or other wine laboratory staff to conduct analyses on wine samples—as described in previous description. The position may or may not require a Bachelor's degree. In general a lab assistant is a training or preparatory position to becoming an enologist or winemaker.

Cellar Master: Oversees inventory, scheduling, and employee relations within the cellar. Often referred to as the cellar manager or supervisor. Usually reports into the winemaker and oversees the work of cellar workers and interns. Duties include assisting the winemaker with winemaking operations, as well as ordering materials, inventory control, computer database management, scheduling employee work, and training and development employees. May or may not require Bachelor's degree depending on the size of the winery, but needs excellent management and organization skills. In small wineries, the winemaker and the cellar master are usually combined into one position.

Cellar Worker: Full or part-time position performing cellar operation work within a winery. Position usually requires all aspects of cellar work including rackings, additions, punchdowns, pumpovers, sorting, and destemming. Workers generally must know how to operate a forklift, and engage in extensive cleaning of the winery and equipment. Ability to lift hoses, barrels, cases and other items usually required.

Bachelor's degree not necessary, but most positions usually require prior cellar experience.

Crush Intern: Entry-level, part-time job to assist with harvest and crush within the cellar. Many wineries hire college students who are pursuing a degree in winemaking or viticulture to serve as crush interns. Duties usually include all responsibilities of cellar worker, but the job only lasts through harvest, which is usually August through November in the Northern Hemisphere. Hours are typically very long, ranging from ten to twelve hours per day.

WINERY SIZE DOES MATTER

It is important to determine whether you would like to work in a small-, medium-, or large-sized winery because the range of job duties can fluctuate dramatically. Though there are a variety of definitions for winery-size, in the US most are classified by the number of cases produced (12 bottles of 750ml wine make up one case). Following is one classification for winery size:

- Boutique = Under 3000 cases
- Small = 3000 to 10,000
- Medium = 10,000 to 50,000
- Intermediate = 50,000 to 250,000
- Large = 250,000 to 500,000
- Super = 500,000 to 1 million
- Mogul = 1 million plus

A boutique winery usually employs very few people (less than five), and often the owner is also the winemaker and vineyard manager. In some cases, however, a boutique winery owner may hire consulting winemakers to manage winemaking operations. A small winery generally hires a full-time winemaker and may also employ an assistant winemaker. In both boutique and small wineries, the winemaker will generally be expected to wear multiple hats and also play the role of enologist, cellar master, vineyard manager and even marketing rep as he/she may be required to go on the road and help to sell wine.

Jobs within medium- to mogul-sized wineries are typically more structured, with clear job descriptions for winemakers and other cellar workers. The larger the company, the more assistant winemakers are employed. For example, mogul-sized companies often have winemakers around the world at their various winery sites, and may also have pools of winemakers who specialize in making a certain type or style of wine, such as red or white wine, sparkling wine, or mass-market everyone day wine verses high-end luxury wines.

Because of the differences in job duties, expectations, and also salaries (larger wineries usually pay higher rates), it is important to think about the type of environment in which you would like to work.

TIPS ON GETTING STARTED

The best way to get started as a winemaker is to make some wine. It is important to experience the winemaking process in order to see if it is something that you feel passionate about. Without a passion for the creative process of winemaking, you will not be successful in this field. There are several ways to practice making wine:

- Volunteer to help at a local winery.
- Purchase equipment and grapes to make wine at home. There are many books and Internet sites to help in this endeavor.
- Purchase a home winemaking kit from the Internet. Many include frozen must or grape juice concentrate to help you get started.

- Take a class in winemaking at your local college or online.
- Join a home winemaker's group
- Attend a winemaker's bootcamp or tour which includes winemaking activities.
- Pursue self-study in winemaking by reading books, websites, and attending seminars or conferences.

HELPFUL CONFERENCES, BOOKS, AND WEBSITES

In addition to making wine, there are also many useful resources to help you learn about wine on your own. If winemaking is truly a passion for you, then reading and studying about it will be fun, rather than a chore. Following is a partial list of some of the wine conferences, books, and websites that will help you get started.

Wine Conferences/Seminars

- **American Society of Enology & Viticulture:** Academic conference on winemaking. Held each summer in various locations.
- **Unified Wine & Grape Symposium:** Largest US wine conference held each January in Sacramento, California.
- **Vin Expo:** Large international wine conference held each year in France.
- **Vin-Italy:** large international wine conference held each year in Italy.
- **Multiple small, regional or state winemaking conferences/seminars:** Identify a specific wine region in which you are interested and conduct a search on the web to find their association website. Most will list local conferences and seminars.

Winemaking Books

- ***The Art of Making Wine*** by Stanley F. Anderson and Raymond Hull
- ***Concepts in Wine Chemistry*** by Yair Margalit, Ph.D, & James Crum, Ph.D., Editor
- ***Concepts in Wine Technology*** by Yair Margalit
- ***From Vines to Wines: The Complete Guide to Growing Grapes and Making Your Own Wine*** by Jeff Cox
- ***Knowing and Making Wine*** by Emile Peynaud—a classic on the topic. Translated from French.
- ***Understanding Wine Technology: The Science of Wine Explained*** by David Bird
- ***The Way to Make Wine: How to Craft Superb Table Wines at Home*** by Sheridan Warrick
- ***A Wine Grower's Guide*** by Philip M. Wagner
- ***Wine Technology and Operations: A Handbook for Small Wineries*** by Yair Margalit, Ph.D

Helpful Websites

- **http://www.oiv.int/uk/accueil/index.php:** Organization of International Vine and Wine, headquartered in Paris, France
- **http://www.practicalwinery.com/:** Magazine for wineries and grape growers
- **http://www.vtwines.info:** Virginia Tech Enology Notes
- **http://www.wineamerica.org/:** Website of the National Association of American Wineries
- **http://www.winefiles.org/:** Database to access to information about wine making, grape growing, and the history of wine
- **http://www.winemakermag.com/:** Online version of the *WineMaker* magazine

- **http://www.winemakersworld.com/:** Discussion forum for winemakers
- **http://winemaking.jackkeller.net/index.asp:** Useful website for beginning and professional winemakers
- **http://www.winepress.us/:** Website which includes information for amateur winemakers
- **http://wineserver.ucdavis.edu/:** Link to UC Davis Department of Viticulture and Enology describing their programs and online resources

JOB HUNTING STRATEGIES

If you obtain a professional winemaking degree from a university, most will assist you in finding an entry-level winemaking position. However, if you obtain a certificate in winemaking or just learn on your own through self-study, attending seminars, and experience, then you will most likely have to begin as a volunteer or cellar worker. Though this option doesn't pay as well, you will be able to obtain valuable experience and hopefully obtain a good reference. It will also link you into the wine community, which is amazingly small and relationship oriented. Through networking and meeting other winemakers, you will eventually be able to identify assistant winemaking positions that will match your career goals. Once you get a few years of winemaking experience on your resume and craft some award winning wines, then you will be able to move onto other wineries which may provide broader learning opportunities.

Another job hunting strategy is to begin as a home winemaker and enter your wine in local contests. If your wine wins some medals, you may receive attention from the professionals and could obtain part-time work in a winery. Finally, if you have the funds, you can start your own winery. This obviously means you need to obtain the proper permits to make and sell wine commercially.

ADVICE FROM WINEMAKERS

Following are excerpts of interviews with four famous winemakers, who each entered the wine industry using different strategies. Their stories and advice are very useful in helping you to understand the various ways in which you can enter and work in the exciting field of winemaking.

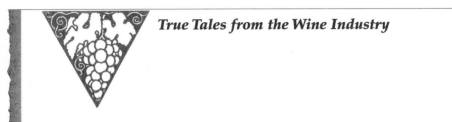

True Tales from the Wine Industry

HEIDI PETERSON BARRETT, CONSULTING WINEMAKER AND OWNER OF LA SIRENA WINERY

Named "the first lady of wine" by Robert Parker and wine-maker for such prestigious brands as Screaming Eagle, Dalle Valle, and Paradigm, Heidi was destined to be a great wine-maker from an early age. Heidi spent many of her formative years in winery cellars, helping her winemaker father, Dr. Richard Peterson. "I was fortunate enough to grow up in Napa Valley," says Heidi, "so I was surrounded by great wine from an early age."

EDUCATION AND TRAINING

Heidi always knew she wanted to be a winemaker. During high school, she worked part-time at Beaulieu Vineyards where her father was a winemaker. When the family moved to Monterrey to start the Monterrey Vineyard winery, Heidi was excited about helping out and learning about cool climate Chardonnay and Pinot Noir.

When it came time to go to college, there was no question in her mind about where she would study. "I applied to UC Davis," she says. "It was the only university to which I sent an application." Heidi obtained a B.S. in Fermentation Science and was assistant to the famous professor, Dr. Anne Noble, who invented the wine aroma wheel. She also did an internship in Germany where she learned the art of making balanced wines.

Upon graduation, Heidi worked for Justin Meyer at Silver Oak, and also worked crush at Lindeman's in Australia. A year later, she obtained a position as assistant winemaker at Bouchaine. The next step in her career was as head winemaker at Buelher Vineyards. It was here that she perfected her winemaking skills, gaining national acclaim for her beautifully crafted wines. In 1988, she launched her career as a consulting winemaker, and has been making wine history ever since with countless awards and record-breaking scores in all of the major wine journals. Her 1992 six-liter bottle of Screaming Eagle Cabernet Sauvignon broke the world record when it sold for $500,000 at the Napa Valley Wine Auction in 2000. In 1994, Heidi started her own winery, La Sirena, which means "mermaid," to honor her love for the sea.

MOST IMPORTANT SKILLS FOR WINEMAKERS

When asked about the most important skills for winemakers, Heidi has some excellent advice: "I think it is very important to develop versatility and a calm temperament. There is a lot of pressure during crush, and as the winemaker, it is critical that you remain calm and be a role model for others. Naturally, another important skill set is a strong background in science and chemistry. Then there is the intuitive or artistic side of winemaking. This is the fun part, where you get to be creative. Over time you develop a gut feel for what is needed to craft a perfect wine. Each harvest and each wine is very different, and it is exciting to consider all the variables at play and develop a creative solution."

As a CEO of her own winery, plus consulting winemaker to many other famous brands, Heidi has also had to develop excellent decision-making skills. "During harvest, I have to visit all of the wineries and quickly assess the situation. My goal is to emphasize the unique characteristics of each vineyard while crafting a beautifully balanced wine. This means that I have to quickly evaluate what is happening during fermentation and make fast decisions on the spot. As a winemaker, this is a skill that comes with time and ex-perience. Each harvest you learn more and more."

Heidi also mentions how important it is to develop team-work skills. "We work as a team at each winery," she says. "At times, it is like a relay race, where each person is handing off a part of the process. It is important to respect one another and keep the team going. I have the utmost respect for the people in the vineyards and the cellars where I work."

MOST CHALLENGING ASPECT OF THE JOB

"One of the more challenging elements of being a wine-maker is to not to over schedule myself. There are so many wonderful wine events—many for special causes and chari-ties—and I want to attend them all. Even though I know it is not physically possible, it is difficult to say no because there are so many worthy causes. At the same time, I realize that in order to keep balance in my life, work, and family that I can't say yes to everything."

BEST PART OF THE JOB

"The best part of the job is the magic that happens with winemaking," says Heidi. "I especially enjoy crush and the blending process. Crush is such an exciting time. Even though it is busy, there is such joy in the air because new wines are being born. Blending is even better, because that is where the magic happens: where two plus two equals five, and the creative synergies come together to create something beautiful. It is where I get to be an artist and add the finishing touches that bring balance to the wine."

ED SBRAGIA, HEAD WINEMAKER AT BERINGER AND SBRAGIA WINERY

As a member of a fourth generation Italian family which settled in the Dry Creek appellation of Sonoma County, Ed grew up with wine in his veins. "In my family," says Ed, "wine and food go together. They are both part of daily life. My father was a winemaker, and so I grew up helping out in the vineyards and assisting with making wine."

EDUCATION AND TRAINING

After spending so many long hours helping in the vineyard and cellar, Ed didn't want to be a winemaker when he first went to college. Instead he wanted to study chemistry. So he

enrolled at Santa Rosa Junior College for his first two years, then completed his B.S. in Chemistry at UC Davis. He then went to work as a research chemist at Gallo in Modesto. After a while, the call of the vineyard was too hard to resist, so Ed went back to school to study winemaking at CSU-Fresno where he completed a Master's in Agriculture Science. From there, he was recruited by Foppiano and then Beringer in Napa Valley. He started as an assistant winemaker, and then was promoted to head winemaker.

Today, after thirty years of winemaking, he continues in his role as head winemaker with Beringer, and in 2005 he fulfilled a dream of launching his own family winery in Dry Creek. Called Sbragia Vineyards, the winery has a stunning view of the tapestry of vineyards spreading over the valley, and Ed is able to make wine from grapes that his father planted over forty years ago. His wife, two sons, and their families also live nearby and help to run the winery.

MOST IMPORTANT SKILLS FOR WINEMAKERS

When asked about the most important skills for winemakers, Ed has very clear advice: "The number one most important thing is to love wine," says Ed. "Wine has to be watched and nurtured as a child, and you don't have much time off. Therefore, it is very important to love wine, because it is what you do every day. For me, each day is a joy, because I wake up and know I will be working with wine.

"A second important skill is a strong technical background in science, chemistry, and microbiology—especially knowledge of yeasts and bacteria. Third, is good practical experience in the cellar. For example, it doesn't hurt to know how to fix a pump. A fourth skill area is business—

especially accounting, finance, and marketing. Finally, one thing I didn't realize when I started out as a winemaker was how much public speaking and media relations you need to do. This includes not only making presentations at winemaker dinners, but talking with wine writers and other members of the media. It is important to get some good public relations training."

MOST CHALLENGING ASPECT OF THE JOB

"One of the more challenging elements is promoting the wine," reports Ed. "Especially with my new winery, I have to travel a lot and meet with distributors, retailers, restaurant owners, and other people who may not have heard about Sbragia Winery yet. Sometimes it takes a lot of energy to describe the benefits of your wine to a retailer who has already listened to fifteen other pitches that morning. But if you really want your wine to sell, you have to work in partnership with distributors and call on accounts with them. You then realize how hard the job of promoting wine can be at times—especially with so many great brands on the market."

BEST PART OF THE JOB

"The best part of the job is being around wine," says Ed. "I enjoy the whole process, from watching the grapes grow in the vineyard, to preserving the fruit quality in the winemaking process, and then seeing people's enjoyment as they drink the wine. Each harvest is like the birth of new children, and I get to help nurture them. It is also exciting to see how they age over the years. I just tasted some of the cabernet I made thirty years ago in Napa, and it was still very fresh

and flavorful. I really get a kick out of crafting the wine and seeing the enjoyment it brings to people."

PAUL BONARRIGO, WINEMAKER AT MESSINA-HOF WINERY, BRYAN, TEXAS

Growing up in the Bronx as a member of an immigrant Sicilian family, Paul Bonarrigo used to build scooters out of the wooden crates in which his grandfather purchased wine grapes. "When my relatives came to America from Sicily," says Paul, "it was Prohibition. But we were allowed to make home-made wine. I grew up with wine on the table, and really enjoyed making scooters out of the used grape crates. My friends and I would attach roller skates to the bottom and have races in the Little Italy section of the Bronx where we lived."

Those early childhood experiences helped shape Paul's career future, and though he also became a physical therapist along the way, today he is most famous for creating one of the most successful wine tourist destinations in the US—the Messina Hof Winery & Resort in Bryan, Texas where he reins as winemaker and owner with his wife, Merrill Hof.

EDUCATION AND TRAINING

"I didn't start out planning to be a winemaker," reports Paul. "First, I went to Columbia University to obtain a degree in

Physical Therapy and then joined the Navy." Paul was stationed in Oakland, California at Naval Hospital and on weekends he visited Napa and Sonoma wine country with friends. "I found myself fascinated with wine again," says Paul. "I even got to help with the '68 crush at BV, and then enrolled in some of the short courses on winemaking at UC Davis."

Wine continued to fascinate Paul even after a transfer to Pensacola, Florida and then eventually to Bryan, Texas where he was recruited to start a new Rehabilitation department. "It was here that I met Ron Perry who was doing his Ph.D. dissertation on grape feasibility in Texas," says Paul. "I encouraged him to plant some wine grapes on our property and it was fascinating to watch and see which grapes performed best in the warmer and more humid Texas climate. It was from that one acre beginning that Messina-Hof was born."

Today Paul and his wife, Merrill, have more than forty acres of grapes on their 100 acre property, farm more than 250 acres in West Texas, and purchase grapes from another ten growers around the state. They produce more than fifty different wines totaling more than 100,000 cases. They are most well known for their late harvest Riesling and port made from the Black Spanish grape and produced naturally, without any brandy.

"It was a great joy to make wine just like my grandfather," says Paul. "The courses I took at UC Davis, plus all of the books and seminars I read helped in my training. But Texas is a unique winegrowing environment, and we've had to learn a lot of it on our own." Paul still works as a physical therapist part of the time, even though Messina-Hof is very successful now. "I enjoy both jobs," says Paul, "and they never seem like work. It's all in your frame of mind!"

MOST IMPORTANT SKILLS FOR WINEMAKERS

"It's important to have a vision of where the wine is going to go," states Paul. "There are many people who understand the chemistry of winemaking, but not the soul of a wine. A truly talented winemaker understands both. It's not just about getting the pH and acidity technically correct, but allowing the wine to evolve into its greatest potential. This requires time and experience."

"Obviously, enjoying wine is another pre-requisite for becoming a great winemaker," says Paul. "I don't know any great winemakers who don't love wine. From this base, you can then develop your palate. It is important to taste many wines and build up a 'palate memory' so you can evaluate and improve your winemaking. We continually taste not only our wines, but the competitors' wines from around the world."

Paul also emphasizes the marketing and sales aspect of wine. "It is important to remember that a winemaker is a public person. Customers want to interact with the winemaker," he says. "If you don't enjoy that part of the job and being accessible to the public, then it will be difficult to be successful." In order to stay close to his customers, Paul conducts many tastings, educational seminars, and invites people to help harvest the grapes. "I am continually asking customers for feedback," says Paul. "I listen and try to incorporate their ideas."

MOST CHALLENGING ASPECT OF THE JOB

"In Texas, our biggest issue is lack of qualified labor." Paul mentions that Messina-Hof has more than ninety employees to help run the tasting room, restaurant, resort, and the many events, including weddings, which they offer to customers. "Texas

doesn't have a university that offers a Bachelor's degree in winemaking like UC Davis," says Paul. "Therefore, people want to come and work with us to learn the industry, but after a few years, they often leave to go to California. This is very frustrating to lose good people. Texas needs more wine education and training."

BEST PART OF THE JOB

"The best part of the job is meeting fabulous people," says Paul. "Wine lovers are some of the most enjoyable people in the world to be around. They are usually well educated; have traveled; they are fun and interested in many subjects. There is nothing more enjoyable than talking with people over a great bottle of wine and delicious food. It makes life whole and satisfying."

Paul admits that another great pleasure is converting beer drinkers to wine drinkers. "You know that Texas was primarily a beer drinking state in the past," smiles Paul, "and it still is to some extent, but you would be amazed at how many people, especially young people in their twenties are adopting wine. This is a good thing!"

MICHAEL BROWNE, WINEMAKER FOR KOSTA BROWNE

Michael Browne grew up in Washington state with dreams of becoming an architect, but when he moved to Sonoma County in his early twenties he became enamored with food and wine. Obtaining a job as a waiter at Equus Restaurant to help pay the bills, he was fascinated by the magic that happened when the right wine was paired with an exquisite dish. Michael was mentored by the head chef and sommelier at Equus and encouraged to visit many local wineries and vineyards during his free time. It was during this process that Michael realized his dream was to be an architect of fine wines.

EDUCATION AND TRAINING

"Once I realized that I wanted to be a winemaker," says Michael, "I immediately threw myself into the process. I read every winemaking book I could get my hands on. I visited as many wineries and vineyards as I could, and when a new job came open at John Ash, I decided to apply because I knew I wanted to be immersed in more opportunities to match food and fine wines."

Michael started as a waiter at John Ash, assisted in the kitchen, and then was promoted to sommelier. It was during this formative period that he met fellow waiter and colleague Dan Kosta, and became enchanted with Pinot Noir. "It is such an amazing grape," he enthuses. "It can take on so many forms. It is very challenging to grow and craft into a wine; but it can be incredibly rewarding when it all comes together. Dan and I began to taste as many Pinot Noirs as possible to understand the amazing range this grape can achieve.

"Then I was fortunate enough to meet Robert Rex of Deerfield Ranch. He was willing to let me work part-time in the cellar and learn the basics of winemaking. After a year of volunteer work, he gave me a job as assistant winemaker. I learned so much in those formative years, through both mistakes and successes. The most important lesson is that winemaking is a long-term craft. It is like learning to play an instrument. You don't just learn it in a year or two. It is a lifelong process. In fact when I had dinner with Aubert de Villane of Domaine Romanee Conti recently—a winery that has been making some of the most prestigious burgundies in the world for over 500 years—he told me that he believes it takes two consecutive lifetimes to be a good winemaker. I most humbly agree, and am honored to learn something new with each harvest."

After a couple vintages with Deerfield Ranch, Michael and Dan scraped together enough tip money to buy some excellent Russian River Valley Pinot Noir and do a couple of barrels of their own wine through a custom-crush operation. When the first batch turned out rather well, they did it again and again, until eventually they obtained a permit to sell their Pinot Noir. In 2001, they partnered with Chris Costello who helped them craft a business plan to grow. It started with marketing to local restaurants, retail shops, and direct to consumer via a mailing list and the Internet. In 2004, Kosta Browne received a 92-point rating and a very favorable write-up from the **Wine Spectator.** Since then, their wines have soared to the tops of the chart, ranking #7 in the world in the **Wine Spectator** December 2006 issue of the top 100 wines. Today they have a customer waitlist of which other wineries can only dream.

MOST IMPORTANT SKILLS FOR WINEMAKERS

When asked about the most important skills for winemakers, Michael is very clear about what matters: "The grape quality always comes first. It is critical to learn about viticulture; how to work in partnership with growers; and to understand how to harvest at optimum maturity. Without quality grapes, you cannot make a high quality wine.

"Next in importance," says Michael, "is learning the skills to insure a healthy fermentation. It is important to have the winemaking knowledge that allows you to make the necessary adjustments to the grapes before fermentation. You must be able to measure acid, pH, sugar, tannins, phenolics, and all of the other variables that go into making a good wine. This is the hard part, because it takes many vintages to experience all of the variables that Mother Nature may bring. That is why winemaking is a long-term craft."

MOST CHALLENGING ASPECT OF THE JOB

"For me, bottling is one of the most challenging aspects of the job. It is very important, but very stressful, because all of the work you've done over the last few years to craft the wine could be damaged if it isn't handled carefully during bottling. We use a mobile bottling line, and there are always *so many different issues to consider. If one small part is not working or is missing, the whole operation must stop. It is so critical to protect the wines from oxygen, too much movement, variations in temperature and other elements. The whole process of bottling is important, but unnerving."*

BEST PART OF THE JOB

"The best part of the job is harvest and crush. It is like the birth of a child. The grapes come in from the vineyard, and as the winemaker, you are there to insure that they are carefully handled and made ready for fermentation. Then the grapes become wine, and as the winemaker, it is your job to craft the new wine into a high-quality final product," says Michael. *"That involves blending, which is also a lot of fun. It is very creative. Finally, I really enjoy just being in the cellar doing cellar work, such as topping the wines; taking measurements; making adjustments; and just being there as the wine evolves into its new and very special state."*

70

Working in the Vineyard

*Hey, you should be thanking us for improving
your cluster-to-leaf balance.*

Chapter 4

ntranced by the beauty of the vineyard and looking for a job where you can spend a lot of time outdoors and close to nature? If so, a position in viticulture may be just the job for you. Vineyard positions require knowledge of viticulture and long hours during harvest, pruning season, and other times of the year where the vines need special attention. These types of jobs also call for a strong farming instinct and the ability to accept the give and take of Mother Nature in terms of sun, rain, hail, frost, fog, and other weather patterns over which you have no control. Yet the beauty of the vineyard and its changing shape and colors through the season can be very inspirational— especially when you realize that your efforts are paying off in healthy vines and a bountiful harvest.

So how do you get a job in viticulture, and what types of positions are available? This chapter describes the various jobs in a vineyard, and the skills and education needed to become a vineyard manager. In addition, it explains the interaction between vineyard owners and wineries, as well as the difference between winery-owned vineyards and independent vineyard operations. Descriptions of the various vineyard management systems are also provided, including traditional vineyard management techniques, as well as organic, biodynamic, and integrated pest management (IPM). Finally, this chapter includes tips on how to get started, helpful resources, job hunting strategies, and advice from vineyard experts and owners.

JOB DESCRIPTION FOR A VITICULTURIST/VINEYARD MANAGER

Simply speaking, a viticulturist is someone who practices viticulture, and usually has received some training or formal education in viti-culture. However, there are many grape growers or vineyard owners around the world who practice viticulture because they own or inher-ited a vineyard and may or may not have formal training. Following are general responsibilities for a vineyard manager position:

- Monitor the vineyards on a daily basis.
- Organize all farming operations including pest control, cover crop, spraying, fertilizing etc.
- Oversee and manage the full and part-time vineyard crew, including training, scheduling, and performance management.
- Create and implement a vineyard plan and budget for the year including pruning, harvest, and all daily vineyard maintenance issues.
- Oversee quality control and inspection systems.
- Communicate with vineyard customers and other visiting clients.
- Work in partnership with the winemaking team.
- Prepare weekly and/or monthly reports on vineyard operation progress and issues.

SKILL AND EDUCATION REQUIREMENTS

In order to obtain a position as a vineyard manager or viticulturist, you must be able to verify that you are able to perform the essential duties described above. In addition, most companies will require that you have prior experience working in a vineyard and managing others. Specifically, they will look for:

- Viticulture knowledge, including vineyard growing techniques, trellis systems, both cordon and cane pruning, suckering, training vines, pest and disease monitoring and control, disease prevention (such as eutypa), irrigation systems, fertilization, rootstocks and clone knowledge, and familiarity with federal, state, and county regulations.
- Good mechanical and maintenance skills for farming equipment.

- Sensory techniques for crop evaluation, including tasting and measurement of acids, pH, sugars, tannins, and phenolic ripeness.
- Computer knowledge including email, Internet research, word-processing, database management, and scheduling software.
- General management skills such as goal setting, training, performance management, labor law knowledge, and motivational techniques.
- Other requirements may include Pest Control Certification, specific equipment certification, and/or basic Spanish.

In addition, most large vineyard operations or winery-operated vineyard prefer a Bachelor's degree from a four-year college in viticulture, agriculture, or a related field such as horticulture or geology. Most of the major universities which provide winemaking degrees also offer degrees in viticulture:

- CSU Fresno, California
- UC Davis, California
- Cornell University, New York
- Oregon State University, Oregon
- Texas A&M University, Texas

There are also outstanding university programs outside of the US, especially in France, Italy, Spain, Australia, South Africa, and other large wine-producing nations.

Finally, there are some excellent programs which offer Associate's degrees or certificates in Viticulture. For example, community colleges near winemaking regions, such as Napa Valley College and Santa Rosa Community College in California, offer such degrees.

THE VINEYARD CAREER LADDER

Figure 1 illustrates the most common career levels in a vineyard. Most people gain experience in the vineyard by working as a harvest intern or part-time worker, which involves assisting with sugar samples and the actual harvest. This is because during harvest, many more hands are required to support the process. This is the case even in operations where mechanical harvesters are used, because employees are still needed to help with the loading, transport, sorting, and coordinating the harvest operations. In some countries, such as the US, many seasonal workers are hired—usually from Mexico—to help with the harvest and pruning operations. In many cases, the same workers return to the vineyard year after year and their skills and knowledge are much valued.

Full-time vineyard workers are usually employed by larger vineyard operations. Their job is to monitor and implement vineyard management programs on a year-round basis. In the winter they focus on pruning and fertilizing the vines; in the spring they are kept busy with suckering, pest and weed control, and sulfur spraying to control powdery mildew. During the summer, they monitor the grapes for verasion (changing color from green to pale green or red/purple), do cluster thinning and leaf pulling, as well as to continue to control for pests, disease, and weeds. However, the autumn is the busiest season because when harvest arrives many workers are called upon to work ten and twelve hour days. **The part-time or seasonal workers** also help, but many hands are needed to conduct sugar samples and then prepare to pick the grapes at the exact time they reach the correct ripeness level for the vineyard clients. In small family-owned vineyards, the owners will often recruit family and neighbors to assist with harvest.

Figure 1: The Vineyard Career Ladder

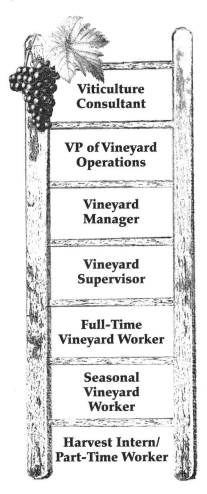

Most vineyards employ either a **vineyard supervisor or manager.** If it is a small vineyard, usually one person assumes this role. It can even be the vineyard owner. For larger vineyard operations, there is usually one supervisor to oversee several vineyard blocks. The supervisor coordinates and oversees vineyard work for both part-time and full-time employees. He/she may report to a vineyard manager who has the responsibility for multiple vineyard blocks. Each set of blocks may have one supervisor and up to thirty crew members during harvest. As described above, the vineyard manager is responsible for overseeing all work in the vineyards.

For large winery or vineyard corporations, a position of **vice president of vineyard operations** is usually created. This person operates at a strategic level and works with other top level executives to implement company strategy regarding the short and long-term plans for the vineyards. For example, there may be long-term plans to graft over to another varietal because one of the current varietals is no longer as popular on the market. In addition, new vineyards may be planted or acquired, or older vineyards torn out and replaced. The VP of vineyard operations is in charge of making sure all of this work is implemented correctly by delegating to his/her vineyard managers. Finally, the VP is usually in charge of vineyard relations with non-company owned vineyards as well, and is responsible for ensuring that farming operations are implemented according to the contract.

At the top rung of the vineyard career ladder is the role of the **viticulture consultant.** This person usually has many years of experience working in vineyards and often has a graduate degree, such as a Master's or Ph.D., in viticulture or a related field. They are usually an expert in solving vineyard issues with pests, disease, and weed control, and can also recommend technology or other solutions that will help the vineyard become healthier and produce higher quality crops.

WINERY-OWNED VINEYARDS VERSUS INDEPENDENT VINEYARD OPERATIONS

It is important to recognize that there are two major types of vineyard operations—those owned by wineries and those that are independently operated by a vineyard owner who sells his/her grapes to a winery or other agent. **Winery-owned vineyards** are usually farmed in a very specific way to meet the needs of the winery. For example, if the winery specializes in Cabernet Sauvignon, the majority of the vineyards will most likely be planted in this varietal and farmed to exacting standards—such as 1.5 tons to the acre, with only the top quality fruit going into the wine. Substandard fruit may be sold to other wineries or used in a less expensive brand. Usually winery-owned vineyards are larger and have a more formal organization structure which includes a vineyard manager, supervisors, and full and part-time employees.

There are thousands of **independently-owned vineyard operations** around the world, with many of them being so small that the vineyard owner assumes the role of vineyard manager and does all of the work, with perhaps some help from part-time workers or friends. The vineyards may be as small as two acres. Very large independent vineyard operations with hundreds of acres, such as Vino Farms in California, have more formal structures with many employees covering all levels in the vineyard career ladder, as well as support functions in administration and marketing/sales. Both types of operations usually farm their grapes according to a contract they have received from a winery. Contracts are usually three to five years in length and describe how the vineyard should be farmed—ranging from how often to drop grape clusters to picking at the correct sugar (brix) level for harvest. The winery will then pay the vineyard owner when the grapes are delivered. If the vineyard owner doesn't have a contract, then he/she must sell their grapes on the open market or with the help of a grape brokerage firm.

MAJOR TYPES OF VITICULTURE

If you are considering a job in viticulture, it is useful to understand the five major types of viticulture that are used throughout the world today. Following are basic descriptions of each of these types of viticulture.

- **Conventional Viticulture:** Vineyard management techniques that are organized around a farming schedule with set timeline for irrigation, fertilizers, pesticides, and other conventional agro-chemicals.

- **Integrated Pest Management (IPM) or Lutte Raisonée:** A vineyard management systems that promotes "monitoring" the vineyard to determine if pesticides, fertilizers, irrigation, and other human intervention is needed. It doesn't depend on calendar-based spraying like conventional viticulture, but adapts to the unique needs of the vineyard depending on the weather, pests, predators or other issues. Then decisions are made with an emphasis on reducing agro-chemicals if possible while still maintaining the health and economic viability of the vineyard. Lutte raisonée is the French term for "reasoned struggle" to describe this farming philosophy.

- **Organic Viticulture:** Vineyard management techniques that do not include the use of any unnatural substance within the vineyard. Therefore all conventional agro-chemicals are banned from the vineyard, but natural substances such as sulfur can still be sprayed on the vines. According to USDA guidelines a vineyard that produces "certified organically grown grapes" must be inspected by a government-approved certifier who inspects the vineyard to verify they have produced the grapes without using most conventional pesticides, sewage sludge or petroleum based fertilizers; ionizing radiation; or bioengineering.

- **Biodynamic Viticulture:** Based on the work of Rudolph Steiner, biodynamics views each vineyard as a living organism which can maintain itself if the soil and environment is nursed back to its natural condition before man intervened with chemicals and other unnatural systems. Viewed by some as an extreme form of viticulture, it involves farming according to the rhythms of the earth, such as planting new vines or pruning when the moon is descending. Biodynamics also includes preparing and administering field sprays made with cow manure, ground quartz and herbs to bring the soil back into balance, and using beneficial insects. Demeter Association, an independent international certifier of biodynamic farming practices, is usually called to validate biodynamic practices. Wine brands such as Benzinger and Grigch Hills in the US, as well as the famous Domaine Leroy and LeFlaive from Burgundy and Coulée de Serrant of the Loire are just a few of the wineries that are distinguishing themselves with biodynamic labeling.

- **Sustainable Viticulture:** An array of vineyard management techniques that attempt to preserve the environment and are socially responsible, while at the same time providing economic viability in the vineyard. In most cases, sustainable vineyards adopt IPM methods, but may also use organic viticulture programs at times. There is also an emphasis on treating workers well and collaborating with the local community. Some vineyard regions have adopted "Codes" of sustainable winegrowing to evaluate themselves. The Lodi Grape Growers Association in California is a good example of a group that has done this well.

TIPS ON GETTING STARTED

The best way to get started on your viticulture career is to gain some experience and knowledge in the subject. Many people think they would enjoy working in the vineyard until they try it and realize how much work it really is. A vineyard always needs to be tended. You cannot go on vacation anytime you want, but must monitor the cycles of the vine to make sure the vineyard is protected from bad weather, pests, diseases, weeds, and other issues. However gaining vineyard experience is not that difficult. Following are a few tips on getting started:

- Volunteer as a part-time worker in a vineyard or apply for a job as a harvest intern. With these types of positions you can receive some basic training and hands-on experience which will tell you if working in the vineyard is the right job for you.
- Read books on viticulture *(see list on pp. 83 and 84).*
- Attend viticulture classes at your local community college.
- Attend viticulture conferences and seminars *(see list on pp. 83 and 84).*
- Schedule and conduct an informational interview with a local vineyard owner. Call and ask permission to meet with them and tour the vineyard. They can provide valuable information on the pros/cons of owning and working in a vineyard.
- Purchase and plant a few grape vines in your backyard. Tending them will teach you much about the cycles of the vine.
- Attend a winemaker's boot camp which includes a vineyard segment.

HELPFUL CONFERENCES, BOOKS, AND WEBSITES

In addition to gaining vineyard experience, there are many useful resources to help you learn about viticulture on your own. Following is a partial list of some of the viticulture conferences, books, and websites that will help you get started.

Viticulture Conferences/Seminars

- **American Society of Enology & Viticulture Conference:** Academic conference on viticulture and winemaking. Held each summer in various locations.
- **Grape Growing Regional Seminars:** Most grape growing regions have a local association that hosts viticulture conferences. Identify a specific wine region in which you are interested and conduct a search on the web to find their association website. Most will list local conferences and seminars.
- **Unified Wine & Grape Symposium:** Largest wine conference in the US. Held each January in Sacramento, California. Includes three days of special tracks on viticulture.
- **University Viticulture Conferences:** Most of the major agriculture universities in grape growing regions, such as Brock University in Canada, Cornell in New York, and CSU Fresno in California, hold annual viticulture conferences.
- **Vineyard Economics Symposium:** Review of economics issues in vineyards in California. Held each Spring.

Books on Viticulture

- *A Winegrower's Guide* by Philip Wagner: A practical guide on how to grow wine grapes.
- *Biodynamic Wine, Demystified* by Nicolas Joly
- *From Vines to Wines: The Complete Guide to Growing Grapes and Making Your Own Wine* by Jeff Cox
- *General Viticulture* by A. J. Winkler, James A. Cook, W. M.
- *The Grape Grower: A Guide to Organic Viticulture* by Lon J. Rombough

- ***Northern WineWork: Growing Grapes and Making Wine in Cold Climates*** by Thomas A. Plocher and Robert J. Parke
- ***Sunlight Into Wine: A Handbook for Wine Grape Canopy Arrangement*** by Richard Smart and Mike Robinson
- ***Vineyards in the Watershed: Sustainable Winegrowing in Napa County*** by Juliane Poirer

Helpful Websites

- **http://www.avf.org/:** American Vineyard Foundation website
- **http://www.agricultureinformation.com/directory/Useful_Resources/Discussion_Forums/:** Online discussion forum for grape growers
- **http://www.asev.org:** Website of the American Society for Enology and Viticulture. Helpful information on both viticulture and winemaking
- **www.brocku.ca/ccovi/:** Website of the Cool Climate Oenology and Viticulture Institute at Brock University in Canada
- **http://www.montpellier.inra.fr/:** Center for Research in Viticulture and Oenology at Montpellier, France.
- **http://www.oiv.int/uk/accueil/index.php:** Organization of International Vine and Wine, headquartered in Paris, France.
- **http://www.practicalwinery.com/:** Magazine for grape growers and winery owners.
- **http://wineserver.ucdavis.edu/:** Link to UC Davis Department of Viticulture and Enology, describing their programs and online resources.

JOB HUNTING STRATEGIES

If you don't have any viticulture experience, the best way to get started is to volunteer to work a harvest. This way you can get experience with basic viticulture work such as obtaining sugar samples and picking grapes. However this type of work is only seasonal and won't pay the bills over the long haul. Therefore, unless you are going to manage your own vineyard, you will most likely need to obtain a certificate or degree in viticulture in order to get a full-time job in one of the larger vineyard corporations or a winery with vineyard operations. Once you've obtained a full-time job then you can work your way up the vineyard career ladder.

Installing and managing your own vineyard is another option. Though it will call for an upfront investment and a minimum of three years before you will have a crop to sell, you can still begin your viticulture career in this fashion. Keep in mind that tending a vineyard is a lot of work and you will most likely have to hire a part-time crew to help you, but managing your own vineyard can be quite rewarding. This is especially the case if you are in an appellation that has strong market appeal and have planted grape varietals that have a good market demand. In general, in order to obtain financing to plant a vineyard, most banks will require that you have a marketing strategy and one or two grape-selling contracts in place with local wineries, as well as crop insurance to protect you against inclement weather and other issues.

ADVICE FROM VINEYARDS EXPERTS

Following are excerpts of interview with three vineyard experts who each entered the field of viticulture using different strategies. Their stories and advice are very useful in helping you to understand the various ways in which you can enter and work in a vineyard operation.

True Tales from the Wine Industry

GORDON PEACOCK, OWNER AND GENERAL MANAGER OF PEACOCK VINEYARDS

Gordon grew up in North Carolina with no premonition that someday he would develop and farm Peacock Vineyards on Sonoma Mountain in the Sonoma Coast appellation. Indeed for the first thirty years of his career he was a medical doctor and didn't even purchase the land on which he would plant his vineyard until 1995. Today Gordon is retired from his first career and is a successful small vineyard owner of two acres of ultra-premium grapes which he sells to boutique wineries and hobby winemakers.

EDUCATION AND TRAINING

"My medical school training provided some of the background in biology and chemistry," says Gordon, "but most of my vineyard education came from reading books and attending seminars." Gordon attended a series of vineyard seminars and short courses at UC Davis, University of Santa Cruz Extension, and through the Sonoma County Grape Growers Association. "Most of the classes were one to two days in length, with the longest being one semester," says Gordon. "I also took hands-on courses in how to prune a vineyard."

The impetus for his second career as a vineyard owner started in 1996, one year after he bought the land and house on top of Sonoma Mountain. "When I first bought the property," explains Gordon, "I had no plans to develop a vineyard. However my wife and I had some good friends in Kentfield who had planted a backyard hobby vineyard. They were so enthusiastic about it that we thought we would give it a try. So in 1997 we planted 115 Chardonnay vines. I had so much fun with those vines that the next year we planted another 250, and then I was addicted and just couldn't stop. Today we have 1,100 vines on two acres that produce around 2.5 tons per acre. We are still quite small as a vineyard, but the grapes we produce are very high quality."

In addition to Chardonnay, Gordon and his wife, Lois, planted Pinot Noir, Syrah, and Cabernet Sauvignon. All of the varietals are doing well, but the Pinot Noir is most popular with the wineries. "Originally, I wasn't planning to sell the grapes," Gordon reports, "but through networking at events sponsored by the Sonoma County Grape Growers, I have met some people who are interested in buying my grapes. Now we have repeat customers."

Gordon also makes homemade wine for friends and family. At this time he has no desire to obtain a permit to make commercial wine. "My joy is in the vineyard," says Gordon with a big smile on his face. "It is therapeutic to work amongst these beautiful vines. I know each and every one of them."

MOST IMPORTANT SKILLS FOR VITICULTURE

"In addition to obtaining the basic knowledge about viti-culture—which anyone can do by attending classes and reading books—I believe the most important skill is vineyard planning," says Gordon. "I think too many people, including myself, jump into planting vines without enough information.

For example, I should have conducted a soil analysis and ripped the soil before planting the vines. I probably should have paid more attention to the clones, rather than just the varietals and rootstocks.

"Vineyard maintenance is very important," continues Gordon, "and I find that I can't fit my mower between all of the rows, because I planted some of them too close. Though everything works fine, I also think I should have done more research on trellis systems. So you see," concludes Gordon, "I think there are a lot of strategic planning skills that go into vineyard design which people should realize before planting their own vineyard."

MOST CHALLENGING ASPECT OF THE JOB

"The most challenging part for me is disease management," states Gordon. "It is very difficult to discover you have a small patch of powdery mildew growing in part of the vineyard. It is the main disease we have in Northern California, and even though we use sulfur and other preventative measures, it still happens occasionally. Then you may lose some crop. Staying on top of it is critical, and that means spending time in the vineyard most everyday." When asked to provide an estimate of the amount of time he spends working in the vineyard, Gordon replied that it probably averaged out to around two hours per day.

BEST PART OF THE JOB

"The best part of the job" says Gordon, "is producing a high quality crop with grapes that are well-balanced in sugar, acid, pH, and phenolics. It is very rewarding to see and taste the end product." His 2005 Pinot Noir recently won a gold medal at the Sonoma County Harvest Fair.

"Another benefit," reports Gordon, "is the joy of spending time outdoors in the vineyard. It may seem strange to say, but working in a vineyard can be very therapeutic. It is peaceful out there with the vines around you, the sound of the birds, and maybe a light breeze—plus the view from Sonoma Mountain out towards the western hills and valleys. You know you are close to the earth and nature, and you feel part of it all in the vineyard. You have a role that is important in helping the vineyard grow and be healthy.

"Finally," says Gordon, "an unexpected benefit is how much my palate has improved now that I've owned this vineyard. I am always tasting the grapes to see how they are maturing. I then taste them in the wines we make, and I am now more skilled at differentiating flavors in grapes and wine. So, you see, there are many benefits to owning and managing a small vineyard."

PAUL DOLAN,
CEO, MENDOCINO WINE COMPANY

Known as the "Godfather of Organic & Biodynamic Viticulture in the US," Paul Dolan is a world-renown expert on the topic and a strong component of sustainable farming practices to protect the environment. As a member of a fourth generation winemaking family, Paul felt the lure of the vine from an early age. "My great grandfather came from Genoa, Italy, in

1881 and helped start the Italian Swiss Colony winery north of San Francisco. He was also known to give away grape-vines and growing contracts to many farmers in Mendocino County where my company is headquartered today. Since my earliest years, wine and vineyards have always been part of the conversation in my family."

EDUCATION AND TRAINING

Even though he grew up in Oakland, CA, Paul knew from a young age that he wanted to work in the vineyards and make wine. However, he decided to obtain some business background first, so he obtained a B.S. in Finance from Santa Clara University, and then spent three years in the military. After that he enrolled at CSU-Fresno to pursue his dream, and obtained an M.S. in Food Science with a viticulture/enology focus. Upon graduation, he immediately went to work as a winemaker at Fetzer Winery in Mendocino County where he spent fifteen years. During this time he became CEO and helped to grow the winery from 30,000 cases to over 2 million when it became part of Brown-Foreman in 1992.

"My viticulture and enology education were very useful for the job," says Paul, "but learning about organic and bio-dynamic was self-taught. It basically started one day in the vineyard when I was tasting Sauvignon Blanc grapes from different blocks. One block tasted much better than the others, and I discovered that it was being farmed organically whereas the others were farmed with traditional methods using pesticides, chemical fertilizers and other man-made products. I was amazed at the difference in quality and taste of the organic grapes, so we began doing some experiments with UC Davis. Over the years and through reading many

books, networking with experts, and trial and error, we developed some very effective and cost-efficient methods to grow grapes both organically and biodyamically."

When asked to define these two types of viticulture techniques, Paul states, "Farming organically is a systems approach where you pay attention to the interconnectivity of things. Your primary purpose is to build the health of the soil, so that it can express itself. In order to do this, you stop using artificial pesticides and similar products, and instead use methods such as cover crops, beneficial insects, and deficient irrigation. It is an ongoing process with ongoing learning, but the results are amazing. The grapes have more concentrated flavors for winemaking and the vines actually produce larger crops, but of higher quality.

"Biodynamic farming uses similar approaches," says Paul, "but incorporates more of a spiritual aspect and connection with the land. It includes the development of natural fertilizers to help balance the soil, and certain farming practices are governed by lunar cycles—very similar to the Old Farmer's Almanac. Biodynamic farming takes a little more time and is more complex than organic. In order for a vineyard to be biodynamic, it needs to be a special piece of property so it can express its 'ego.' Like children, vines need a good environment and nutrients to grow. Our responsibility as wine grape growers is nurturing the environment so the vines and grapes can express themselves."

MOST IMPORTANT SKILLS FOR VITICULTURE

When asked about the most important skills for a viticulturist or wine grape grower, Paul said that obtaining a solid background and knowledge of viticulture practices is im-

portant. "There are many excellent university and community college programs that can provide viticulture knowledge," states Paul.

When it comes to specific knowledge about organic and biodynamic winegrowing, however, it is more difficult. "As yet, there is still no formal degree program in this area," reports Paul. "But people can learn about it by reading books on the subject. Many local grape grower associations also offer seminars and information on the topic. Another method to obtain knowledge in this area is by networking with people who are doing organic and biodynamic viticulture, and if possible, working in the vineyards with them."

"In the end," says Paul, "the most important skill is a passion for the land and a curiosity to learn about how to grow better quality wine grapes. I always like to differentiate between the terms grape grower and winegrower. The former is usually someone who is focused on producing the largest quantity of grapes for economic gain, whereas the winegrower is focused on creating the best quality grapes for the wine."

MOST CHALLENGING ASPECT OF THE JOB

"I think for most people the most challenging part is giving up the past," muses Paul. "This is because many vineyard owners have been farming the same way for a long time. They are used to using pesticides to control weeds, irrigating on set schedules, and other traditional farming methods. It can be uncomfortable to let that all go and embrace organic or biodynamic methods. It is really a process of exploration.

"Another issue has to do with the increased amount of time you need to spend in the vineyards. Though organic and *biodynamic farming doesn't cost any more than traditional, it does require you to be more vigilant in the vineyards. You have to spend more time managing under the vine and using special mowers and cover crops to control weeds. However, once you see and taste the results, you realize how much better this method is."*

BEST PART OF THE JOB

"The best part of the job" says Paul, "is knowing that you are producing a better quality product—and you will be able to taste that quality in the grape and in the wine. It is for that reason that you can often sell your organic or biodynamic grapes for a higher price." He pauses and a smile lights up his face. "But the most satisfying part is knowing that you are making the grapes and the environment healthier. There is great satisfaction in this, because you know you are living in integrity and respect with yourself and the environment. You are contributing to the world in a good way."

LUCIE MORTON, INTERNATIONAL VITICULTURE CONSULTANT, VIRGINIA

As one of the most respected viticulture consultants in the world, Lucie Morton was first introduced to grapes as a child on her grandparents' farm in King George, Virginia on the banks of the Potomac River. "They had a lovely garden planting

of Concords, Caco, and Niagara planted in the late 1920's," says Lucie. *"Allegedly, it was in response to Prohibition, but more likely for the fresh fruit and jams it would provide."* When her parents moved to the farm in the late 1960s, they asked Lucie if she would be willing to manage the family farm. *"Since I had just graduated from college in a big city,"* reports Lucie, *"and had discovered that I preferred life in the country, I welcomed the opportunity.*

EDUCATION AND TRAINING

Lucie admits that in the beginning she didn't have formal training in viticulture. "With a Bachelor of Arts degree and very little viticulture knowledge," says Lucie, "I naively oversaw the planting of 1800 vines — eight selected French-American varieties plus an undisclosed nursery "bonus" of two more hybrids and ungrafted Zinfandel. It was exhausting and sweaty work, and it soon became apparent to me that blindly following viticultural dictums from A Wine-Growers Guide *was not going to offer sufficient guidance for a commercial venture."*

Lucie then began investigating universities to pursue a post-graduate degree. "Neither UC Davis nor Cornell had programs that seemed to fit our situation of wanting to make European style wines in Virginia, so Europe seemed like a better choice," reports Lucie. "By a wonderful set of circumstances, I landed at the Viticulture Department of the Ecole Nationale Superieure d"Agriculture Montpellier as a student of a great team of teachers and researchers including Jean Branas, Pierre Galet, Francois Champenol and Denis Boubals. Even better was being selected to participate with the French, Swiss, Spanish, and Italian students in a seven month graduate program where our teachers were the leading European research scientists. The travels and academic rigor of that time forever shaped my appreciation for the diversity and complexity of viticulture even within a relatively small locale. I learned (and am still learning) that to be successful, winegrowers must embrace and balance a triad of tradition, art and science."

MOST IMPORTANT SKILLS FOR VITICULTURE

Lucie concurs that viticulture requires a variety of skills. "I think some of the most important skills in the vineyard are being observant, curious, and informed," says Lucie. "My ampelography training taught me to really see vines—not just look at them, but see what is there. Then you need to figure out what the vines are telling you. There are so many variables and changes that occur over a season and over the years."

Lucie also recommends staying up to date with the latest research and practices in viticulture. "I get at least five US trade magazines, two foreign journals, and have been a member of the American Society of Enology and Viticulture (ASEV) for over thirty years," states Lucie. "In fact, I still go back over old issues when I want to review research literature on a specific topic."

Finally, Lucie recommends getting to know other people in the industry, both in the US and abroad. "I think it is very important to have a good network, or 'grapevine,' of colleagues with whom to exchange experiences and ideas. It's nice to be able to pick up the phone or send an email and get a different point of view or suggestion from a good friend in another vineyard location."

MOST CHALLENGING ASPECT OF THE JOB

"Working in the vineyard can mean long sweaty hours, and the potential of disease or weather that can destroy a crop," says Lucie. *"It is a reality of farm work, and that is why you always have to be observant and set-up smart practices and contingency plans to deal with these issues. Since I focus on sustainability and quality in the vineyard, I am concerned that my clients find the right enological path for their grapes because it is not fun to see lovely grapes treated poorly."*

BEST PART OF THE JOB

"I enjoy the challenge of solving problems and achieving goals," says Lucie. *"In my case, I focus on all the issues surrounding sustainability with the goal of achieving the desired wine quality. Once you've planted a well-designed vineyard with the right plant material and trained a good team, then you move on to what I call the 'fine-tuning' stage. Fine-tuning in my work means tasting wines and analyzing what more you can do in the vineyard to make the wines you hope for."*

Lucie also admits that another aspect of her work that she enjoys is consulting in viticulture and educating others through articles, books, and seminars. Indeed, she has published more than twenty articles on viticulture and three books: Roots for Fine Wine: Rootstock Selection Beyond Phylloxera; Winegrowing in Eastern America; *and* A Practical Ampelography.

Wine Marketing, Sales & Public Relations for a Winery

You paid three goats for this? Robertus Parkerus only rated it LXXIV.

Chapter 5

ine marketing and sales is considered by many in the wine industry to be one of the most crucial functions for winery success. This is because you can make a high-quality wine, but if you can't market it well and convince people to buy it, then the long-term sustainability of your winery is at risk. This is even more true today in our highly competitive global wine market with more than 10,000 wine labels for sale in the US and thousands more in other wine countries that have not yet been exported. Therefore, developing an expertise in wine marketing, sales and public relations can be a lucrative career choice.

So how do you obtain a job with a winery in their marketing, sales or PR departments? First, it is important to gain an understanding of the different sales channels for wine, which is why this chapter begins with a big picture overview of how sales and marketing works in the US wine industry, as well as some information on the international aspects.

BIG PICTURE OVERVIEW OF WINE MARKETING & SALES

Since wine is an alcoholic beverage, the production, distribution, and sale of wine is regulated in most every country in the world. Some countries, such as Canada and Sweden, have implemented government agencies to sell wine. Other countries, such as the US, give each State the right to determine how wine sales will be regulated; whereas countries with more open wine markets, such as the UK and Australia, allow direct negotiation between winery, retailer and consumer. Because of this, there are different wine laws and regulations in different countries, states, and even some counties in the US, which have decided to remain "dry" and not allow any alcohol sales. It is for this reason that wine marketing and sales can often be quite complex for newcomers to the industry. However, in general, there are four major sales channels for wine. These are illustrated in Figure 1.

Figure 1: Four Major Wine Sales Channels

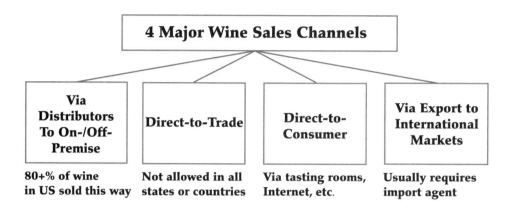

It is important for anyone desiring to enter wine marketing and sales to have a basic understanding of how these four channels work, as the job functions, skills, and experience for each channel are quite different. Some of these are described in more detail in other chapters.

Wine sales via a distributor is the most common method to sell wine in the US, with more than 80% of the wine sold in this fashion. This is because many states have laws requiring that wineries sell wine to distributors, rather than directly to trade establishments such as restaurants, wine shops, and grocery stores. This is referred to as the three-tier system, with the first tier being the winery, the second tier the distributor, and the third tier the retailer *(See figure 2)*. The other reason is that many wineries prefer to work with distributors, because the distributor usually manages all of the logistics of transporting wine from the winery to the retailer, and also assists with tax reporting, marketing, and has a network of contacts to help sell the wine.

In the three-tier system, retailers sell wine in both on- and off-premise establishments. On-premise refers to trade accounts in which the wine is consumed "on the premise." Therefore, restaurants, hotels, wine bars, and cruise ships fit this category. Off-premise includes all

Figure 2: Three Tier System

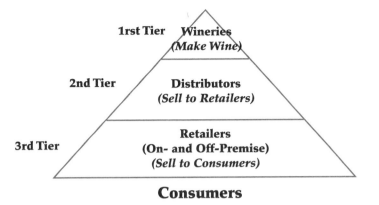

trade accounts in which the consumer purchases the wine and takes it "off premise" to be consumed. Grocery stores, wine shops, and retail establishments such as Costco and Beverages & More fit this category.

Direct-to-trade is the channel in which wineries are allowed to sell directly to on- and off-premise establishments. As previously mentioned, this is not permissible in every country or state. However, where it is allowed, such as in California, winery sales reps will call on restaurants and retail stores to sell wine, and will often contract with transportation companies in order to deliver the wine. This is usually a more profitable channel for wineries as there is no "middle person," such as a distributor to take a portion of the profits. On the downside, it requires the winery to hire more personnel or consultants to service accounts. For a small winery, this may not be feasible, or they may need to limit the number of direct to trade accounts because they do not have the volume to support larger retailers.

The direct-to-consumer channel generally flows through tasting room sales, Internet sales, wine club, mailing lists, telemarketing, and special events at the winery or other location, such as a charity event. Direct-to-consumer is considered to be the most profitable channel for wineries, as there is no need to share part of the sales revenue with distributors or retailers. On the flipside, overhead costs—especially to run a tasting room—can be quite high. More information on this channel can be found in Chapter 6 "Direct-to-Consumer Sales at the Winery."

The fourth channel, **selling wine via export** to international markets, is another viable option for wineries who wish to establish their brands in other countries. In the US, the largest export markets are the UK, Germany, Canada, and Japan. Wine sales through export require a long-term commitment and strategic plan, as margins are often smaller in the beginning as the brand is getting established. Other logistical issues also must be considered, such as currency exchange rates, insurance, shipping, taxes, different labeling and compliance requirements. Finally, most countries require a winery to work with an import agent who can help distribute and sell the wine internationally. Therefore, identifying and building a trusting relationship with a good import partner is crucial.

PRICING, MARGINS AND PROFITS: WHICH CHANNEL?

Wine pricing is a very controversial topic in the industry. Obviously the wine needs to be priced at a point that will allow the winery to recoup material and production costs and also turn some sort of a profit. At the same time, the wine must be able to compete with others in its same category. Therefore, in general, if it is a low-priced wine of less than $10 it will usually be sold in a grocery store where the margins are much lower for the winery, distributor and retailer, but because it usually involves a very large volume of wine, profitability can be quite good. This is the way most popular branded wine is sold—via the distributor channel. However, if the wine is priced in the luxury or cult category, it will most likely be sold via mailing list, exclusive wine shops, or in a fine restaurant. Volume will be much lower, but margins will be higher, so profitability can also be high through these channels.

Determining which channels to use to sell wine is an important part of wine marketing strategy and should be determined at the executive team level within a winery. In most cases, larger wineries will have different brand categories and pricing so that they can participate in all four channels. Whereas, a small family run winery producing only 5,000 cases may choose to sell 100% direct-to-consumer.

It is also important to understand the general margin mark-ups by channel. In selling via distributors to on- or off-premise, the winery will first price the wine by case. This will include all of their costs, plus their profit margin. This is referred to as FOB, or Freight On Board. The case of wine is then sold to the distributor, who generally adds an additional 30% to the price, and in turn sells it to a retailer. If off-premise, an additional 30% is usually added and that will be the final cost to the consumer. If on-premise, the mark-up is usually higher—at least double the retail price in restaurants to help cover additional costs of services, glassware, etc.

In addition to margin, distributors will often negotiate case discounts with the winery and/or the retailers—or vice-versa. Sometimes distributors bundle wine and provide additional discounts or incentives for purchasing multiple brands. The whole process can get quite complex.

When a winery sells direct-to-consumer, they usually pocket the distributor and retailer mark-ups and sell for the same price as the wine would in a store, or perhaps with a small discount. This is because they do not want to undercut their distributors and retailers, as that would damage the relationship. At the same time, this allows them to increase profitability.

Therefore, depending on the size of the winery for which you work, you may be involved in selling to all four channels, or to just one or two. In large global wine corporations, they often have separate divisions to support each of the four channels. Understanding which customers you serve, margin and profitability levels, discounting practices, and common promotions is very important in succeeding in wine marketing and sales.

JOB DESCRIPTIONS FOR WINE MARKETING, SALES AND PUBLIC RELATIONS

Before jumping into job descriptions, it is helpful to begin with some basic definitions of wine marketing, sales and public relations. They are all related to one another, and must work closely together—however, they are quite distinctive functions.

Wine marketing can be defined as "the performance of business activities that direct the flow of wine from the winery to consumers." Some people refer to marketing as "preparing the ground," whereas sales is "harvesting the crop." Wine marketing is concerned with the marketing mix, or the Five P's of product, price, packaging, placement, and promotion. Marketing works closely with sales to obtain feedback on how well the marketing strategy and mix are working in different client accounts.

Figure 3: The Five P's of Wine Marketing

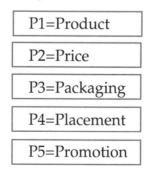

| P1=Product |
| P2=Price |
| P3=Packaging |
| P4=Placement |
| P5=Promotion |

Table 1: *Major Job Responsibilities in Winery Marketing, Sales & PR*

Wine Marketing	Wine Sales	Wine PR
• Based on winery strategy, prepare annual marketing plan for each wine brand/category with clear, measurable goals. • Determine specific marketing mix for each brand (Five P's), with special emphasis on placement in channels. • Create and monitor budget against goals. • Work in partnership with sales, PR, and wine production. • Monitor relationship building in key accounts. • Evaluate and measure progress against goals. • Conduct consumer research. • Assist in identifying new prospects for sales. • Stay abreast of competition in the industry.	• Build positive relationships with client base and distributors. • Engage in sales activities to meet sales quotas and long-term goals. • Service accounts, including resolution of any issues. • Prospect for new clients. • Assist marketing to implement new promotions within client base. • Manage depletions database. • Manage sales reporting processes. • Gather customer feedback and make suggestions to marketing. • Work in partnership with marketing, PR, winery production, and other sales reps. • Stay abreast of new developments in the industry.	• Assist in developing clear and positive winery mission, vision, and values to communicate to stakeholders. • Develop an annual PR plan with clear, measurable goals. • Identify opportunities to communicate to stakeholders about winery developments. • Prepare and distribute press releases as needed. • Develop positive relationships with wine writers, press, and other key constituents. • Develop charitable giving plan based on winery strategy. • Create and monitor budget. • Assist with event management. • Provide oversight for online communications, including website, blogs, vlogs, customer emails, etc.

Wine sales is the presentation of a winery's products and unique attributes for the purpose of making sales and building customer relationships. It is concerned with the following activities: prospecting, relationship-building, information gathering, selling, servicing, and communicating. People who work in wine sales also provide customer feedback to marketing about how well the Five P's are being implemented, and make improvement suggestions.

Public relations is a special subset of promotion, and one of the most important processes for small- to medium-sized wineries that may not have large marketing budgets. It can be defined as building good relationships with the winery's various stakeholders (customer, shareholders, community, press, wine writers, online, etc.) by obtaining positive publicity, managing unfavorable events, and creating a good corporate image.

Table 1 highlights some of the major responsibilities found in the job descriptions for a wine marketing rep, wine sales rep, or public relations representative.

SKILLS, EXPERIENCE AND EDUCATION REQUIREMENTS FOR WINE MARKETING

In speaking with wine marketing experts in both small and large wineries, the majority identify the following list of critical skills in order to succeed in the job:

1. Marketing Expertise: It is important to have some education, training, and or experience in marketing before you will be considered suitable for hire by a winery. Many wineries prefer to hire people who have worked a few years as a distributor, as they will be familiar with the wine industry and what is happening in the market. They will also understand how the Five P's of the marketing mix play out in on- and off-premise accounts, as well as the basics of marketing management and budgeting. In some companies, this may also include using marketing skills in online environments such as blogs, digital video, online advertising, and social networking sites.

2. Wine Industry Knowledge: Since wine is such a highly regulated product with multiple laws and issues in terms of production, distribution and sales, most wineries prefer to hire people who have a knowledge of how the wine industry works in the US with the three-tier system. If the job includes international wine marketing components, then familiarity with those markets is generally preferred.

3. Passion for Wine: Many experts say that without a passion for wine—and especially how it is made and tastes—that you cannot succeed in the wine industry.

4. Creativity & Innovation Skills: Marketing requires creativity and the ability to come up with new break-through ideas for wine promotions. However, creativity requires innovation, which is the ability to translate creative ideas into practical use. The most successful marketers can do both and are continually searching for ways in which they can differentiate their brand from the competition and achieve a sustainable advantage.

5. Excellent Written and Oral Communications: Even though a marketing rep may not be speaking face-to-face with customers every day, as is required in wine sales, excellent oral and written communications skills are still required. Wine marketing includes report writing, promotion development, and communication with other departments, consultants and vendors who support the marketing function.

6. Strategic Planning Skills: Wine marketers need high-level planning and visioning skills in order to create long-term marketing plans and goals, and then to track progress against goals.

7. Excellent Follow-Through Skills: Once the annual plan has been implemented, it is critical that marketing reps follow-up on all components, track results, make necessary revisions, and compare against budget.

8. Ability to Multi-Task: Most wineries require the marketing department to handle a large variety of job duties, and the ability to multi-task and work well with sales, PR, production, finance, and a multitude of external marketing suppliers, such as graphic designers, merchandisers, and promotion support consultants. Furthermore, in a small- to medium-sized winery, there may only be one person to manage all of the marketing, sales, and PR functions. This requires a high level of multi-tasking ability.

9. Marketing Management Skills: Many people don't realize how much report writing, budgeting, and general administrative work is required by marketing experts. The ability to handle all of the management portions of a wine marketing job, which includes human resource management when you move into higher levels, is very important.

In terms of experience, almost every winery requires prior wine marketing or sales experience before they will hire you. The easiest way to do this is to work for a wine distributor for a year or two (see Chapter 7 "Wine Marketing & Sales with a Distributor"). Occasionally some of the larger wineries will hire experienced brand marketing people from other industries. For entry-level marketing rep position, a few wineries will hire a recent college grad with a Bachelor's in Wine Business or Marketing. See the Tips on Getting Started section.

In terms of education, the majority of wineries require a minimum of a Bachelor's degree from a four-year college in Marketing, Wine Business, Sales, Management, or a related field. For those desiring to move higher up into the executive ranks of wine marketing, most firms prefer an MBA. Following is a representative career ladder for wine marketing in a larger winery.

Figure 4: Wine Marketing Career Ladder

SKILLS, EXPERIENCE AND EDUCATION
REQUIREMENTS FOR WINE SALES

In general, sales in any industry requires a different skill set than marketing, but there are some areas that overlap. In wine sales, most experts will agree that the following skills, experience, and education are very important for the job.

Required Experience

1. Sales Experience and Expertise: Not everyone can succeed in sales. It takes a certain type of personality to relish the challenge of interacting with customers everyday in order to build relationships and achieve the sale, as well as to handle rejection. This is especially true in wine sales, which can be very competitive. A knowledge of how to "do sales," including prospecting, understanding consumer needs, presenting the product, asking for and closing the sale, follow-up, etc. is mandatory.

2. Passion for Wine: A love of wine, with solid knowledge of how it is produced is very important to succeed in wine sales. In addition, the winery sales rep must be able to clearly articulate what makes his/her wine so unique compared to the competition. He/she must also be able to describe all varietals and/or brands within the winery portfolio.

3. Wine Industry Knowledge: Wine sales reps need to have an equally strong knowledge of the special nuances of the wine industry—just as wine marketing reps. Again, knowledge of competition, the three-tier systems, regulations, and staying up-to-date on new promotions as well as new product and packaging introductions is critical.

4. Excellent Interpersonal Communication Skills: It goes without saying that exceptional communication skills are required of anyone working in sales. This includes the ability to "read" the body language and reaction of customers, adjust sales style to match the needs of others, and problem-solve to ensure the customer is satisfied. Wine sales reps also must communicate and partner with distributors, as well as winery employees.

5. Sales Management Skills: Once the sale is made, experienced sales people realize that the work has just begun. Now they need to service the account, which means placing orders, following-up, tracking shipments, resolving issues, reviewing depletion reports, budgeting, and many other sales management issues.

Most wineries prefer to hire experienced wine sales reps, rather than train on their own. One exception is Gallo, who does recruit and train university grads with an aptitude to succeed in the field. Again, working for a distributor before applying for a job in winery sales is another good path to consider.

It is important to note that most small wineries do not hire full-time sales reps, but instead rely on their distributors to handle sales. Some wineries will also hire consultants or brokers to act as their sales force. Medium to large wineries generally have an in-house sales force, and may also supplement with consultants/brokers. Together they work in partnership with their distributors to sell wine.

Required Education
Wineries generally prefer to hire sales reps who have a four-year Bachelor's degree in sales management, wine business, marketing, communication, psychology, or a related field. Following is a representative career ladder for wine sales in a larger winery.

Figure 5: Wine Sales Career Ladder

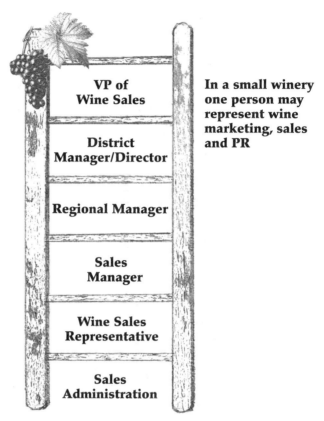

VP of
Wine Sales

District
Manager/Director

Regional Manager

Sales
Manager

Wine Sales
Representative

Sales
Administration

In a small winery
one person may
represent wine
marketing, sales
and PR

SKILLS, EXPERIENCE AND EDUCATION REQUIREMENTS FOR WINE PUBLIC RELATIONS

It is important to mention that usually only larger-sized wineries have a full-time public relations professional. The role of public relations in small- to medium-sized wineries is usually also handled by the marketing manager, and/or it may be outsourced to a PR firm. Furthermore, the event management portion of PR may be implemented by the hospitality staff in the tasting room, but PR is still responsible for getting the word out to the public to insure the event is well-attended. It is for this reason that in small wineries, the PR function works closely with whoever is handling wine club events (who may be the same person).

In the wine industry, the term "trade" is often attached to the title of PR professional, because they handle relations with the "trade," a term used to describe wine writers, buyers, educators, and any other stakeholders who can influence consumer perception about a wine or winery. Skills required to succeed in wine PR are similar to other industries with some exceptions.

1. Public Relations Expertise: Obviously in order to obtain one of the few and coveted full-time wine PR positions, public relations expertise and experience is required. This includes knowing how to contact and network with the appropriate press, wine writers, and other key stakeholders, as well as skills in writing press releases, managing media crises, budgeting, event oversight, and other important PR functions.

2. Online Social Networking Skills: Increasingly, some PR professionals are being asked to assume new job responsibilities regarding the winery's online presence and image. This may include answering customer emails; responding to/or creating a company blog or digital videos; and monitoring social networking sights to respond to comments or questions consumers may make or have about the winery. This calls for an advanced level of online communication knowledge—especially how to respond diplomatically in an online environment.

3. Passion for Wine: A love of wine, with solid knowledge of how it is produced, is equally important for PR as it is for wine marketing and sales. PR professionals often interface with food writers as well, so food/wine matching knowledge is important.

4. Wine Industry Knowledge: Public relations professionals should be familiar with the wine industry value chain, competition, and social issues such as responsible drinking and environmental awareness.

5. Excellent Written and Oral Communication Skills: Marketing, Sales or PR skills are critical for PR professionals as they spend much time writing press releases, other company documents, and usually manage website communications. They also should have media training and know how to talk to reporters both on and off camera. Networking, diplomacy, and excellent interpersonal skills are another important part of oral communications for PR.

6. PR Management Skills: Public relations professionals need to have good planning and management skills to structure the annual PR plan, set goals, manage the budget, and oversee event/charity management cost/benefit analyses. In addition, they must know how to handle a crisis and interface with multiple stakeholders within the winery and local community.

Required Experience

In terms of experience, larger wineries which do hire full-time PR professionals usually require PR experience at another company. However, small wineries are often open to hiring part-time or intern PR grads, especially if they can assist with event management during busy seasons.

Required Education

In general, for education, wine PR professionals are expected to have a four-year Bachelor's degree in public relations, communications, event management, marketing, business, or a related field. Following is a representative career ladder for wine PR in a larger winery.

Figure 6: Wine PR Career Ladder

TIPS ON GETTING STARTED/JOB HUNTING STRATEGIES FOR WINE MARKETING, SALES AND PR

Following is a list of tips to help you get started in your wine marketing, sales or PR career:

1. Obtain Prior Experience: It is almost impossible to obtain a job with a winery in wine marketing, sales, or PR without prior experience. A few wineries will hire you if you have performed one of more of these functions in other industries, but the majority prefer wine industry experience. Some of the most effective ways to do this are getting a part-time job doing wine sales in a tasting room, being a PR or marketing intern for a winery, or working for a distributor in either merchandising or sales.

2. Conduct Informational Interviews: Schedule informational interviews with successful people in winery marketing, sales and PR positions. Ask how they got started and what advice they may have for you. Remember, during an informational interview, you are only supposed to ask for information, not a job.

3. Network in the Wine Industry: Join local winery associations and attend wine conferences so you can learn how the industry works and meet people who can provide advice on where there are winery openings.

4. Monitor Wine Job Websites: Once you've obtained your wine industry experience, monitor websites which have job postings in the wine industry. Get your resume in shape to highlight your wine experience and skills. Then submit it.

5. Obtain a Degree in Wine Marketing: There are now wine marketing certifications and degrees available at a few universities (see list below). Consider pursuing one in order to help gain the necessary background and credentials.

EDUCATION PROGRAMS FOR WINE MARKETING, SALES & PR

Following is a partial list of some of the institutions offering degrees in wine business, marketing, sales and public relations.

- **A.S.** in Wine Business & Marketing, Santa Rosa Community College, Santa Rosa, CA
- **A.S.** in Wine Marketing & Sales, Napa Valley College, Napa, CA

- **A.S.** in Wine Marketing, Walla Walla Community College, Walla Walla, Washington
- **B.S.** in Wine Business, Sonoma State University, Rohnert Park, CA
- **B.S.** in Wine Business, Charles Stuart University, New South Wales, Australia
- **B.S.** in Wine & Viticulture, Cal-Poly University, San Luis Obispo, CA
- **MBA** in Wine Business, Sonoma State University, Rohnert Park, CA
- **MBA** in Wine Business, Bordeaux Business School, Bordeaux, France

HELPFUL CONFERENCES, BOOKS, AND WEBSITES

Following is a list of useful resources to help you learn more about wine marketing, sales and PR.

Wine Marketing & Business Conferences/ Seminars/Associations

- **Academy of Wine Business Research Conference:** Sponsor an academic wine marketing and business conference every two years in a different wine producing country. http://www. agro-montpellier.fr/awbr/
- **London International Wine Fair:** Wine trade show in the UK. Held annually each Spring. http://www.londonwinefair. com/
- **National Wine Marketing Conference:** Host national wine marketing conference in various US locations on an annual basis.

- **Unified Wine Symposium:** Largest wine conference in the US. Held each January in Sacramento. Includes multiple wine-related topics as well as tastings. http://www.unifiedsymposium.org/
- **Vin Expo:** Large international wine conference held every other year in Bordeaux, France. www.vinexpo.com
- **Vin-Italy:** Large international wine conference held each year in Verona, Italy. www.vinitaly.com
- **Various regional wine trade associations:** Offering seminars in wine marketing, sales and/or PR.

Books on Wine Marketing, Sales & Public Relations

- *The Brand Gym: A Practical Workout for Boosting Brand and Business* by David Tyler
- *Brand New World* by Scott Bradbury
- *Marketing Management: The Big Picture* by Christie L. Nordhielm
- *Marketing Public Relations: The HOWS That Make It Work* by Rene A. Henry
- *The New Rules of Marketing and PR: How to Use News Releases, Blogs, Podcasting, Viral Marketing and Online Media to Reach Buyers Directly* by David Meerman Scott
- *Sales and Service for the Wine Professional* by Brian K. Julya
- *Spinning the Bottle* by Harvey Posert & Paul Franson
- *Successful Wine Marketing* by James Lapsley and Kirby Moulton
- *Travel and Tourism Public Relations: An Introductory Guide for Hospitality Managers* by Dennis E. Deuschl
- *Wine Marketing: A Practical Guide* by C. Michael Hall and Richard Mitchell
- *Wine Marketing & Sales: Success Strategies for a Saturated Market* by Paul Wagner, Janeen Olsen and Liz Thach

Helpful Websites on Wine Marketing, Sales & Public Relations

- **http://www.awbm.com.au/:** Link to Australian online wine industry news
- **http://www.erobertparker.com/:** Link to the Wine Advocate by Robert Parker
- **http://www.harpers.com.uk/:** Link to U.K. wine and spirits trade news, plus coverage of key European wine business
- **http://www.jancisrobinson.com:** Link to Jancis Robinson's viewpoints on wine
- **http://www.wineandspiritsmagazine.com/:** Link to Wine & Spirits Magazine, an excellent sources of news in the wine industry.
- **http://www.winebusiness.com/:** Link to Wine Business Monthly, US based online wine industry news
- **http://www.winemag.com/:** Link to Wine Enthusiast magazine
- **http://www.winespectator.com/:** Link to online version of Wine Spectator, one of the largest and most popular wine enthusiastic magazines.

ADVICE FROM WINE MARKETING, SALES & PUBLIC RELATIONS EXPERTS

Following are excerpts of interviews with experts in wine marketing, sales, and public relations. They offer helpful insight into the daily responsibilities of their jobs, as well as what they enjoy most about working in the wine industry. Two large publicly traded wineries and one medium-sized family run winery are represented.

True Tales from the Wine Industry

STEPHANIE GALLO, SENIOR DIRECTOR OF MARKETING, E. & J. GALLO WINERY

Born into a pioneering wine family, Stephanie Gallo was given the freedom to carve her own career path. "My parents never put any expectations on me to join the family business," explained Stephanie. "Instead, they encouraged me to follow my passion and make my own choices."

Stephanie was clear on one thing: She had an inner drive to pursue a career in marketing. Even as a child, Stephanie was fascinated by product labels and spent hours thinking of creative ways to redesign them. Early in her career, after interviewing with an array of consumer goods companies, Stephanie realized that selling cereal or soap simply did not spark her interest.

"The more I learned about marketing, the more I realized how important it is to be passionate about your product," she said. Stephanie eventually followed her parents' advice and her own passion toward the one product that ignites her enthusiasm: wine.

"Wine is a very special product because it connects people to each other, particularly in this era of telecommuting and virtual communication," explained Stephanie. "I feel very fortunate to market a product that is often part of our most joyful and memorable moments. It is hard not to be passionate about wine."

EDUCATION AND TRAINING

Recognizing that marketing requires strong critical thinking and communication skills, Stephanie pursued a Liberal Arts degree as an undergraduate at the University of Notre Dame. Exposure to a variety of disciplines gave Stephanie a broad perspective. Today, as a marketer, she relies on her liberal arts background to draw ideas from diverse sources.

Stephanie's career in the wine industry began with a sales position at a Chicago distributor that carried wine from several producers, including Gallo. Stephanie saw an inherent value in learning the fundamentals of sales in an entry-level position. "I believe every marketer must spend time selling his or her own product," she said.

After three years in wine sales—first as a sales rep and later as a district manager and key account manager—Stephanie honed her business acumen at Northwestern's Kellogg School of Management.

Armed with an MBA in marketing, Stephanie joined E. & J. Gallo Winery as an entry-level marketer, writing back label copy and creating retail promotions for the Turning Leaf brand. She gained experience developing advertising campaigns and eventually played an integral role in strategic planning for several brands.

Today, Stephanie is Senior Director of Marketing at the Winery, where she manages a staff of fifteen and oversees Gallo's "popular price" portfolio, including Gallo Family Vineyards Twin Valley, Barefoot, Turning Leaf and Redwood Creek.

MOST IMPORTANT SKILLS FOR WINE MARKETING

Stephanie cites a mix of essential skills that sets talented wine marketers apart from their peers: 1) Passion for your

industry and your product; 2) Genuine interest in meeting the needs of consumers; 3) Strategic thinking coupled with the ability to execute ideas; 4) Leadership that provides visionary direction and motivation; 5) Innovation and the courage to take risks.

First and foremost, Stephanie believes passion for your industry and the product you sell is fundamental to success in marketing, particularly in the wine industry. "Wine is a lifestyle. The best wine marketers are immersed in that lifestyle. Their personal and professional lives often intersect, because of an innate passion for wine—whether it's about integrating food and wine, learning to cook or entertaining with wine," explained Stephanie. "That passion translates into the work we do every day."

Second, according to Stephanie, successful marketers are motivated by a genuine interest in understanding consumers' needs and a strong desire to meet those needs. Wine marketing poses a unique challenge, because opinions about wine are highly subjective. Since consumers have difficulty articulating why they like or dislike a particular wine, marketers must be naturally inquisitive.

Stephanie advocates using consumer research as a starting point for understanding consumers' needs, but she emphasizes that intuition should inform every decision. "Understanding today's wine consumer requires getting out there. It's about developing an intuitive sense of consumers' needs. It means interacting with consumers in uncontrolled environments," said Stephanie. "Whether in the wine aisle of the grocery store or at a wine tasting event, I constantly ask consumers what they think of a brand or a particular wine."

Third, Stephanie values strong strategic thinking skills, balanced by an ability to turn ideas into action. "Some marketers are great at the strategic piece and can visualize opportunities that others don't see, but they lack the ability to implement the plan. Others can execute ideas, but fail to think strategically," explained Stephanie. "Highly successful marketers excel at both."

Fourth, Stephanie emphasizes the importance of strong leadership skills. Wine marketers are charged with developing a vision and motivating others to generate buy-in and enthusiasm for a campaign. "In the wine industry, we work with production teams, distributors, sales reps, retailers and many other partners—most of whom do not report directly to marketing," explained Stephanie, "It is the job of the wine marketer to demonstrate leadership and inspire these cross-functional teams to bring a strategic vision to life."

Lastly, Stephanie is an ardent proponent of innovation. She advocates taking risks to push innovation and creativity forward, even when conventional wisdom might suggest a more traditional path. "Great innovation in marketing is about choosing the road less traveled," said Stephanie. "It's about zigging when everyone else zags. It's about seeking truly unique ways to fill white spaces in the marketplace."

Stephanie believes innovation requires more than average creativity to foster out-of-the-box thinking. "True innovation is what brings a brand to the next level, and the courage to take risks is the X factor that sets great marketers apart from the pack," she said.

123

MOST CHALLENGING ASPECTS OF THE JOB

Prioritizing which creative ideas to implement is one of Stephanie's greatest challenges. "Our marketing team may generate fifty exciting ideas, but we can't necessarily execute all of them," said Stephanie. "Prioritizing key projects and letting go of some of those great ideas is challenging. My job is to maximize our resources and bring the most innovative concepts to the forefront."

Stephanie also cites the dynamic nature of the wine industry as an ongoing challenge. "Our industry is constantly changing," explained Stephanie. "As priorities continually shift, we have to be flexible and responsive to our consumers' needs."

BEST PART OF THE JOB

Stephanie finds several aspects of her position rewarding: working with her family, selling a product for which she is so passionate, developing her staff and seeing the results of her hard work.

"I love working with my family—my brothers and cousins—every day. The energy that comes from working toward a common goal brings us closer together as a family. I also feel fortunate to sell a product that connects people and allows them to slow down and enjoy life's best moments," said Stephanie.

"I find it highly rewarding to develop my staff and watch them grow personally and professionally. Most of all, I love a good challenge—taking risks, finding the undiscovered opportunities, bringing innovation to market and being part of a brand's growth."

The notion that something can't be done may be Stephanie's most important motivator. "I do enjoy proving people wrong by succeeding at a concept that no one thought would work," said Stephanie. "If you tell me something can't be done, I'll find a way to make it happen."

PATTY HELD-UTHLAUT, DIRECTOR OF MARKETING & PR, STONE HILL WINERY

Patty Held-Uthlaut grew up in Hermann, Missouri, at her family's winery, Stone Hill. Established in 1847, Stone Hill is one of the oldest wineries in the US and specializes in Native American varietals such as the Norton grape. "When my parents bought the winery in 1965," says Patty, "my two brothers, sister and I all learned to help with everything from harvest, to assisting in the cellar and talking with customers." But it was the customer relations part of the job that won Patty's heart. Today, along with her brother Thomas, Patty oversees all marketing, sales and public relations activities for their three different winery locations in Hermann, Branson and New Florence, Missouri.

EDUCATION AND TRAINING

"Since I enjoy interacting with people," recounts Patty, "I decided to pursue a degree in Marketing at Tulsa University in Oklahoma where I had received a scholarship. However,

after one semester, my brother talked me into transferring to Fresno State University in California where I enrolled in their winemaking program."

Making the most of two enology/viticulture scholarships, Patty received her B.S. with cum laude distinction and moved to upstate New York to work as assistant winemaker for Taylor Wine Company. Here she was responsible for more than 1.5 million gallons of wine, and received the Governor's Cup award for her Vidal Blanc ice wine. However, Patty's dream of working with customers at her family winery was calling to her, so she returned to Hermann, Missouri and took over retail sales, special events, and wholesale distribution. Today, along with her brother, they handle all marketing, sales and PR for the winery with a staff of around fifty employees who work in the three tasting rooms, restaurant, advertising, web support, and other key functions. All together, Stone Hill Winery employs 150 people and produces around 100,000 cases per year.

"Training as a winemaker has been especially helpful in my marketing and PR role," reports Patty. "Many times I speak to wine writers who want all the details of winemaking and viticulture, and I can provide it. I guess I've come full circle back into customer relations, which I really enjoy." Patty notes that she has supplemented her winemaking expertise with much self-study and reading in marketing, as well as attending many wine conferences and seminars on the subject.

MOST IMPORTANT SKILLS FOR WINE MARKETING & PR
"Being in charge of marketing and PR for a medium-sized winery requires good organization skills and the ability to

multi-task," says Patty. "I wear many different hats and am constantly juggling a dozen different projects and events."

Another important skill set includes good planning ability in order to create an annual marketing and sales plan, as well as follow-up in terms of daily sales, depletion reports, progress on marketing campaigns, and follow-through with the many details required to successfully implement all of the events scheduled at the winery. "Since we are located in Missouri," says Patty, "we focus on destination marketing to get visitors to the winery. This means we constantly plan special events, including weddings, concerts, grape stomp, etc.

"Hiring the right people to implement all of the marketing programs is very important," says Patty. This includes not only their full-time staff, but working with marketing consultants such as label design firms and their brokered sales reps.

Finally, Patty mentions how important the traditional skills of friendly interpersonal communication, good writing and speaking are. "We always try to hire outgoing, friendly people. I can teach them wine knowledge—and we offer a lot of training—but we hire for a positive attitude."

Patty concludes with a bit of wisdom her father always shared with her when she was growing up. "He had a favorite saying: 'Never argue or cross anyone who buys ink by the gallon.'" Because of this, Patty does everything possible to ensure that Stone Hill Winery embraces all visitors with a very positive and warm welcome.

MOST CHALLENGING ASPECT OF THE JOB

"The most challenging part is trying to keep all of the balls in the air at the same time," reports Patty. "We have so much

going on and the three wineries are open seven days a week. That means that work-life balance is not always possible." Patty mentions that her solutions to address this issue are to exercise as much as possible and take at least one day a week off from her responsibilities.

BEST PART OF THE JOB

"The best part of the job for me is serving wine to someone who is not familiar with our winery or Missouri wines. It is very exciting when they recognize the quality of our wines. Then I have made a new friend and created a new Missouri wine drinker. This is very gratifying," smiles Patty.

"The other great part of my job is the fact that since this is a family winery, I get to be with my family every day. Not everyone has this opportunity. I am very lucky!"

JIM RUSSELL, SENIOR VP OF SALES, ICON ESTATES, CONSTELLATION

Jim Russell was introduced to wine sales early on in his childhood. While growing up, he listened to his step-father talk at the dinner table about the excitement of selling wine at Calloway Winery in Southern California. "I grew up in Orange County," says Jim, " and knew at an early age that I wanted a career in sales." That clear focus has paid off, because today Jim is in charge Icon Estates, the fine wine *division of Constellation Brands, the largest wine company in the world.*

EDUCATION AND TRAINING

"I chose University of Southern California to obtain my degree," reports Jim, "because, at the time, they were the top local university to offer a B.S. in Sales & Marketing." After graduation Jim followed in his father's footsteps and obtained a job selling wine at Callaway Winery.

The job soon grew into a much larger one when Callaway was purchased first by Hiram Walker and then Allied Domecq. "I successfully worked through a long series of acquisitions and mergers," says Jim, "and ended up spending twenty-four years with them in the end." The M&A experience not only honed Jim's skills in being flexible, but gave him a strategic perspective on international wine sales and marketing.

"Eventually, I decided to move back into a smaller winery," says Jim, "and took a job as VP of Sales and Marketing with Rosenblum Cellars." He greatly enjoyed working closely with Kent Rosenblum and the shareholders, but after a year was soon lured away by Icon Estates. "The opportunity to oversee three-million cases of some of the most famous wines in the world, such as Robert Mondavi Winery, Simi, Estancia, Franciscan, Mount Veeder, Tintara and many others, was just too good to pass up."

Today, Jim holds the position of Senior Vice-President of Sales for the fine wine division of Constellation, Icon Estates, with more than eighty people reporting into him, including a structure that encompasses divisional VPs, channel directors, regional directors, district managers, and analysts.

MOST IMPORTANT SKILLS FOR WINE SALES

Wine sales for a major winery include both strong distributor relationship skills and good sales management abilities. "In the US wine industry," says Jim, "we have to work within the three-tier system, so understanding that system and knowing how to work well with distributors is critical. We generally don't hire anyone unless they have previous experience working within the three-tier system and have good wine knowledge."

In addition to calling on accounts with distributors for both account maintenance and new development, sales professionals must stay up-to-date on new promotions, track case depletions and meet sales goals. "Professional sales management skills and interpersonal communication skills are a must," reports Jim," however at the same time, we offer our sales force excellent advanced training in the areas of presentation skills, management, and wine/food culture."

Jim says that, in general, they prefer a Bachelor's degree, and that it is very important if you want to move up in sales management. "In the end," says Jim, "all of these skills and experience are important, but I find that having a passion for wine is the most critical. Sales professionals who have a passion for our products, and a deep desire to learn more about the winemaking practices and cultures of our fine wine estates, are the ones who excel."

MOST CHALLENGING ASPECT OF THE JOB

"The challenges of the job are very similar to sales in other consumer product companies," says Jim. "There are many changing variables over which you have no control, such

as the economy, competitors, and changing grape supply issues."

Another matter common to most sales jobs is the travel and time away from home. "In the wine industry," says Jim, "you also have to work many evenings and weekends, because we are calling on restaurant accounts and participating in consumer events. The hours can be long, but on the flip side, no two days are very alike so you never get bored."

BEST PART OF THE JOB

"I think the best part of the job," says Jim, "is working with a very high level of professionals at some of the top wine estates in the world. There is so much diversity in products, settings, and culture, as well as new vintages and promotions. You never stop learning. It is continually inspiring."

JIM CAUDILL, TRADE PUBLIC RELATIONS, BROWN-FORMAN

Jim Caudill grew up in Detroit, Michigan, knowing from an early age that he wanted to write for a living. The son of an autoworker father and a 5th grade teacher mother, he never dreamed that he would some day handle wine trade public relations for one of the largest wine and spirits companies. "In the 8th grade, I wanted to be a newspaper reporter," reminisces Jim. "But that led to investigating community

events and soon I became very interested in the field of public relations, although it wasn't really called that at the time." Today, Jim manages the wine writer and wine trade relationships for Fetzer, Bonterra, Sonoma-Cutrer and many other brands.

EDUCATION AND TRAINING

"I received my B.A. in Journalism at Wayne State University," says Jim, "and immediately got a job with a local newspaper. I really enjoyed investigating stories, interviewing people, and then writing up the results. Being in the community and interacting with people was very enjoyable for me, so when I was recruited to work for the Michigan Department of Education doing polling and community relations—and at a larger salary—it seemed a reasonable next step." Jim continued to work in educational public relations for seven years before he was recruited by a national PR Agency and transferred into food and tourism.

"The benefit of working for large PR firm is that you get to work on different types of accounts in diverse industries," says Jim. "My major account for some years was Fireman's Fund Insurance Companies, which led to a transfer to San Francisco. From there I was placed on other accounts and eventually ended up doing public relations for food, wine, hotels, and restaurants." This is where Jim found a perfect match between his writing and community relations skills and his new found passion for wine and food.

In 1996 he was recruited by Kendall-Jackson to head up their PR efforts, and then in 2003 he was invited to join Brown-Forman. Along the way, he picked up a Master's in Communication and has started an MBA program.

MOST IMPORTANT SKILLS FOR
WINE PUBLIC RELATIONS

According to Jim there are several important skill sets to becoming a successful wine PR professional. "The first is knowledge of and appreciation for wine and food culture," says Jim. "This is because you frequently talk to wine writers about both food and wine. In addition, you need to be familiar with all of the technical details of viticulture and winemaking."

Second is a clear grasp of PR basics. "This means," says Jim, "that strong communications skills are critical. You have to be good at writing, interviewing, researching, and communicating interpersonally with the press, employees, and consumers." Furthermore, PR has to work closely with the marketing department to collaborate on key initiatives, and the PR professional may be called upon to assist sales by calling on clients in the field to serve as the winery representative.

In addition, Jim mentions that an understanding of event management and conflict resolution skills are important. "Most PR professionals have to understand how to do community relations work, including charity and special events. In addition, they may have to resolve consumer issues, including web communications such as e-mail responses and blogging," reports Jim.

He mentions that most wineries prefer to hire someone who already has wine industry experience, such as having been a harvest intern or experience in the tasting room. For the most part, in small- to medium-sized wineries with less than 100,000 cases the PR function is usually combined with marketing, however in larger wineries it is a separate department.

MOST CHALLENGING ASPECT OF THE JOB

According to Jim, the most challenging part of a job in PR is work-life balance. "You are expected to be available 24/7," says Jim. "Often you have to take both early morning and late evening phone calls, as well as work events on the weekend. Even if you are not at work or on vacation, the PR professional is always on call in case of an emergency at the company. This is because you are the spokesperson."

BEST PART OF THE JOB

Despite the long hours, Jim says he really enjoys his job. "I don't even think of it as a job," says Jim. "It's more of a lifestyle—and a really great lifestyle at that. I get to travel around the world and consume great food and wine—plus the people you meet are wonderful. I never thought that as the son of a Detroit autoworker that I would be doing these things. It is a wonderful life style."

Direct-to-Consumer Sales at the Winery

We've been making the finest wines since 1965—
Before that we really didn't give a hoot.

Chapter

K, let's have a show of hands. Who's bellied up to a tasting room bar before? My suspicion is you're holding this book in one hand, and raising the other. For most visitors to wine country anywhere in the world, a great part of the experience is visiting the wineries, tasting wines, and participating in tours, wine and food pairings, and special events. Those functions are handled by the direct-to-consumer staff of the winery.

Direct-to-consumer sales can include any of the following types of activities:

- Hospitality/Retail
- Culinary
- Special Events/Wine Education
- Wine Clubs

For most wineries, hospitality/retail and wine clubs are the core of the direct-to-consumer channel. Others have small- to mid-scale culinary operations, ranging from pre-prepared foods to full-service restaurants. Some wineries also host a variety of special events and wine education programs to entice guests to visit (and spend!). We'll expand on this in a moment.

Why do wineries have direct-to-consumer sales functions as part of their winery? Simple—this channel offers the highest profit on wine sold. Wine purchased at the winery isn't transported or warehoused (off-premises), and doesn't incur any of the costs associated with working with distributors or retailers. These are all factors that cut into the potential profit of a sale.

Direct sales also don't rely on large-scale advertising to pull consumers in, instead focusing on marketing the winery to local concierges and tourist publications, some print advertisement (targeted at potential visitors to wine country), capitalizing on any public relations activities, and, perhaps most important, word-of-mouth from previous winery visitors and current wine club members.

Wine club sales may incur shipping fees, and costs of producing print pieces like newsletters and mailings, but these costs pale in comparison to the advertising and operating costs associated with selling wine through national distribution channels. Club sales are guaranteed, high-margin revenue, ringing the winery's cash register with each shipment.

Direct-to-consumer sales, as mentioned in Chapter 1 "Introduction to Wine Careers," are a primary sales channel for small wineries, and can be a very important one for some medium-sized wineries, for two reasons. First, as with any industry, size is important. Small- to medium-sized wineries often have challenges getting the attentions of either distributors or retailers that they need to sell their wines.

Second, selling through those channels has hard costs (like those mentioned above) as well as soft costs (time, and possibly the headcount required to manage a national sales process). Many small wineries simply aren't willing, or can't afford, to have their profit on sale cut so much. Medium wineries may choose to pursue a dual strategy, selling some larger-production wines nationally, while selling the higher-priced, smaller-quantity wines through a direct channel.

Some wineries produce in such small quantities, and have such buzz around their wines, that they don't need to look to national distribution to sell through each vintage. They can easily sell through 250 or 500 cases of a highly desirable wine right at the winery door.

Large wineries, while having direct-to-consumer functions, tend to focus much more on selling through distributors in the US. So while many large wineries have hospitality operations at different sites, as well as wine clubs, their direct-to-consumer focus varies between providing high-margin revenue; building the image of the brand through direct consumer contact; and providing locations and trained staff to wine-and-dine key decision-makers like distributors, wine press, and buyers from major customers.

Within the direct-to-consumer channel, there are two main sub-functions: hospitality/retail, and wine clubs. The rest of the chapter will focus on careers in those two areas. Hospitality and retail jobs focus on the operations of a winery tasting room. There are a number of **entry-level** roles in tasting rooms. Titles vary, and include **tasting room specialist, hospitality specialist, hospitality/winery representative,** and **sales associate.**

JOB DESCRIPTION FOR ENTRY-LEVEL HOSPITALITY/RETAIL

The responsibilities of these roles are fairly consistent across wineries. They include:

- Pouring wines for visitors to the winery.
- Sharing the winery's history, and explaining the wines poured.
- Selling! Selling wines, merchandise, wine club memberships, wine education programs, and special events.
- Answering questions about wines and merchandise sold in the tasting room.
- Operating cash registers or POS systems.
- Stocking shelves, floor displays, and taking inventory of wine and non-wine merchandise.
- Assisting customers in the packing, carrying, and shipping of wine.

- Answering questions about the local area, including referrals to other wineries, hotels, restaurants, and local activities.
- Washing and drying glasses.
- Pouring wines at offsite events like festivals and fairs.
- Working special events.
- Presenting the brand image positively through all of the activities listed above.

Some wineries have tour guides. These wineries have both the right kind of properties to make a tour interesting and enjoyable for patrons, and a hospitality program which includes tours. Tour guides are responsible for leading groups of anywhere from five to thirty-five people on tours of the winery. They will also take part in the duties described above.

SKILL AND EDUCATION REQUIREMENTS FOR ENTRY-LEVEL HOSPITALITY/RETAIL

Requirements of these roles are also fairly consistent. They include:

- High school diploma or GED
- Being at least twenty-one years of age
- Strong customer service orientation
- High personal energy and enthusiasm
- Excellent communication skills, particularly verbal, including over the phone
- Public speaking ability, especially for Tour Guide roles

Wine knowledge requirements vary from winery to winery, but having some is always a plus. Depending on the nature of the winery, and the personality of the brands it sells, you may not need to know much of anything about wine, or you may be expected to have a solid foundation of wine knowledge.

In general, wineries that produce luxury, boutique brands will likely look for individuals with more wine knowledge. Employees in these types of tasting rooms are often selling to a higher-income, if not a more knowledgeable, wine consumer. In this circumstance, wine knowledge is helpful, as you may be asked to explain how the winery's Cabernet Sauvignon compares to the wines of Bordeaux, or the Super Tuscans of Italy. These wineries may look fondly on the "wine geek" that wants to work for them.

Wineries that produce more commercial, premium wines, or have a more casual, lighthearted brand, will often take an applicant with energy, enthusiasm, and a willingness to learn, over a "wine geek." These individuals are typically a better fit with the winery's target consumers, as well as their brand. They will be more appealing when chatting with tasters at the bar than someone with lots of knowledge, who could come off as a bit stuffy.

Previous experience requirements vary. They include:

- Previous hospitality industry experience; high-end restaurant, retail, or special events experience usually preferred
- Previous winery tasting room experience (ranging from required at some wineries, to desirable but not required at others)
- Public speaking experience for tour guides

Even if you don't have a background in wine, some wineries will take career changers—such as people from financial services, high tech, and health care—who have genuine passion and interest in their brand and wine. Obtaining a job in hospitality/retail is as much about the skills you bring as it is about where you've worked before and what you know about wine.

Most wineries staff up for the tourist season, which runs Memorial Day to Labor Day (and sometimes beyond in Northern California). Start looking for newspaper advertisements and web postings in late February. Late winter/early spring is a great time to visit wine country. It's also an opportune time to find out about job openings and possibly speak to hiring managers at the tasting room.

Many wineries also employ part-time or on-call staff. On-call employees are generally available to work during especially busy weekends or events, or to cover a shift on short notice in the event of a staff shortage. These roles work particularly well for individuals seeking the benefits of being associated with a winery (including discounts on the wines), but require a lesser commitment.

Career options in hospitality/retail vary by winery, and are particularly influenced by the size of the tasting room operation. Small wineries will often have very flat organizational structures, including a staff of fifteen or less tasting room specialists and a tasting room manager. There may be a single lead role or supervisor.

Let's talk about the non-management roles first.

JOB DESCRIPTION FOR MID-LEVEL HOSPITALITY/RETAIL

Larger tasting rooms may have multiple levels of tasting room specialists or tour guides. **Advanced roles** will pick up additional duties such as:

- Pouring and selling reserve and library wines, typically in specialized settings (special rooms, sit-down tasting environments).
- Conducting tours for VIPs, including celebrities, influential members of the wine media and press, distributor principles, and other special guests.

- Conducting wine education and other special consumer programs for guests.
- Training new staff.
- Opening and closing duties; other responsibilities associated with managers on duty (MODs) including cash handling and approving breaks and lunches.

Other specialized roles may include:

Special Events: These roles are responsible for the different events held at the winery. They can include winemaker dinners, new release parties; barrel tasting events; participation in festivals and inter-winery association events; weddings; and even concerts and galas. Roles can range from that of on-call support for the event (setting up, serving, and breaking down) to managerial roles (developing, planning, and managing event activities for the winery). A great way to break into working these special events is to work with one of the many catering operations or restaurants in wine country.

Culinary: Some wineries have active, thriving culinary operations that complement their wine sales. These activities range from small deli counters that sell pre-prepared foods to full-scale restaurants to culinary programs. Roles vary accordingly, from individuals with food handling experience acting as salespeople behind deli counters, to complete chefs who develop dishes to best complement the wines being sold, and to create a complete wine country experience for guests. Culinary roles can be located by networking through culinary programs, such as the Culinary Institute of America and the California Culinary Academy.

On-Site Wine Club Representative: These roles are responsible for selling the wine club program to visitors, answering questions about the club, and providing specialized service to club members who visit the winery. At some wineries, the wine club representative handles both the tasting room duties described earlier and the wine club duties described later in this chapter.

Merchandising: These roles are responsible for the buying and display of non-wine merchandise in the tasting room. They work with the tasting room staff to ensure that the look and feel of the room presents an image consistent with the brand positioning for the winery. Pure merchandising roles are rare, and quite specialized. A previous background in merchandising for high-end retailers and destinations is most desirable.

Shipping and Receiving: These roles are responsible for the movement of large quantities of wine from on-site warehouses. This may involve using forklifts, dollys, and hand trucks. Job duties may also include overall inventory and wine ordering responsibilities.

Beyond these roles, advancement in hospitality/retails means moving into the world of people and operational management. Titles for these types of roles include tasting room, hospitality, or retail supervisor; tasting room, hospitality, or retail manager; or director of hospitality.

JOB DESCRIPTION FOR HOSPITALITY/RETAIL MANAGEMENT

Management roles at these levels mirror those in any retail business. Job duties include:

- Managing the day-to-day operations of a tasting room.

- Hiring, training, supervising, and as required, disciplining and discharging staff.
- Setting sales goals and quotas.
- Developing consumer programs and promotions to drive foot traffic and sales onsite.
- Developing and managing budgets, including labor and operating budgets for the tasting room, up to full P&L responsibility for the operation.
- Ensuring customer service standards are met, including resolving escalated customer service issues.
- Responsibility for the appearance and safety of grounds, including site and building maintenance, and signage.

Titles, and their respective duties, can vary widely from winery to winery. Supervisor roles are generally more traditional "working supervisors," and spend a lot of time on the sales floor or behind the tasting room bar with the staff.

Manager and director roles typically pick up the budgetary, program development, and site/ground responsibilities, and spend at least half of their time tending to these administrative responsibilities. A director may also be responsible for more than one tasting room, if the family or company owns multiple brands and properties.

SKILL AND EDUCATION REQUIREMENTS FOR HOSPITALITY/RETAIL MANAGEMENT

Experience requirements for management roles typically include:

- Bachelor's degree, typically in business, hospitality, or equivalent.

- At least five years of retail, hospitality, special events, restaurant, or winery work experience.
- For supervisors, at least two years previous experience leading or managing staff.
- For managers, at least four years previous people management experience, with exposure to budgets and program development.
- For directors, at least seven years previous people management experience, with budget development and P&L responsibility being a common expectation.
- Strong communication skills, both written and verbal.
- Strong people and relationship skills, including the ability to effectively interact with a broad and diverse group of people, both internal employees, and external visitors.
- Good financial skills, including the ability to read and understand budgets and other financial documents.
- Knowledge of different retail practices, including merchandising, consumer programming, and promotions.
- Wine industry experience is typically a plus; however, high-end retail or restaurant experience will also get a long look from many wineries.

Figure 1: Hospitality Career Ladder

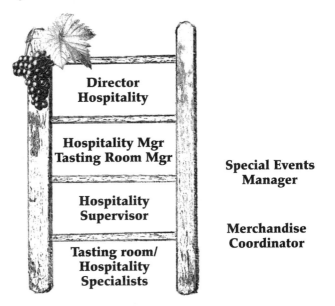

Hospitality/retail is where you get the greatest contact with wine consumers. The roles are much like that in other industries.

One major exception for those coming from more traditional retail or restaurants is the hours. While weekend work is typically a requirement (particularly for newcomers), evening hours are rare. Most tasting rooms open no earlier than 9AM, and close no later than 6PM during the summer season. Hours are often reduced in the off-season, varying by geography, but typically December to April. Evening events are infrequent.

Working in hospitality/retail is a great way to break into the wine business. It gives you the opportunity to get to know more about wine, its consumers, the overall industry, and the region you work in. Above all, it provides a great opportunity for you to start networking in the business.

Keep in mind, however, that working hospitality is not necessarily your ticket into a great job in sales, marketing, or winemaking. While individuals can—and do—move from the tasting room into the boardroom or the cellar, it's not a typical path. Most individuals interested in working their way up through the industry find hospitality to be a worthwhile first step. However, they often find themselves networking hard; acquiring additional education and credentials in the industry; and moving to a different winery, in order to take the next step in their wine career.

WINE CLUBS

Imagine this. You're visiting a beautiful winery on a gorgeous summer day in wine country. You're sipping the third or fourth wine in what's been an amazing lineup. Your host behind the bar is friendly, gracious, and knowledgeable. It's one of those moments you'd like to have go on forever. And, in a way, you can—by signing up for the winery's wine club!

That's the simple premise on which wine clubs operate: the promise of regular communication from the winery, and shipments of two to six bottles of wine anywhere from two to six times a year. You continue to hear about the winemaker, rave press reviews, events at the winery, and the latest vintages of your favorite wine—all delivered right to your doorstep.

The majority of wine clubs rely on a simple but effective method for gaining members. They sign you up when you visit the winery. For those familiar with direct marketing, wine clubs are incredibly efficient. Rather than buying lists of potential consumers and spending time deciphering who to mail to, the winery just opens the tasting room doors and the most highly qualified prospects they could hope for walk right up to the tasting room bar.

Most wine club businesses have four key components to their operation:

1) Acquiring new club members
2) Developing and managing club marketing strategies
3) Choosing, packaging, and shipping wines to consumers
4) Customer service for existing club customers

ACQUISITION

Acquisition is often driven through the winery's tasting room. Hospitality staff is trained to bring the club up as part of their discussion with guests. Some clubs also purchase lists from traditional direct marketing businesses, and send out direct mail pieces to entice new membership. Email is an increasingly common communication vehicle, and can also be used to acquire new members.

As mentioned above, some wineries will have a staff member who specializes in selling to promote the wine club to tasting room visitors. This role can either be a specialized member of the hospitality staff, or the wine club manager wearing another hat. They may attempt to sign up members both in the tasting room, at festivals, or at offsite events where their wines are featured.

Some clubs have telephone customer service professionals who engage in targeted calling of qualified prospects (individuals who have left their contact information at the winery after a visit, on a website, or are members of another club) to acquire new members.

CLUB MARKETING STRATEGIES

The marketing strategies used to maintain contact with club members and encourage sales can range from the simple to the complex.

At their simplest, clubs ship new releases to members and include a folksy newsletter which shares recent goings-on at the winery, good reviews and scores, tasting notes for the wines, and possibly a calendar of events.

At their most complex, clubs will have detailed contact strategies which rely on a combination of emails, special member-only events at the winery, and calls from customer service professionals—all in an effort to retain club members and generate additional sales.

SHIPMENT SELECTION AND FULFILLMENT

Choosing the wines to be shipped to club members can be more challenging than it first appears. Most club members sign up with two primary expectations. First, they expect to receive wines of a certain quality and stature. Second, they expect the cost of each shipment to fall within a predictable range (ideally the one they committed to when they joined the club). Wineries are simultaneously trying to maximize revenue, and meet member expectations and retain them in the club. They also have to make sure they have enough inventory of highly desirable wines to ship to club members while still having sufficient quantity on-hand in the tasting room to pour for site guests. When supply is limited (as it often is for sought-after wines), it becomes a very delicate balancing act.

Logistically, managing a two to six bottle shipment to hundreds (if not thousands) of club members is a rather daunting task. Besides the physical aspects of staging, packing and shipping so much wine, there is also the legal aspect. Currently less than half of the states in the US allow direct wine shipments to their residents (a legacy of Prohibition). While the trend is slowly swinging in favor of direct shipments, wine clubs need to be careful to ensure they're shipping only to legally authorized addresses. Some states also place limits on the quantity of wine which may be shipped in a year, further complicating legal compliance.

Many clubs choose to outsource this part of the club business. Three large outsource partners are Wineshipping.com, AmbrosiaWine. com and New Vine Logistics.

WINE CLUB ROLES

Wine clubs offer a number of different career options. Typical roles include **customer service representative** (CSR), **on-site club representative, e-commerce/web specialist** or **manager,** and **wine club manager.**

JOB DESCRIPTIONS FOR CUSTOMER SERVICE REPS

As with any direct business, there are invariably customer service requirements to manage. Club customer service requirements include answering questions about wines, the winery, upcoming events, and club policies; taking phone orders for additional wine; changes of address; billing questions, including issues of expired and declined credit cards; complaints and issues with shipments; and canceling membership in the club. **Customer service representative** roles will be found in mid- to large-sized wineries with large wine club operations. Duties and responsibilities are consistent with any CSR role, and include:

- Providing customer service to inbound customer calls, which includes answering questions about wines and the winery; knowledge of club policies and procedures; and resolving complaints and issues.
- Placing targeted outbound calls to club members and other prospects to solicit sales and membership in the club.
- Entering and updating information in the wine club membership database or customer relations management (CRM) system.

SKILLS AND EDUCATION FOR CUSTOMER SERVICES REPRESENTATIVES

Requirements are also consistent with other CSR roles, and will include:

- High school diploma, GED or equivalent
- Minimum two to four years previous work experience in customer service, particularly in a call center environment
- Strong telephone customer service and verbal communication skills
- Ability to remain calm and diplomatic under pressure
- Familiarity with Microsoft Office applications and experience working with CRM software packages
- An understanding of common wine terms and concepts is helpful

JOB DESCRIPTIONS FOR E-COMMERCE/ WEB SPECIALISTS

E-commerce/web specialist or **manager roles** focus specifically on the winery's Internet presence. They manage website design, e-commerce software and sales, and email communications. While many clubs combine e-commerce and their club channel, some wineries offer customers the opportunity to purchase directly via the Internet without joining a club. The infrastructure required to maintain an e-commerce channel is essentially the same as for a club—both require a through and up-to-date understanding of interstate shipping laws, and the ability to fulfill customer shipments.

The difference between "pure" e-commerce and club e-commerce is primarily contact strategy. Pure e-commerce is more of a "pull" and relies on the information provided on a website. Club e-commerce is both "push" and "pull" combining emails to club customers with information provided on a website.

E-commerce roles are highly specialized, and are usually found in larger wine companies with multiple clubs, or at wineries that have a very strong e-commerce focus. Duties and responsibilities include:

- Designing, developing and maintaining brand and/or club websites.
- Management of the e-commerce functionality of brand and club websites, including interfacing between the websites, CRM software, and any in-house or third-party fulfillment system.
- Development and execution of online contact strategies, including email blasts (eblasts), targeted email campaigns to select club members and periodic refreshing of online content.
- Ensuring legal compliance with all appropriate federal and state laws regarding interstate commerce and alcohol sales.
- Management of subordinate developers or outside free-lancers.

SKILLS, EXPERIENCE & EDUCATION REQUIREMENTS FOR E-COMMERCE/WEB SPECIALIST

Requirements for these roles include:
- Bachelor's degree in marketing, communications, IS/IT, or equivalent.
- Three to seven years experience in website design and e-commerce, preferably with another wine club, high-end retailer, or similar company.

- Proficiency in relevant web technologies including HTML, Java, and Flash, and the ability to use them to deliver mass Internet communications.
- Strong written and verbal communications skills.
- Wine knowledge helpful but not required.

JOB DESCRIPTION FOR WINE CLUB MANAGERS

Wine club manager roles are the core of wine club operations managing both strategy and tactics for the club. They are oftentimes the public face of the club to members as well. Duties and responsibilities include:

- Developing member acquisition strategies for the club, including training tasting room personnel on how to sell the club; developing written promotional materials about the club; and purchasing lists or engaging in targeted direct calls to prospective club members when applicable. Manage attrition of club members to within targeted levels.
- Developing and executing member contact strategies, including determining number and frequency of club shipments, newsletters and other mailings, and online contacts including emails.
- Managing a P&L for an assigned club, including revenue targets and margin responsibility; analysis of previous campaigns and tactics to determine which generate the best return; development of new revenue-generating ideas.
- Selecting wines for shipments.
- Authoring or managing the creation of club collateral including newsletters, winemaker letters, emails and website copy.

- Developing and executing, or managing the execution of club special events.
- Partnering with the e-commerce, customer service, and hospitality functions within the winery to achieve all of the above.
- Managing customer service representatives, on-site wine club representatives and e-commerce professionals, as well as external fulfillment agencies and freelancers.

SKILLS AND EDUCATION FOR WINE CLUB MANAGERS

Requirements for these roles include:

- Bachelor's degree in marketing, business, direct marketing or equivalent.
- Minimum five to seven years in direct marketing, including retail direct marketing, database marketing, or equivalent.
- Strong project management skills, including the ability to handle multiple deadlines and pressure.
- Strong financial and quantitative analysis skills, including the ability to develop detailed contact strategies and forecast revenue and margins.
- Strong written and verbal communications skills, including previous experience writing copy for direct mail or e-commerce materials.
- Ability to act as the public face of the club, including hosting club events and representing the winery at functions.
- Strong knowledge of wine and wine terms highly desirable (and will need to be developed within the first year if the candidate does not possess them initially).

You will occasionally see a director role which oversees all of the above wine club functions, usually for a large wine company with a number of different brands and clubs. In some wineries, one director or vice president oversees both hospitality and wine club programs.

Figure 2: Wine Club Career Ladder

TIPS ON GETTING STARTED/ JOB HUNTING STRATEGIES

If you want to work in a direct-to-consumer sales position in the wine industry, consider some of the following steps:

Visit Wine Country: How cool is it that you can hunt for a job and go wine tasting at the same time? Visiting the wineries is your best look at exactly what your job might be like were you to land a role at that winery. You can also use your visit to bone up on the history of the winery, learn more about what it's known for, and about its wines. If you're looking for a wine club role, it's equally valuable, as you'll be able to meet some of your prospective club members. You may even get to meet real club members while onsite, and chat to them about their experience with the club.

Virtual Visiting: Most wineries have good consumer websites that provide you with great information about the winery, the wines, and an idea of how the winery likes to market itself to its customers. Visiting them is a must, particularly for individuals looking for wine club roles.

Timing is Everything: This relates particularly for hospitality jobs. Make sure you take the seasonal nature of the industry into account when planning your job search. While wineries will hire as-needed throughout the year, the bulk of the hiring will be done in the spring as wineries get ready for high season.

Put People First: Your people skills will be given a hard look no matter what role you're looking for in direct to consumer. Review the interviews from this chapter. Understand what's important to succeed. Make sure you profile your ability to be an effective part of a team, your communication skills, and above all, your ability to deliver wine country hospitality!

Play Favorites: As mentioned in the interviews, there are so many great wineries it's almost silly not to focus on ones you would love to represent. Focus your search on wineries you would love to represent. It'll help you in the interview process, and it will help you succeed once you're actually in the job.

HELPFUL CONFERENCES, PUBLICATIONS & WEBSITES

Direct to Consumer Conferences/Seminars

- **Tasting Room Profitability Conference & Trade Show**
- **The Wine Club Summit**
- **Wine Industry's Direct-to-Consumer Symposium**—Sponsored by Free the Grapes (www.freethegrapes.org)
- **Wine Industry Technology Symposium**—The only annual conference designed exclusively to foster wine industry technology solutions.

Books & Trade Publications

- **CRM News**
- **Direct Marketing Monthly**
- **Practical Winery & Vineyard Magazine**
- **Vineyard and Winery Management**
- **Wine Business Monthly**
- **Wines**
- **Wines and Vines**
- **Wine Marketing and Sales,** Paul Wagner, Janeen Olsen, Ph.D., Liz Thach, Ph.D.

Helpful Websites

- **http://www.craigslist.org:** An excellent site for wine job searches
- **http://www.crm-daily.com:** CRM (Customer Relations Management) News
- **http://www.the-dma.org:** The Direct Marketing Association's website
- **http://www.winebusiness.com:** *Wine Business Monthly*
- **http://www.winestyles.net:** A website that utilizes a "Style System" of classifying wine.

ADVICE FROM DIRECT-TO-CUSTOMER SALES EXPERTS

Following are three interviews from individuals who currently work in the Direct-to-Consumer channel.

True Tales from the Wine Industry

JOHN MCGREGOR, GENERAL MANAGER, MCGREGOR FAMILY WINERY

John McGregor is the second generation of a small, family-owned winery in the New York Finger Lakes region, which sells its wines almost exclusively through the direct-to-consumer channel.

McGregor Family is a fascinating story for students of the New York wine industry. It's also a great story of how a small, family-owned winery got its beginnings—and how it continues to this day.

John describes McGregor Family Winery best. "We're one of the first vineyards really in the Northeast US to have decided to give it a go with vinifera grape vines. Back in '71 my parents purchased this land with another investor.

"Walter Taylor was actually the reason that we—my family—ended up getting into the wine business. He would have some dinners with customers, with some of the people who were members of his newsletter, which my parents were. One late evening he just shared this idea with my father that he envisioned the Finger Lakes in the future being an

outpost of small family vineyards and wineries. My dad took that idea home with him, and really couldn't shake it. He thought to himself, 'I'd really like to be part of something like that, and that would be a great thing.' It's really from the seeds that Walter Taylor planted in my father's head is how this ultimately began.

"We produce fifteen to 20,000 gallons of wine a year. We're literally 99% on-premise sales/direct-to-consumer sales. That was really a direction we've always felt we wanted to be in. We weren't quite there, when I first started. For the first year, I was doing on-the-road sales, [and] it became quickly apparent to me that my efforts needed to be focused on growing business at the winery.

"Twenty years ago my parents formed what was probably one of the first wine clubs in America, in 1985 or 1986. They started this because they realized when they would have a good customer come to the winery, 'how am I going to keep in contact with them? How am I going to keep in touch with them when I have a really good vintage at the winery? Because I know they're going to like it.

"When I started here we had a few hundred households [in the club]. Now we have over 1100."

EDUCATION AND TRAINING

"We lived an hour away from the vineyard. It was largely a weekend and summer venture for most of my childhood. I never really got pushed into it; it was just something that was always part of my life.

"I didn't spend my time as a child thinking this was something I was going to do, I didn't go to school to study business, or viticulture, or enology. I've taken literally zero

education for what I'm doing now. Actually, my profession is as an archaeologist. I got my Master's down in Binghamton, NY. My Master's work was in the Sonoran desert, in Northern Mexico.

"I would work my nine to five doing archaeology around the state Monday through Friday, and then I'd oftentimes come down to the winery and help out here on the weekends. As time went on I'd come down and see how hard my parents were still working—it just dawned on me how tired they were. I literally just called them one evening—my wife, at the time fiancé, was willing to move up to this area—and said, 'Well, what do you think about retiring? I'm going to quit my job and I'll take over the business for you.' [laughing] Very naively! 'No big deal, I'll just come in and take care of things for you.'

"I always had a pull towards this land, though. It's something that, when it seemed like it was no longer going to be run by family, I started realizing just how much this place meant to me, having grown up here, having planted a lot of the vines and tended to them. It became clear that it was just something I had to do.

"What helped was growing up in the wine business. I didn't have the know-how to run a business by itself, but I watched how the winery had grown, what my parents were doing—I didn't prep myself too much. I immediately started trying to read more, and taste more. There was also a fair amount of winging it. There was also a fair amount of guidance in the first years from my parents."

MOST IMPORTANT SKILLS FOR DIRECT-TO-CONSUMER PROFESSIONALS IN WINE

"One of the things is just an outright honesty and caring for your product, truly believing in what you're doing. Making sure you're worried more about having pride through the day than the dollars at the end of the day. I just can't stress that enough. You've got to like what you're doing and you've got to be sure that you approach it with honesty.

"We always feel here the wine sells itself. My staff is here to sell wine, but they don't have to sell it. They need to be here to provide a comfortable experience for people, something that is memorable, where they truly in a genuine way are looking the customers in the eye and saying I care about what you have to say, I'm interested in what you're doing in this region."

"You can tell people all day long about what they are supposed to taste in the wine, how good it is, how many medals it has. Let the wine speak for itself for the most part, and provide an atmosphere that is conducive to one enjoying wine—that's the approach for the most part that we like to take.

"Coming from an anthropological background has helped me enormously, just in terms of understanding or embracing the diversity of people. For my staff and anyone I hire new, on our fridge in the kitchen here I've got a postcard with a chimpanzee dressed up to the nines with a big smile, holding up a glass of wine. Underneath I wrote a caption that says, 'Never pre-judge your customer.' That's rule number one here. Rule number two says, 'See Rule Number One.'

162

"The more time goes on the more blinders I put on myself. I'm not as concerned about what my neighbors are doing with their wineries or their wines. I'm not as concerned about what the industry says is the next big varietal—it's almost a blind passion in knowing in what you're doing is right, [and] it'll translate to your business growing and succeeding."

MOST CHALLENGING PART OF THE JOB

"Keeping up with the work! Being a family run business, a lot of times it's a one-man band with things. Getting pulled in so many directions is pretty tough. It's easy to get over-consumed with your business. It's very easy to get wrapped up when you own your own business."

BEST PART OF THE JOB

"The wow factor—just standing back and watching customers, whether they've been a customer of ours for ten years or whether this is their first time visiting. Watching them experience one of our wines for the first time, [and] seeing how pleasantly surprised some people are, how overjoyed some people are. To have someone actually use one of my wines for their wedding or something of that caliber just blows me away—that you're actually choosing wholeheartedly to incorporate something that my family and staff have toiled over [for one of your special occasions]. I'll never get tired of those moments happening. That's to me what it's all about. That's the end of a good day.

"[Wine is] totally unique from other industries. Our competition also happens to be our acquaintances, our friends. We share customers. We're always recommending the next

winery down the road. I've never been in any business where there have been so many positive networking opportunities, and true openness to talk about each others' business and to help each other out. There's a lot of sharing, a lot of cross-pollination going on. I find it phenomenal."

ADVICE FOR PEOPLE LOOKING TO START THEIR WINE CAREER

JOHN'S DO'S:

- *"It's important that if you're starting from scratch, that you somehow educate yourself—whether that's with books or interning at a facility [where] you like the way they do things."*
- *"Trying out things from different perspectives, [even] if you have no business experience with the wine business. Try getting as much diverse experience as you can before taking the plunge yourself."*
- *"Remember that there's not just one way to do it. How many wineries have you been to that are identical to the ones next door?"*
- *"Find out what you want out of the business. What are you getting into it for? What do you want out of it?"*
- *"Play around. Maybe instead of chomping down and buying twenty acres, maybe you should start with an acre for five years or so and say, "Is something I can really follow through on?" Because this is something you're going to dump a lot of money into—this industry—before you get anything out of it, particularly if you take the avenue of grape-growing and winemaking."*

- *"Get involved as much as you can in the wine industry [where] you're planning on starting a winery in. Get to know the people, [and] find out the history of the area that you're entering. How did the region grow? Who's there now that wasn't there twenty years ago? Who's there twenty years ago that's not there now and why? How are your neighbors successful?"*

JOHN'S DON'T:

- *"[Don't] be naïve about it. It's not the "Falcon Crest" scenario—it's hard work! It's a lot more work than one could imagine."*

MIRYAM CHAE, DIRECTOR, CONSUMER RELATIONSHIP MARKETING, FOSTER'S WINE ESTATES AMERICAS AND TOM JOHNSON, DIRECTOR, HOSPITALITY, FOSTER'S WINE ESTATES AMERICAS

Miryam Chae and Tom Johnson are the dynamic duo who manage the direct-to-consumer functions for Foster's Wine Estates.

Miryam came from direct marketing in other industries, including working for KPMG, Frankel & Company, and United

165

News and Media (Miller Freeman). Tom's background is in retail, having previously worked at Macy's, The Disney Store, and Target. Tom's family also owns a small winery in Alexander Valley.

They've both been promoted twice in their four-plus years with the company, and currently hold the top jobs in this facet of the business. When asked how they got into the wine business, they provided fairly similar—yet different—answers.

MC: [Laughter] How do I say it politely? You poached me, you stole me, you enticed me, you sent random emails to me... No, you saw my resume on the DMA (Direct Marketing Association) website, and shot me an email and asked if I was interested.

TJ: The Foster's job description came across my wife's desk—she was with an executive placement company—and, so I wasn't looking for a job, but the job met with my skills, and here I am later on!

EDUCATION AND TRAINING

TJ: In my role as hospitality director, we're dealing with people every single day. They're usually people on vacation that have come to find your site. They want to be entertained and educated and talked to about wines, [as well as] share what they know about wines, so mine is relationship-based. I did go to college for history and social science. Even in my retail background before Foster's, I used more of what I learned in the fraternity world—about building relationships and talking to people and using my social skills—in my business life every single day than what I learned in school.

MC: See, I'm exactly the opposite. I actually got a business degree with an emphasis in marketing, which for what I do on the consumer direct marketing side, you have to have a basis, an understanding, of how you're going to communicate with your consumer. Coming in here, I think the most important thing I've had is management training—going to a really good management development program [has] allowed me to manage my team through change, through difficult times, and through the financial issues.

MOST IMPORTANT SKILLS FOR DIRECT-TO-CONSUMER PROFESSIONALS IN WINE

MC: For me, it was relationship-building. I wouldn't be here today if it weren't for the relationships I've been able to build in the company.

TJ: I would say relationship-building as well. But, to be honest, the success I've had at the sites was due to the fact that I brought to the table some practical and business knowledge as well, and hard work ethic. The person that was working the hardest and doing the best job within this organization has been promoted, which is great. The ones who can make it happen and have a positive, can-do attitude have been rewarded.

We have over 200 employees in the hospitality organization. Dealing with the people part of the business first, making sure that you're talking to your people, doing pulse checks with your people, making sure that they're in the right mindset to get the job done, making sure they're able to motivate their people and their teams to be successful. If they're not successful—

MC: Consequently, you're not successful!

TJ: Absolutely.

MC: Yeah, I think it's the same thing. The one thing I've realized [is] you're only as successful as your people are. The most important item you should focus on is ensuring that they're happy in their current role, that they have the tools that they need to do their job—promoting their talents, making them feel like they're cared for, rewarded and someone is here to listen to them.

TJ: To drill it back down into why someone would be successful in a hospitality business, you [need to] look at the hospitality staff. A lot of times this is their second career, this is their retirement career, this is their fun career, this is their weekend job to relax and to get away from their other job. So you have some very talented individuals who are working for you for a lot of different reasons. We have authors, we have professors, we have former CFOs who are taking direction from a former liberal arts major from Chico State! [Laughter] If you do it the right way they will be successful for you.

BEST PART OF THE JOB

MC: I think it's the people. For us, our lives are driven by the numbers. There's always a number we're watching, a number we're trying to meet. We don't make that number unless our people are driving to meet it. So they're the best part of it.

TJ: I've had the jobs from hell. No matter how tough this job is, it's not that bad! We're not here curing cancer. It's—

MC: Fermented grape juice!

TJ: [Laughter] That's right! It's fermented grape juice.

We're talking with people who've spent their hard-earned money to come see us, to come taste our wines. I love getting behind the bar to talk to those people and see what they're all about. I love that we have so many diverse people that we work with, back to Miryam's point—it's the people. Every singe day, my day is different—that keeps it exciting and fun as well. You can never plan your day because it goes in so many different directions.

MC: And you have to like that! It's a new challenge—every day brings something new. We call each other and laugh about it, and say, 'OK, let's keep going!' It's not a big deal—you handle it, you move on. But you have to have that personality, or else it doesn't work.

TJ: The last part of that is in the Hospitality field it's all about guest service. We are talking to guests, we're branding the brand—if you look at it the right way, if you do the guest service, the retail will come.

MC: It's funny about that. In my team's world, they use mostly email to communicate. We obviously work very closely with Tom's team as well, so I have to teach new people to pick up the telephone to talk to his team, because that's how they prefer to interact. You have to understand how the recipient hears your message.

MOST CHALLENGING PART OF THE JOB

MC: [Laughing] The people!

TJ: Absolutely! It's true! It's not having the right fit, and working through that. When we do get frustrated, when we do pull our hair out, it's because there's a people issue that's a mismatch, a bad fit.

MC: They don't understand the vision, don't understand

what the business is trying to achieve, and are almost oper-ating on their own agenda. This is very much a team-based environment. You can't have that—you can't have someone being a renegade and going off and doing their own thing. It just doesn't work that way.

ADVICE FOR PEOPLE LOOKING TO START THEIR DIRECT-TO-CONSUMER CAREER IN WINE

MIRYAM AND TOM'S DO'S:

- *MC: Be yourself [in the interview]. I need to know who you really are. I need to be able to see you in a real life setting with my team, with Tom's team. I don't judge people on whether they have wine industry background. I know I can teach someone that.*
- *TJ: When approaching whomever it is that they're ap-proaching, don't be overzealous, don't be 'I'm your guy, I'm a sommelier, I've passed this and that.' Know the brand, know the pronunciations.*
- *MC: Know what [the winery]'s known for. Do a little research.*
- *TJ: There are so many great brands out there within the wine industry. Go after a brand that you're very, very passionate about. Some of our best employees are the ones who live and breathe that brand. They smile when they talk about the brand.*
- *MC: They genuinely say, 'If I didn't work here, I'd be a wine club member here.' Passion is a huge 'do.'*

MIRYAM AND TOM'S DON'TS:

- *TJ: Think that you want a wine country job because it's easy, that you get to just stand there and talk and pour wine all day long. That's not the case. Standing there and pouring wine and talking all day is a hard job: you're on your feet, hustling, you're lifting sixty pounds of wine, you're on-stage all day.*

- *MC: We're in such a small environment that negativity doesn't fly. It's just really disruptive. The common thread for the people we've seen aren't a good fit—part of it is they weren't able to build relationships with people around them, part of it is the negativity rubbing people the wrong way.*

- *TJ: Don't be afraid to take a job that isn't necessarily what you're looking for. The industry is a fast-moving one—if you're successful at what you do, the cream will rise to the top.*

Wine Marketing & Sales with Distributors & Importers

My new boss is 25—I've got Barolos older than that.

As explained in Chapter 2 "Overview of the Global Wine Market and Key Issues," there are multiple tiers within the global wine industry. Two of these tiers are made up of distributors and importers.

The role of the distributor varies based on the wine industry you want to enter. If you want to work in the alcohol beverage industry in the United States, distributors play a very specific, and very important, role. To properly understand their role, you need a brief history of Prohibition, and how it evolved into the "three-tiered system."

A VERY BRIEF SUMMARY OF PROHIBITION

Prohibition, for those unfamiliar with it, is shorthand for the prohibition of alcohol in the US that took place from 1920 through 1933. The 18th Amendment to the Constitution banned the manufacture, transportation and sale of alcoholic beverages. There were limited exceptions for medical and religious purposes. The Volstead Act, passed shortly before the 18th Amendment became effective, gave power to the IRS to regulate enforcement of the 18th Amendment.

Prohibition was the result of successive waves of temperance movements that had their roots back in the early 1800s. The twenty years surrounding the beginning of the 20th century were marked by technological advances in the production of beer and liquor, as well as a corresponding dramatic rise in the number of saloons. Some sources suggest there were as many as one saloon for every 150-200 people during this period.

Many of these saloons were owned by distillers and brewers, who sought to provide additional outlets for the marketing and sale of their products. This seemingly logical vertical integration led to the aggressive marketing of alcoholic beverages and fierce competition between competing producers for customers. Additionally, many saloons could only sell the products produced by the brewery or distiller who owned them.

Some saloons also provided other "entertainments" for their customers, such as cockfighting, prostitution, and gambling. Many in the temperance movement and elsewhere found these entertainments to be morally offensive. Those involved in the movement advocated for complete abstinence from alcohol as the basis for a moral, virtuous, productive life, and in turn saw saloons as the root cause of many societal ills.

Prohibition, dubbed "the Noble Experiment" by Herbert Hoover, was expected to usher in an age of moral, responsible behavior, if not a more productive society. Unfortunately for its advocates, Prohibition had several unanticipated side-effects. Popular support was dramatically overestimated. By the mid-1920s, illegal saloons, or "speakeasies," had become an entrenched and well-patronized social institution. As with any item which people want and is difficult to obtain, the illegal production and sale of alcohol became an extraordinarily lucrative business. Some of the most famous gangsters of the time, including Al Capone and "Bugs" Moran, made much of their living on the illegal manufacture, sale and distribution of alcohol. And while Prohibition reduced the consumption of alcohol—at least initially—by the mid-20s, more and more Americans were beginning to ignore the law and seek out ways to quench their thirst for alcoholic beverages.

By the late 1920s, even hard-core supporters of Prohibition were forced to admit that Prohibition was a failure. In 1933, the 21st Amendment to the Constitution was passed, which repealed the 18th Amendment. It's a note of historical curiosity that Prohibition is the only Amendment to the Constitution to have been repealed. The 21st Amendment made alcohol manufacture, sales and distribution legal once more, and left the regulation of the industry to the states.

Prohibition decimated the fledgling US wine industry, which had begun to emerge in the second-half of the 1800s. Few wineries survived. Those that did stayed alive by producing sacramental or medicinal wine, or finding other creative ways to sell their fruit. It has taken most of the 20th century for the US wine industry to recover from Prohibition.

AN EQUALLY BRIEF SUMMARY OF THE THREE-TIERED SYSTEM

One of the longest-lasting legacies of Prohibition is the laws that govern the manufacture, sale and distribution of alcoholic beverages.

Despite repealing Prohibition, lawmakers were still leery of the "tied house"—a situation in which a brewer, distiller or vintner could control not only the manufacture, but also the distribution and sale of alcoholic beverages. In their view, this was the source of many of the pre-Prohibition ills.

Detailed legislation was left to the states. However, the 21st Amendment contained provisions preventing the creation of tied houses. Thus in most states, the supplier, distributor, and retailer of alcoholic beverages were separated.

This resulted in what we know today as the Three-Tiered System. The **first tier** is comprised of **suppliers:** vintners, brewers, and distillers. The **second tier** is the **distributors**—also referred to as wholesalers. The **third tier** is made up of **end retailers:** grocery, club, independent liquor stores; restaurants, hotels, and anywhere other than the brewery or winery where you may purchase alcohol.

The role of the distributor is to act as a buffer between the end retailer and the supplier. Distributors purchase wine and other alcoholic beverages from suppliers. They in turn sell those products to end retailers. Depending on the state and the distributor, they may play a significant role in the transportation, warehousing, and even marketing of the product. They also play a key role in some states in collecting excise taxes on alcohol.

The intent of the three-tiered system is to eliminate the social ills of the tied house, promote competition among suppliers (wineries), and allow state and local governments to collect revenues by taxing the sale of alcoholic beverages.

You may be thinking—correctly—that this arrangement sounds very similar to distributor and third-party broker relationships you're familiar with in other industries. In terms of the core functions, that is likely very true. The difference is the legally mandated nature of the relationships, *and* that the laws governing that relationship vary significantly from state to state. In some states, the state itself may directly control either the distribution or retailing of alcoholic beverages. These states (Pennsylvania and New Hampshire are two examples) are frequently referred to as control states. Other states, like California, allow for direct intrastate sales from wineries to retailers and restaurants. Discounting, advertising, and promotion of wine are similarly regulated—and may similarly be different from state to state.

For your purposes, distributors provide yet another avenue for entry into the wine business.

DISTRIBUTORS

There are over 150 distributors in the US. Each distributor is licensed to operate in different markets, and represents different suppliers in those markets. There are four large players: Southern/Glazer's Distributors of America, The Charmer Sunbelt Group, Young's Market Company, and the Republic National Distributing Company (RNDC).

Many sales professionals in wine get their start working for a distributor. Distributors are the true "feet on the street," calling on customers in specific geographic areas, selling and assisting in the marketing of the products they represent.

While many supplier sales organizations require previous experience (either with another supplier or distributor) to be considered for hire, many distributors are willing to hire new college graduates or individuals from outside the wine industry. These individuals typically start in merchandising roles or sales representative roles, depending on previous experience and skills.

JOB DESCRIPTION FOR DISTRIBUTOR MERCHANDISERS

Merchandisers are the core entry-level role in many distributor organizations. Their role's main responsibility, as the name suggests, is to go to customers' retail outlets and, once there, stock and display merchandise on the sales floor of retail stores to attract the attention of prospective customers.

Merchandisers are typically responsible for the following:

- Placing price and descriptive signs on backdrops, fixtures, merchandise, and the floor (where legally permitted).
- Preparing, constructing and maintaining product displays according to schematics, directions and standards.
- Presenting promotional activities and suggestions to customers.
- Surveying the account for merchandising opportunities.
- Using sell sheets and point of sale (POS) materials to improve the display and representation of wines on the sales floor.
- Maintaining updated account information for all assigned accounts, and using the information to plan and execute their day.

- Submitting daily activity report and merchandising reports.
- Preparing and maintaining required paperwork, reports and records.
- Reporting competitive activities and pricing as it occurs to immediate supervisor.
- Managing the supply of POS materials needed for balancing accounts.
- Lifting cases and bottles of wine throughout the day.

SKILLS, EXPERIENCE AND EDUCATION REQUIREMENTS FOR DISTRIBUTOR MERCHANDISERS

To secure a job as a merchandiser, you will likely need to meet the following requirements:

- High school diploma or GED at minimum; undergraduate college degree usually preferred
- Previous sales experience is typically desirable; experience in retail sales and merchandising a plus.
- Strong written and verbal communication skills.
- Effective relationship skills, including the ability to create collaborative partnerships with customers.
- High work standards and self-motivation.
- Valid driver's license
- Physically capable of lifting multiple cases of wine (up to twenty-five) throughout the course of the day.
- Basic knowledge of wine, particularly wine terms and varietals, a plus.

JOB DESCRIPTION FOR DISTRIBUTOR SALES REPRESENTATIVE

The core sales role at a distributor is a **sales representative.** This position is typically the next step for someone who has been in a merchandiser role. As a sales rep, you will truly "carry the bag" and call on accounts. These roles are typically responsible for the following:

- Achieving sales growth, specifically through assigning quotas and business plan objectives, in an assigned sales territory.
- Soliciting business by personally visiting sales accounts. Garnering interest of prospective buyers by explaining the merits of represented products and how they would benefit the account.
- Preparing price quotes, taking orders, and scheduling delivery dates and service obligations for existing accounts.
- Producing weekly and monthly reporting of results, risks and opportunities.
- Investigating and resolving customer complaints in accordance with their company policy.
- Familiarizing established accounts with new products and developments.
- Driving depletion of represented products through new product distribution, achieving desired product placement at retail or on-premise sites, and providing sales support materials (display materials, menus, table tents, etc.) to accounts.
- Keeping information on competitive products, promotional matters, sales techniques, pricing and marketing policies. Informing company of competitive activity and conditions that could affect company interests.

- Attending evening promotional events for products, including pouring wines, developing customer contacts, and other related duties.

SKILLS, EXPERIENCE AND EDUCATION FOR DISTRIBUTOR SALES REPRESENTATIVE

To secure a sales rep role, you will likely need to meet the following requirements:

- Undergraduate college degree
- One to three years of previous general sales experience; a big plus if in the alcohol beverage industry.
- Previous experience in retail beverage or on-premise sales a plus.
- Strong written and verbal communication skills, including the ability to effectively present to individuals and medium-sized groups.
- Effective relationship skills, including the ability to create collaborative partnerships with customers.
- Very strong time management and organizational skills, including the ability to create daily, weekly, and monthly market plans that maximize time and results.
- Valid driver's license
- Physically capable of lifting multiple cases of wine (up to twenty-five) throughout the course of the day.
- Knowledge of wine, particularly wine terms and varietals.
- Knowledge of the territory, including key accounts, a plus.

Advancement within a distributor from this point onward will vary based on the size of the distributor and your goals. There are two typical paths leading out from a sales rep role. Following is a typical career ladder for distributor sales roles.

Figure 1: Wine Distributor Career Ladder

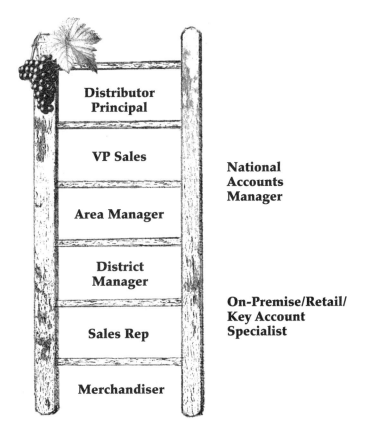

DISTRICT MANAGER

The first path is perhaps the most traditional, which is vertical advancement in broad market selling. Individuals who are successful as sales reps will often be offered the opportunity to move into a management role, which will involve responsibility for a larger territory and supervising a team of sales representatives. A common title for this kind of role is **district manager.**

District managers typically have spent at least two to three years as sales reps, where they had proven their ability to achieve sales goals, manage their time and territory effectively, and create strong relationships (both externally with accounts and suppliers and internally within the distributor). As a district manager, they will take on enhanced responsibilities including:

- All aspects of people management for a team of one to five sales reps, including setting quotas, assigning territories, training new sales reps, and providing coaching and feedback to team members.
- Regular reporting to senior distribution management.
- Partnering with distributor managers from supplier partners to align plans for achieving distribution and case goals.
- Overseeing the execution of programming for targeted accounts.
- Acting as a point of escalation for any customer service issues that sales reps cannot resolve on their own.

AREA MANAGER

The career path from a district manager upward involves gaining responsibility for more territory, moving from supervising sales reps to managing a team of district managers, and gaining enhanced responsibility for setting quotas, managing budget, interacting with supplier/distributor management personnel, and developing strategy for their territory. They will have more involvement in supply chain management, ensuring that they are able to balance inventory levels with maintaining appropriate stock on hand to fulfill account needs, and addressing issues as they arise. They will also have more involvement in negotiating pricing and deal structures with suppliers. Titles for these roles vary from distributor to distributor. A common title is **area manager.**

VICE PRESIDENT OF SALES

From the area manager role, your next step will be into senior management with a distributor, likely with a **vice president of sales** title. This would involve managing the sales staff and efforts for a large geographic territory.

The final step from a VP of sales position is to become a member of the leadership team or ownership group of that distributor. You'll need the following key skill sets as you advance through these more senior levels of management:

- Strong people management skills, including the ability to manage managers.
- Strong financial management skills, including the ability to develop budgets and growth goals, and to manage to agreed budget targets.
- Ability to develop relationships with senior-level individuals at supplier organizations and accounts, as well as internally within the distributor.
- Ability to partner with specialist organizations within the distributor to achieve account and territory goals.
- Excellent negotiating skills.
- Strong understanding of industry and consumer trends.
- An advanced degree, such as an MBA, may be highly desirable for the highest levels of distribution management.

CHANNEL SPECIALISTS

The second way you can advance your career within a distributor is by specializing in a specific sales channel, such as retail, on-premise, or fine wine selling. These roles can exist both as lateral and promotional opportunities. Some distributors may require experience in a channel-specific role before allowing upward advancement past a certain level. Common titles for channel specific roles include:

- **Key Account Specialist**
- **Retail Specialist**
- **On-Premise Specialist**
- **Fine Wine Specialist**

These roles will be focused on specific sales channels—for instance, retail grocery and chain accounts in an assigned territory, or the restaurant and bar trade within that same territory. **Channel specialists** will have similar responsibilities to sales reps. The primary difference is the responsibility for executing channel-specific programming. For example, a **retail specialist** may ensure that specific promotional programming and pricing are being executed within key retail accounts, making sure that represented products are receiving feature and display activity in line with their objectives. They may directly or indirectly oversee the efforts of Merchandisers to achieve those objectives.

An **on-premise specialist** may engage in wait staff training at key accounts to ensure that the servers and bartenders are able to speak knowledgeably about specific products that are being featured on the list or in a by-the-glass pour. They may also work with the account to prepare a progressive wine list, provide promotional materials to enhance sales, and talk with the culinary staff about ideal food and wine pairings.

Fine wine specialists may call on fine restaurants (often referred to as 'white-tablecloth') and high-end specialty retail stores. They will often have substantial wine education and experience, and use it to persuade sommeliers, influential wine buyers, and chefs to sample—and ultimately purchase—represented fine wines. They may attend consumer events as an expert and speak with consumers about the wines being poured.

All channel specialists will be focused on gaining increased distribution of represented products at targeted accounts. The goals for placement may be set by the distributor themselves, or in partnership with the supplier.

These roles are also where the marketing aspects of distributors are most frequently seen. Distributors are not normally engaged in the building of brand image, developing packaging, creating new varietals or line extensions (though they may certainly provide robust feedback to their supplier partners about the need for any and all of the above). They will often partner in the development of trade marketing activities. These roles are often responsible for presenting those programs to accounts and executing them.

SKILLS, EXPERIENCE AND EDUCATIONAL REQUIREMENTS FOR CHANNEL SPECIALISTS

Key skills required for channel-specific roles include:

- Typically three to five years previous wine sales experience.
- Strong wine knowledge, particularly for roles focused in on-premise and fine wine. A certification from a reputable wine education association, such as a MW, MS, CWE, or a WSET certification, may be highly desirable or required (see Chapter 9 "Wine Writers and Educators" for more on these certifications).
- Passion for the wine industry and represented products.
- Ability to effectively interact and influence key decision-makers at targeted accounts.

- Very strong project and time management skills, including the ability to deliver multiple projects on tight deadlines.
- Previous experience working as a retailer, in the on-premise, or at a supplier may be highly desirable.

NATIONAL ACCOUNTS MANAGER

At the most senior levels, you will see **national accounts manager** roles. These roles are responsible for making calls on either the regional or headquarters buyers of major national accounts. Examples of these include Safeway, SUPERVALU, Kroger, Walmart, Costco, OSI Restaurant Partners (think Outback Steakhouse), Starwood Hotels & Resorts Worldwide, and Marriott International. These examples should provide you with a sense of the size—and value to the distributor—of these large accounts.

National accounts managers will partner with such accounts, as well as with the national accounts managers of their supplier partners, to increase the placement of represented products on shelves, on wine lists, and behind bars of these accounts. They will also develop and execute account-specific programming. They will look at category and consumer trends to determine needs and develop solutions for those accounts. They will likely have a substantial budget which they will manage to achieve these results.

Based on the size of those accounts, they will have a substantial role in achieving financial goals for the distributor, and will have heavy interaction with supplier personnel, who rely similarly on results at these accounts to meet their goals. National accounts manager roles may also directly or indirectly supervise channel specialist personnel at the distributor.

JOB ROLES & DISTRIBUTOR SIZE

As mentioned previously, the availability of many of these roles will depend heavily on the size and complexity of the distributor in question. At the largest distributors, there will be more specialization, and more steps in the career ladder.

At smaller distributors, many roles are combined and levels collapsed. A smaller distributor may choose to focus more on the on-premise or independent liquor channels based on their size and the types of brands they represent. Therefore, a sales rep at that distributor may carry out many responsibilities of an on-premise specialist at a larger distributor. Similarly, a smaller distributor that focuses on the retail chain channel may not have merchandisers or key account specialists, and therefore may ask their sales reps to perform many of those functions in addition to their traditional duties. In this instance, there may be three levels to the career ladder: sales representative, manager, and head of sales.

Wine knowledge, and passion for brands, may be more important at a smaller distributor who may be representing 200-300 SKUs (stock-keeping units), than at a larger distributor, where a Sales Rep may represent a portfolio of more than 20,000 SKUs.

The market in which the distributor operates will affect the types and availability of roles. The Northeastern US is an independent retail market (based on the state laws there) with strong on-premise markets in places like New York City, Boston and Philadelphia. In contrast, Florida, Texas, and Illinois are large retail chain markets, and the distributor roles available in those markets will reflect that. You will see more on-premise focused roles are more common in major metropolitan areas that have a lively restaurant scene, and less so in smaller, more rural markets.

Many distributors have a strong promote-from-within bias, so successfully moving up to senior management roles requires working your way up from entry-level positions. Relocation may also be required for advancement, whether to an adjoining territory, nearby metro area, or to a different part of the US.

IMPORTERS

Importers are, as the name suggests, organizations that specialize in bringing wines from other countries into the US. If you have ever tasted French, Italian, Spanish, Chilean, Australian, New Zealand, or a similar non-US wine, then rest assured that it passed through the hands of an importer. There are five different types of importers:

- **Spirits-based:** Examples include Remy Amerique and Diageo.
- **National Specialists:** Examples include Foster's Group (Australian), Empson USA (Italian), Jorge Ordoñez (Spanish), and Martine's Wines, Inc. (Freench).
- **Full-Service National:** Examples include Wilson Daniels Ltd., Kobrand Corporation, Terlato Wine Group, and Vineyard Brands.
- **Distributor Importers:** Examples include Frederick Wildman and Sons, Ltd and Shaw-Ross International Importers.
- **Local:** Examples specific to Napa wine country include North Berkeley Imports, Oliver McCrum Wines, and Exclusive Imports, Inc.

Understanding the role of importers can be confusing, as they can wear a number of different hats. At a minimum, an importer represents one or more suppliers from another country and acts as their agent. They work in the importing country to expedite the movement and sale of the suppliers' wines. Importers are sometimes a separate entity, adding a fourth tier to the system. In turn, those importers work with a distributor network of their selection to effectively market and sell their suppliers' wines.

Distributors may sometimes operate as importers and perform both functions. Some distributors may specialize in imported wines. Larger distributors tend to have an imports division that coordinates the selection, marketing and distribution of imported wines.

Retailers sometimes double as importers by bringing wines into the country specifically to sell at their wine shop (state law permitting).

Depending on the size and sophistication of the supplier whose wines are being imported, an importer may play a role in marketing the wines, including partnering with the supplier to develop a target market, recommend pricing, and collaborate on packaging.

It's difficult to describe a "typical" role at an Importer, based on these complexities. Many roles will resemble distributor sales roles, particularly that of the sales rep and the various sales manager titles.

You will find roles at an importer focused on the logistics and administration of importing alcoholic beverages into the US. As you would imagine, there are practical details of arranging for the proper quantities to arrive in a timely fashion at the appropriate location. This is in turn complicated by the legion of legal requirements (and paperwork!) required to secure licenses and manage customs requirements in both the exporting and importing countries. These roles require strong organizational, computer, and administrative skills, and familiarity with the various regulations in both the exporting and importing countries.

If the importer takes a strong role in the marketing of the supplier's wines, you may find brand or marketing manager roles similar to those described in Chapter 5 "Wine Marketing, Sales & Public Relations for a Winery."

You will also find roles responsible for the selection of supplier relationships, the partnership and management of those relationships, and the selection of specific wines from the supplier's portfolio to bring to market. These are typically **senior-level roles**—a principle, partner or senior manager at a smaller importer or an executive role at a larger importer/distributor—and will combine a strong knowledge of wine with a keen understanding of both the market from which the wines are being imported and the market in which they will be marketed and sold.

There are typically few **entry-level roles** within an importer. It's highly recommended that you gain experience with a distributor or supplier in the industry prior to seeking out opportunities in this specialized niche. See the interviews later in this chapter with Geoff Labitzke of Young's Market Company and Larry Challacombe of Global Vineyard Wine Importers for an idea of the backgrounds of two successful individuals who currently work in wine importing (the former with a distributor and the latter with an importer).

TIPS ON GETTING STARTED/ JOB HUNTING STRATEGIES

Following is a list of tips to help you jumpstart your career in distributor sales or as an importer:

- **Start in the Trade:** Many individuals working at distributors got their start by working in retail at a liquor store, wine shop, or as a server at a restaurant or banquet facility. Working for these customers of distributors and importers—particularly if you progress to being a wine buyer—gives you a great opportunity to get to know the world of wine sales from the customer's perspective. It also gives you great opportunities to build your wine knowledge and your understanding of what drives buyers to purchase certain wines; to learn how wine succeeds (or fails) at retail or in restaurants; and to network.

- **Network, Network, Network:** While distributors will advertise on the web and in local newspapers for merchandiser or sales rep roles, your best bet is networking. If you currently work in the trade, offer to buy lunch for the distributor rep who calls on your store. Pick their brain about what it's like to work as a sales rep or merchandiser. Ask their advice on how to get started in the business. For importers, you will often need to network into these organizations—and your networking skills will be key to your success as an importer.

- **Take a Step Back:** If you have sales experience in other industries, and have progressed your career, you may be expecting to come into the distributor at a district manager (or higher) level. That's probably not a realistic expectation. Most distributors will require you to start as a sales rep and demonstrate your ability to translate your sales skills to the wine business.

- **Learn About Wine:** The level of wine knowledge required to get a job will vary based on the specific role within the distributor or importer. Generally speaking, it can't hurt to have more wine knowledge. Be careful, though, that you promote your selling, organizational, business, and networking skills equally when speaking with potential employers. Join local wine clubs, visit wine country, and read about wine. And above all else—pop some corks!

- **Refine Your Sales Skills:** For many larger distributors, the key criteria to secure a sales rep job will be your ability to sell. Many distributors are willing to invest in training a new sales rep or merchandiser about wine. It's harder to make the jump if your sales skills are lacking.

HELPFUL CONFERENCES, PUBLICATIONS & WEBSITES

Following is a list of useful resources to help you learn more about careers in distributor sales.

- Several job websites including **www.craigslist.org, www.winejobs.com, www.hotjobs.com, www.careerbuilder.com** and **www.simplyhired.com,** list job postings with distributors and importers.

- **Wine & Spirits Wholesalers of America** is the trade association for alcohol beverage distributors. WSWA also hosts a major distributor trade show each year. (www.wswa.org)

- Check the websites of some of the major distributors like **Southern/Glazer's Distributors of America (www.southernwine.com** and **www.glazers.com), Young's Market Company (www.youngsmarket.com), The Charmer Sunbelt Group (www.charmer-sunbelt.com),** and the **Republic National Distributing Company (www.rndc-usa.com).**

- Wine columns in major national newspapers, such as *The Wall Street Journal* and *The New York Times,* as well as in most regional newspapers and trade publications, including *Wine Spectator.*

- Reading *Beverage Industry News, Wine Business Monthly,* M. Shanken's *Market Watch,* and *Patterson's: The Tasting Panel Magazine* for general industry information.

ADVICE FROM DISTRIBUTORS AND IMPORTERS

Following are four interviews with professionals to provide you with an idea of the backgrounds of successful individuals who work currently in wine distributing and importing.

 *True Tales from the Wine Industry*

BRUCE HERMAN, SENIOR VICE PRESIDENT, SALES, FOSTER'S WINE ESTATES AMERICAS

Bruce Herman is a thirty-plus year veteran of the wine indus-try. He's worked on the supplier and distributor sides of the business with organizations like United Vintners (formerly Diageo), Mirrasou Vineyards, Schieffelin & Somerset, Young's Market Company, and Foster's.

Education and Training

Bruce's answer about how he got into wine is disarmingly honest: "I came out of college and needed a job."

Bruce goes on to say, "I was a history/political science major. United Vintners was looking for college-aged young men or women to start as merchandisers. I started as a merchandiser for a year, and then I was asked if I wanted to become a salesman. I said, 'If I'm going to become a sales manager, then maybe I should start as a salesman and un-derstand that.' I said, 'That's great—when do I start?'"

The rest, as they say, is history. Bruce's journey has led him from Bergen County, NJ to Macon, GA to the San Francisco Bay Area. "The only thing I thought would be cool about Macon, Georgia," remembers Bruce, "is that that's where the Allman Brothers were from."

He's held national sales manager and SVP sales roles at Mirrasou, Shieffelin & Somerset, and currently at Foster's.

While building his sales career, Bruce also achieved his MBA in Strategic Leadership from Dominican University. His final paper was a business plan on establishing a fine wine and premium selling organization within a larger distributor—a plan he ended up putting into practice by starting The Estates Group within Young's Market Company.

Bruce learned about wine from several sources, including leveraging people he knew. He got to know Eddie Keston at Westwood Beverage by calling on him, and ultimately taking a second job working for him on weekends. "Eddie was considered one of the wine gurus, and said, 'Do you want to work here?' I answered, 'Under one condition.' He said, 'What's that?' I answered, 'At the end of every Saturday, you'll open a bottle of wine and teach me about it.'"

DIFFERENCES BETWEEN SUPPLIER AND DISTRIBUTOR SALES ROLES

Because Bruce has worked both as a supplier and a distributor salesperson, he was asked what the differences are between working in sales at a distributor versus at a supplier. He replied, "Distributor salespeople have a very challenging environment, just like supplier salespeople do. But distributor salespeople are on a daily basis much more focused on the customer than supplier salespeople are. Not the consumer, but the customer. So they're out there calling on accounts.

"Distributors also have a much larger portfolio of products from which to choose, which has its advantages and its disadvantages. When I first became a distributor salesperson, what I liked about it was, 'Oh, so you don't like this Char-

donnay? I've got about forty-five others!' As a distributor, I could represent 200 Chardonnays.

"About ten years ago, the average distributor in a major metropolitan area had 4,500 SKUs. Today, with all the consolidation at all these levels of supplier and distributor, there are distributors in markets who have 20,000 SKUs.

"The distributor life is more of [that of] a fireman. This account's got an issue, this account didn't get his order, this account has a party coming in and they need to have X, my order didn't show up today, this account has suppliers in, this guy isn't happy, that guy isn't happy—so you're spinning a lot more plates than a supplier."

MOST IMPORTANT SKILLS FOR SALES PROFESSIONALS IN WINE

"Fundamentally, to be very frank about it, it is to try to walk away from almost every instance and every experience and have a little voice that says, 'What have you learned from this interaction? What have you learned about the business? What have you learned about what you're trying to do? What have you learned about the relationships with the people you're either managing, or your colleagues, or that you're reporting to?' Always trying to be observant of what's going on, what happens. Being a good student of whatever you're doing in whatever industry you're in.

"I spent a lot of time learning about wines, learning how distributors work. I was never the supplier who came in and knew it all. I was always interested not only in what I needed to get done on behalf of the brands I represented, but I wanted to understand how the business worked for the person on the other side of the table.

"So that worked throughout my career. There's a lot of learnings out there.

"Intellectual curiosity—trying to find out, 'How can I make this better?'

"Trying to be a good listener. You miss a lot if you don't listen and observe."

MOST CHALLENGING PART OF THE JOB

"It's a very difficult business. There's a lot of things that are fun. Wine is an intellectually fun and interesting business. You meet a lot of interesting people. You're never at a loss for conversation with anybody. But what the most challenging thing is in our business is that it's not a branded business. It's capital intensive. There isn't a huge amount of resources.

"We've taught our customers throughout the years to try something different, not necessarily to be loyal. It's incredibly competitive. We don't like to think of it this way, but it's essentially a commodity business. There are so many brands or wines that are completely interchangeable. We've taught everybody, 'Oh, if you really want to get into this and enjoy it, sure, switch! Drink Chardonnay now, drink red wine five minutes later, try it from here, try it from there, whatever price point you're comfortable with.'

"You're dealing with an agricultural product. So you have to have long planning. Nature usually doesn't cooperate. There's either too much or too little. It's hardly ever just right for any extended period of time.

"We have pricing pressures. We have inability to price sometimes.

"One day, all of a sudden, everybody's drinking Pinot Noir, and you haven't planted it. It can take three to four years to catch up. And by the time you do, you find everyone's on to Sauvignon Blanc. Or you planted it in Napa, and now everyone is drinking Spanish wines.

"It's hard to put your feet up on the desk and say, 'I got it. I've got it all.' But that's probably what keeps me interested."

BEST PART OF THE JOB

"I like making things work. I get a huge amount of satisfaction from having issues, problems—call them opportunities—and then walking away and sitting back with people and solving them.

"I also like people. I wouldn't be happy sitting behind a computer screen all day.

"Obviously, I like results. I get a charge when we move from Point A to Point B—and you can actually measure it. I think when you're in sales, you feel good when you actually see something happen. It's not just all the theory, and 'let's sit down and talk all the time.' To me, there has to be some action connected to that."

ADVICE FOR PEOPLE LOOKING TO START THEIR SALES CAREER IN WINE

BRUCE'S DO'S:

- *"You have to be willing to take rejection. You have to allow good days and bad days to roll off your back. You have to realize the worst thing anyone can say to you is 'no'—and how bad is that?"*

197

- *"You have to enjoy the moment that you've made the sale, and feel good about that."*
- *"You have to have intellectual curiosity and want to deal with people."*
- *"You have to feel comfortable in alien environments, because your office is your car. Every time you have contact with different customers you're always walking into their home, their environment, and you have to be comfortable in those situations."*
- *"I want somebody who knows how to listen, because somebody who just talks will never ask for the order at the right time or know what the customer's wants and needs are."*
- *"In the wine business, you need to come back as a juggler in your next life."*

BRUCE'S DON'TS:

- *"Never end the day without making a sale. Generally, if that meant I had to make another call, I'd make another call, until however many it took so that I'd never go home and end the day without making a sale."*

GEOFF LABITZKE MW, CORPORATE VICE PRESIDENT, FINE WINE, YOUNG'S MARKET COMPANY

Geoff Labitzke has been in the alcohol beverage business, with a strong emphasis on wine, for almost thirty years. He has worked as a retailer with Bradley's Liquor, as an importer with Vineyard Brands, and as a distributor with Wine Warehouse and Young's Market Company.

Geoff is also one of a small number of people in the US who has achieved the Masters of Wine credential.

EDUCATION AND TRAINING

Geoff's career in wine started early. "I was working in a liquor store right out of high school. I basically ran out of beer to try when I was in college, so ended up buying wine for that store, and ended up running the store shortly thereafter. So I started in retail, all facets from stock clerk, to beer buyer, to wine buyer, to running the store.

"I had an internal desire to add to my wine knowledge and to advance my career. When I was at Bradley's Liquor, I knew my next step was into wholesale. I was constantly asking questions. I sat down several times with people who were in management positions in wholesale operations. I'd sit down to lunch with them and say, 'I want to make this step, what would you recommend?'

"I was constantly listening to books on tape on sales, and reading books on sales and so forth. [When] I was working at Bradley's Liquor, I was going to college at the same time. I was taking a lot of marketing courses and sales management courses at community college and at Cal State Fullerton.

"I went to work for a larger store in Southern California called Hi-Time Cellars. I was assistant liquor buyer, was on the wine team, wrote the wine newsletter, was involved in events—it was the most important account in Orange County at the time. That gave me a wide audience of usually the top salespeople from any given wholesaler [because] they were the ones calling on that account. I made a lot of connections with higher level people, and eventually had an opportunity to take a sales opportunity for a wholesaler called Wine Warehouse.

"Historically, there hasn't been a lot of education and training in our industry. A lot of folks are hired into the industry as sales reps and work their way up within the industry with no real education requirement involved. It tends to be the better salespeople get promoted and advance within their company. That's not to say education isn't required, but historically, that hasn't been the road for people to achieve the key positions in our industry. It's only recently, within the last five years, where you've had larger companies hiring people with MBAs.

"On my own time, I pursued advancing my wine knowledge through the Society of Wine Educators. I also achieved the Master of Wine credential."

MOST IMPORTANT SKILLS FOR DISTRIBUTOR SALES PEOPLE

Geoff cites basic sales skills—particularly time management and organizational skills—as critical to success. "It's a lot easier to take someone who has strong sales skills and sales experience and teach them about wine than [it is] to teach someone who's not an organized sales person, who may have a lot of wine knowledge, [to be a salesperson]."

MOST CHALLENGING PART OF THE JOB

"There's been a huge amount of consolidation in the industry. It's very difficult for large wholesale operations to make a profit because of increased gas prices, increased logistics prices, constant costs going up, and demands by large suppliers to achieve goals, which we're achieving.

"The biggest challenge in that whole thing is how do you allocate your time? The business is getting much more consolidated. There are new brands that have to be developed every year—every year a company is coming out with two to three new brands.

"You have to appropriately adjust your time to address the key concerns of the large suppliers that generate a large amount of profitability, while still paying attention to the smaller suppliers who may be the larger suppliers of tomorrow, or who may simply be [providing] the types of products that are important to your accounts.

"The biggest challenge is to allot time to do right by all the people you're partnered up with."

BEST PART OF THE JOB

"Making programs grow is the most exciting part of what I do right now. One of the things that I'm in charge of is our direct imports Bordeaux program. It's kind of like I'm a supplier company within a company. I'm selecting the wines, working on the back of the house logistics, out working with salespeople, making presentations to key accounts, showing salespeople how to sell the wines—basically creating a program within the wholesale organization. That's probably the most exciting part of my job right now. It's rewarding when you can really make selections and have those be well-received, and create a program that grows and works in the marketplace.

"I do instruction in-house and a fair number of consumer events and tastings where I'm speaking in front of groups of various sizes, and that's very rewarding as well."

Advice for People Looking to Start Their Distributor Sales in Wine

GEOFF'S DO'S:

- *"Get a job working at a top wine retailer, where there would be a lot of wholesalers coming in and making presentations, where you could actually meet people and ask questions on how to get into the industry."*
- *"Pick up the phone and make some phone calls. Ask, 'Can I take you to lunch and ask you a few questions?' That's something not a lot of people are doing. People are sending out blanket resumes and talking to headhunters, but they're not talking to the people who are doing the hiring."*

GEOFF'S DON'TS:

- *"If you're entering in the wine business, you should not look at it as you're entering it for a lifestyle choice. It's very easy to get caught up in the glamour part of the business at the expense of achieving company objectives." "Underestimate the value of time management. Nobody sits down and teaches you how to manage your time. As a wholesaler, you don't own the accounts, and you don't own the suppliers. Time is really your only resource. You can spend a lot of time getting caught up talking to guys that you really like about products that you really like, and not achieving results."*

LARRY CHALLACOMBE, GENERAL MANAGER,

Global Vineyard Wine Importers Larry Challacombe is an industry veteran who's worked on the producer, supplier/ importer and retail ends of the wine business. As General Manager of Global Vineyard Wine Importers, he acts as the national representative of a group of small, premium, family-owned wineries from Chile and Argentina. Larry holds a Master's degree from University of Southern California and is the founder of Global Vineyard Importers.

EDUCATION AND TRAINING

"I, like a lot of college people, really had no idea what I wanted to do," says Larry. "What started it for me is that [during] my first two years of college I went to University of California Davis, and I took—as a lot of people—did a couple of enology and viticulture classes. At the time I barely even knew what viticulture and enology were, but [they] seemed like fun classes to take, and it opened the door to at least an interest.

"I graduated from UCLA. What happened at UCLA is there [were] recruiters coming by, as with most colleges, and one of the recruiters coming by was with Gallo. It wasn't some well-researched plan I had. I started my first job selling on the street."

Larry then moved into the marketing side of the industry, first with Christian Brothers, and then with Heublein after it was acquired by Christian Brothers. "I became a real corporate guy for a number of years when I worked for Heublein. I was surrounded by a lot of really bright, knowledgeable, hardworking people that I'm still in touch with, many of whom are in senior positions in the industry today. It was just a wonderful network, not just from a business point of view. I was able to taste with André Tchelistcheff for three or four years when we brought him back to Beaulieu Vineyard when I was heading up marketing with BV."

Larry then experienced the smaller winery side of the business as the executive director of the Oregon Wine Advisory Board. From there, he held additional roles as vice president of Marketing for C. Mondavi & Sons (Charles Krug & C.K. Mondavi wines), Director of Marketing for the West-

ern Schieffelin & Somerset Company, and Vice President of Sales & Marketing for A.G. Ferrari.

"So, at least for me, it sounds like a lot of jobs, and maybe it was, but each gave me a part of the puzzle which helped me start this import company seven years ago."

MOST IMPORTANT SKILLS FOR WINE IMPORTERS

"What you have to do in anything you do, certainly as an importer, you have to always be showing your value-added," Larry says. *"You have to show why you should insert another middle man in between the producer, the winery, and the distributor. Everyone's taking their cut, and the price is going up at every level.*

"There are a lot of ways to be an importer. We act as the national representative for our wineries. We buy the wine from the wineries and we store it at a warehouse in California.

"You have to be willing to hustle, because no one is asking for another wine. Anyone in the industry would, I'm sure, tell you the same thing. There's more competition than there's ever been in this industry, and to make it that much more competitive, most of it is pretty good.

"You have to create a need. You do that partially by what's in the bottle. Just as importantly, you have to work your tail off as if you were starting any other business, and have to be willing to go out to your distributor and explain why in the world they should bring in another wine from your part of the world, because even the smallest distributor out there likely has your category covered with something else. If you can even get a conversation with them, you've got to show

them in pretty short order what makes it special. So you've got to be persistent.

"You have got to have at least enough capital to grow. And you can't be everything to everybody if you're a small importer. If you come in with the mentality that you're going to compete with Woodbridge or Sutter Home, and that's your audience, I think you're just bound to fail, unless you're huge and extremely well-financed. You have to be able to nibble at the edges.

"The only part that's different—if you're in the part of the industry like I am—where you do deal with the fine wine people, you do need to speak the language. And you do have a much higher chance of success if you really honestly sincerely believe in what you're talking about."

MOST CHALLENGING PART OF THE JOB

"The toughest thing—and this is no disrespect intended towards anyone, we try to treat our distributors like gold, because they are the people who buy our wine—we understand that we're not their top priority. Their top priority is all the wine in their warehouse. And it often doesn't matter as much if they sell this or sell that, their job is to go out and sell wine. That's where the persistence comes in. You sometimes have to call a number of times, and sometimes have to communicate from a number of different angles.

"It goes back to what Robert Mondavi termed years ago, 'share of mind': to have whatever piece of their mind you can get. And a lot of people are competing for that same mind. It takes a lot of organization, luck, and getting them excited. But it's trying to get beyond the clutter and get their

attention is probably the biggest challenge for everyone, big or small."

BEST PART OF THE JOB

"Finding great little properties that you can grow together, that they're really good people, that they're as passionate about that as you are—or more so, since they're the grower—and bringing that into the US, and getting your distributors excited about it. And then seeing it unexpectedly on the shelf or on the wine list at a top restaurant. You just happen to in Chicago or New York and just happen to see Ricardo Santos Malbec, which is our Argentinian wine.

"I think that's very fulfilling. What makes it very fulfilling for me is that I really like to expose consumers to not just the mainstream. I find it more interesting to help get someone who was just drinking Chardonnay and Cabernet who starts saying, 'Oh, let me try something different, a Malbec, or a Carménère,' and like it."

Advice for People Looking to Start Their Career as a Wine Importer

LARRY'S DO'S:

- *"You've gotta make sure that wine is a business like everything else. Just because you like to visit wineries and you like to drink wine, doesn't mean that it's something that is going to be something that's just a lot of fun and a lot of drinking wine."*
- *"Fine wine is part of it, but it's the minority of it. You have to be willing to just dig in and run a business. If you want to start a small importer, you're running*

a small business, and that'll be most of your time. You've gotta know that sales and marketing will be the main parts of it, don't worry about business cards, don't worry about fancy offices, don't worry about anything like that. Find great wine, and find ways to be effective in your sales and marketing. And with everything else, you find a way to cram it into your nights and weekends."

LARRY'S DON'TS:

- *"If you don't pick fine wine to import—not just fine wine, but wine that has the right package, the right price, that will grow in the market—and put together a pretty darn good sales and marketing strategy, you're just not going to make it."*

CURTIS EATON, ACCOUNT SPECIALIST, DOMAINE SELECT WINE ESTATES

Curtis Eaton is a great example of someone who was bitten by the wine bug early in life. He's worked in restaurants, in retail, as a supplier, and now as a distributor, all in the wine business. Along the way he's experienced the California, New York, and Bordeaux wine regions.

Curtis' story is also a great example of how people who are serious about the business often take a number of dif-

ferent (sometimes upwards, sometimes lateral, but always forward) steps in advancing their wine career.

EDUCATION AND TRAINING

"Out of high school, I started working at a private country club. We did fine dining there. By the time I was twenty-one, I was the captain in the dining room. We had an interesting wine list, and it caught my attention. So I caught the bug that way.

"After that passion developed, I went on to attain an Associate's degree in hotel and restaurant science. But having a passion for wine, I decided to move up to San Francisco, to the City College of San Francisco. During my fourth semester, an opportunity to work for one of the top fine wine retailers [as an intern] came up.

"Right around that time I was also taking a lot of French, and was able to arrange an internship in Bordeaux. Upon graduating with the Associate's degree, I did an internship with the Maison de Bordeaux and Bordeaux Superiore. I worked with their Marketing department with a focus on tourism and local marketing towards English-speaking visitors.

"After that internship, I came back and enrolled in the wine business degree at Sonoma State University. I went back to Bordeaux again and did the internship the second summer and at Vinexpo. I worked at Buena Vista during that time in the tasting room. I graduated from Sonoma State and went to work for The California Wine Company. During that time I started out as an Associate Marketing Director, and eventually worked my way towards National Sales Manager."

Curtis' current role is as an Account Specialist for Domaine Select, a small distributor and importer in New York State specializing in fine, artisan wines from around the globe.

MOST IMPORTANT SKILLS FOR DISTRIBUTOR SALES PEOPLE

Curtis views all of his assorted experiences—educational, internship, and work experience—as vital to developing the skills that have made him successful as a distributor salesperson.

"Exposure is, I think, the most critical aspect, whether that's through education or to the business side of the wine industry, or just working either through retail or in a restaurant with wine. Being able to understand how wine ends up in the customer's hands, and how it starts at the winery, and being exposed to various facets of the distribution chain.

"Ultimately, no matter where you end up, the object is to get the wine to the customer's hands, and how it gets there is the important part.

"When you work for a small artisanal distributor, you're talking more about what makes the wine unique [versus at a large distributor]. But you're still looking for 'pours and floors.'"

MOST CHALLENGING PART OF THE JOB

"The flip side of working with smaller brands is that you're trying to fight your way into distribution with wines that don't have brand recognition, that don't have brand awareness, who may not even be getting media scores in spite

of their quality. And you're fighting for the life of these brands against the large competitors who have wineries that are well-established, that have brand recognition, that have media scores and media attention. So you're working harder to make those wines visible to the consumer, and it's two to three times harder because at every level you're trying to convince the buyer and the gatekeepers why this is more special than what they've been working with and already know."

BEST PART OF THE JOB

"I'm working in a business that sells a product whose culture revolves around fine food, dining, [and] the finer aspects of what we consider luxury living. We're dealing with a luxury good and a certain fine lifestyle.

"Secondly, I like being able to be closer to the brands [in a smaller distributor focused on artisan wines], taking ownership. I like the personal satisfaction of when you achieve success that you are really making a difference in getting wines that you really believe in into peoples' hands, and you are bringing them enjoyment by doing so."

ADVICE FOR PEOPLE LOOKING TO START THEIR DISTRIBUTOR SALES CAREER IN WINE

CURTIS' DO'S:
- *"Be willing to work at a restaurant, retailer or at a distributor to gain perspective."*
- *"Form a strategy that allows you to be as close to wine as possible. Find out what local wine clubs there are around. Even if it's not an industry wine group, you're*

going to find people who are interested in wine. Get involved with wine as closely as you can on a regular basis."

- *"You've really got to look at the [wine industry] lifestyle and really want to live it. There are some great parts of it, but sometimes you have to wake up and get dressed at 8:00 a.m. in the morning to ride around with someone you've never met to go sell your wines."*

CURTIS' DON'TS:

- *"Passion means nothing without perseverance. If you're going to make the jump, you need to set yourself up to maybe take a step back and recognize you need to understand the world of the wine industry. You can't come in with the concept that, 'I'm going to make a lateral move,' either in title or salary. You need to persevere and maybe even pay your dues. Your sales skill set will allow you to rise to the top."*

Wine Marketing & Sales with a Retailer:

Wine Shops, Wine Bars, & Restaurants

No, no white wine, just a couple cases of '64 Chateau Beychevelle back there between the beans and diapers—five bucks each.

Chapter 8

Intrigued by managing your own wine bar, or educating and selling wine to customers in a wine shop or restaurant? If so, a job in wine marketing and sales in a retail environment may be the career for you. If you frequently find yourself describing the merits of a wine to friends, making recommendations on which food to serve with wine, and enjoy tasting wines from around the world, then the world of wine retail may be quite rewarding. Jobs range from part-time positions at specialty wine shops; to wine buyer for high-end grocery stores; to master sommeliers at five-star restaurants. Salaries can extend from hourly wages with sales commission and/or tips to high-end six figure incomes, with many levels in between. Wine retail is one area of the wine world where entry can be relatively easy, but obtaining the top jobs can be extremely competitive. Yet almost all of these types of positions include the perk of having the opportunity to taste wines from many different producers, rather than just one winery or region.

So how do you obtain a job in wine retail? This chapter describes the various types of jobs in this category, ranging from wine shops, gourmet grocery stores, wine bars and restaurants. It also explains the necessary skills, experience and education to obtain both full- and part-time work in these types of establishments, as well as how to work your way up the wine retail career ladder. In addition, it includes tips on how to get started, helpful resources, and job hunting strategies. This chapter ends with four fascinating interviews with experts in the field who share their advice on how they got started and what it takes to succeed.

JOB DESCRIPTIONS IN WINE RETAIL

Professionals in wine retail are engaged in educating customers about wine and assisting them in selecting the best wine for their needs. In most cases, customers want to match the wine with food, so wine retailers usually need to have some food/wine matching knowledge.

Table 1: Off- & On-Premise Wine Retail Establishments

OFF-PREMISE *(Buy wine & drink off-premise)*	ON-PREMISE *(Buy & drink wine on-premise)*
Wine Shops	Wine Bars
Liquor Shops	Casual Restaurants
Gourmet Grocery Stores	Fine Dining Restaurants
Large Chain Grocery Stores	Bars/Pubs
Multi-Retailers	Cruise Ships/Trains/Planes
	Special Events

In most countries wine retail is divided into the two categories of off-premise and on-premise—also referred to as off-trade and on-trade (see Table 1). Off-premise refers to establishments in which consumers purchase the wine and drink it offsite, such as wine shops, grocery stores, or large multi-retailers which sell wine along with many other consumer goods. On-premise refers to enterprises in which consumers purchase the wine and drink it onsite, such as restaurants or bars. General descriptions and major job responsibilities for each of these types of wine retail businesses are as follows:

Off-Premise Wine/Liquor Shop: Stores which are devoted to selling wine and may also include liquor and spirits. Wine selection is usually larger and more diversified than in grocery stores, with multiple price points and wines from many different countries as well as local representation. Job responsibilities include researching, tasting, and buying wine. This is usually done through distributors, but some countries and states may also include buying directly from winery owners, as well as wine buying trips to foreign countries if you are the owner or an experienced employee in a larger shop. Job duties also include inventory control; tracking sales and margins; sponsoring promotions; and other special events, such as wine dinners, tastings, educational seminars, online sales specials, etc. If management level, the position also incorporates employee hiring, training and management, as well as accounting, tax reporting, and other general business duties. See Esquin's interview at end of this chapter. Other well-known wine stores include K&L, Kermit Lynch, and Bev-Mo in California; Specs in Texas; Applejack's in Colorado; and the Wine Library in New Jersey.

Off-Premise Boutique Grocery Store or Small Chain: Small gourmet grocery stores with a wine section or small specialty grocery chains with wine (see Oliver's Market interview at end of this chapter). With smaller stores, there is generally one person responsible for purchasing wine, but may also include assistants who help stock wine aisles, educate, sell, and conduct consumer tastings and other grocery store events. Wine selection is usually more specialized with an emphasis on local wines and/or unique types of wine, such as Italian wines in an Italian-themed grocery. Responsibilities include meeting with wine distributors and other sellers to taste and purchase wine; stock shelves; sponsor promotions, such as local advertising; track inventory and financials; process paperwork; and manage human resources if multiple staff are employed in-store.

Off-Premise Large Grocery Chain or Multi-Retailer: Large regional or national grocery store chains such as Safeway or multi-retailers such as Cost Plus, Costco, Tesco, Walmart and Target, sell wine in addition to other consumer products. Wine selection is often limited to well-known brands with retail prices points less than $25, as well as barcode scanning mechanisms. One or two people may be responsible for stocking shelves and managing promotions at a single store, with assistance from wine distributors. However, the wine buyer is usually a regional or corporate position who buys for more than one store, negotiating discounted prices in return for larger volumes sold. In big chains, such as Costco, a VP of wine division position may be established at headquarters with regional wine buyers responsible for various stores. Top wine buyers will not only be responsible for purchasing but will often be held accountable for profit margins.

On-Premise Wine Bar: Establishments that specialize in selling wine by-the-glass, flight and bottle. May also sell beer and spirits, and most often some type of small food dishes, such as appetizers, tapas or select entrees. Wine selection usually includes both local and worldwide wines. Some wine bars may specialize in a certain type of wine, such as Spanish wines or a varietal like Pinot Noir (see Noah's Wine Bar interview at end of this chapter). Job responsibilities include tasting and purchasing wine; proper storage (often with gas to protect by the glass wine); promotions and special events, such as music and bands, to attract customers; creating a unique and relaxing environment; tracking inventory; monitoring margins; and handling all management and administrative responsibilities, including food safety and quality issues. These establishments often hire full- and part-time staff to assist at the wine bar—a good entry-level position.

On-Premise Casual Restaurant: Restaurants which serve entrees ranging from $10 to $30 and offer wine to customers. May be a small local restaurant or a large casual chain, such as Olive Garden. Wine selection is usually limited, with less than fifty choices and an emphasis on well-known brands and local selections. In a small local restaurant, the owner often purchases the wine and asks wait staff to help sell it, sometimes without providing wine training. Wine may be listed on a table tent, chalkboard or on a wine list. Larger casual restaurants usually have a dedicated wine buyer at the regional or corporate level, with someone designated as responsible for wine sales at each store. Wait staff are usually trained on wine, including its benefits, how it enhances food, and how to sell it—a good entry-level position for wine sales. Wine buyer or wine management positions with larger casual chain restaurants require more sophisticated skill and experience level, which include tasting, purchasing, promotions, financial accountability, inventory tracking, staff management, and general administrative duties.

On-Premise Fine Dining Restaurant: Restaurants which serve entrees from $30 and up and offer a large and/or sophisticated wine selection to customers. Generally considered to be four- or five-star dining (two- or three-star in the Michelin Guide). Wine selection is typically quite large—from 200 brands into the thousands— with price points ranging from $25 to $10,000 per wine. The position of sommelier (pronounced suh-mal-'yAy)—or wine steward—is usually always present in these types of fine dining establishments. General responsibilities include tasting, purchasing, storing, and tracking wine; financial accountability; promotions; wine list development; food and wine pairings; and training other wait staff. In very high-end establishments, such as The Breakers in Florida (see interview at end of this chapter) or the Bellagio in Las Vegas, multiple sommeliers are available to assist guests with wine selections.

Other On-Premise Establishments: Wine is also sold on-premise on cruise ships, airplanes, and trains, as well as in bars, pubs, hotels, and at special events such as a charity auctions. These types of establishments offer additional employment opportunities for wine retail professionals and include many of the major job responsibilities described earlier.

EDUCATION AND SKILLS REQUIREMENTS

In terms of education, wine retail is one of the easiest career entry points for the world of wine. A college degree is usually not necessary for part-time and full-time wait staff positions in restaurants and bars or for sales positions in wine shops, grocery stores or multi-retailers. However, if you want to move into management or executive positions, or work in a fine dining establishment, then a college degree is usually required, and in some cases an MBA or a certified MS (Master Sommelier) is preferred. Fortunately, there are some excellent Bachelor's degrees in hospitality, restaurant/hotel management, and wine business that can help you prepare for advanced positions in wine retail. Following is a partial list of universities offering these types of degrees:

- Johnson & Wales University, Providence, Rhode Island
- Cornell School of Hospitality, New York
- University of South Florida, Sarasota, Florida
- The George Washington University, Washington, DC
- Sonoma State University, Rohnert Park, California
- Many community colleges also offer Associate's degrees in these areas, e.g. Napa Valley College.

If your career goal is to become a sommelier in a fine dining restaurant, it is highly recommended to pursue one of the wine certifications which provide education towards this end:

Court of Master Sommeliers: Certifies at four levels, each requiring coursework and an exam—Introductory, Certified, Advanced, and Master Sommelier. The MS level is very difficult to obtain only

124 MS's have been awarded worldwide within the last twenty years. (http://www.mastersommeliers.org)

Culinary Institute: Offers wine classes and exams to become a Certified Wine Professional (CWP) Level 1 or Advanced Level 2. Available in New York and Napa. (http://www.ciaprochef.com/winestudies)

Wine & Spirits Education Trust (WSET): Provides several wine certifications ranging from a one-day Level 1 Foundation Certificate to much more lengthy certifications at the Intermediate, Advanced, and Diploma levels. Requires completion of examinations. Available in most major cities around the world. (http://www.wset.co.uk/)

MAJOR SKILLS NEEDED FOR WINE RETAIL

In examining major skills areas, all types of wine retail jobs require some basic knowledge and ability. However, as you move up the career ladder into managerial positions, additional competencies are needed. The three basic skills that all wine retail professionals require are as follows:

Wine Knowledge: A basic understanding of grape varietals, wine regions of the world, viticulture, and winemaking processes is necessary in order to succeed in wine retail. This is especially important in wine shops, wine bars and high-end restaurants, but is also very useful in part-time wait staff positions in casual restaurants.

Wine/Food Matching: Since so many customers purchase wine to pair with food, it is important for wine retail professionals to have a basic background in food and wine matching theories. At the entry-level in a casual restaurant, it can be as simple as pairing white wine with white meat or spicy food with a fruiter wine such as a Riesling. In more sophisticated settings, such as specialty wine shops or high-end restaurants, staff training is usually available (including tastings of wine with food) so that staff can communicate to customers with more confidence.

Customer Service & Sales Focus: Since wine retail is about selling wine and creating return customers—who will in turn encourage new customers to visit your establishment—a customer service focus is mandatory. With wine sales, this is not as simple as giving the customer what they ask for, because many customers don't know what wine they want. Most are quite intimidated and overwhelmed by selecting a wine and need assistance. At the same time, they don't want to be lectured to and made to feel like a fool. On the flipside, there are many sophisticated customers with solid wine knowledge who want to be recognized and praised for this. Therefore, learning how to "read customers" and gauging their wine knowledge calls for quite refined customer service and sales skills on behalf of the wine retail professional. Usually, this includes asking questions; clarifying and confirming; and making recommendations (followed by praise for the customer's wise choice). Good customer service also includes follow-up to see how the customer liked the wine—which can be done in both on- and off-premise settings.

If your career goal is to advance into the management and executive levels of wine retail, then you will need to obtain additional skills and competencies. These include:

Retail Management Skills: In any industry, retail management calls for a very sophisticated focus on margins, employee relations, and customer service. In general, margins are tight in retail businesses, so purchasing and inventory tracking require extreme scrutiny in order for the business to be successful. Employee turnover is usually much higher in retail than in other industries, primarily because starting salaries are often low and commission-based. Therefore, this requires good recruiting, training, and motivational skills so that talented staff stay with the store/bar/restaurant. This in turn creates a positive domino effect, as cheerful employees provide great customer service, which then brings customers back again and again. Without this strong skill set in retail management, most wine retail businesses will struggle.

Advanced Tasting Skills & Wine Knowledge: Sommeliers and professional wine buyers are required to have a very sophisticated wine palate and advanced wine knowledge about wine regions of the world and vintage variations. This all comes with time and practice, but is critical in order to advance up the career ladder. Many sommeliers and wine buyers are so good at this that they are asked to be wine judges in national and international competitions. This type of honor reflects well on their retail establishments.

Wine List Development: In restaurants and bars, sommeliers and managers will be required to develop skills in creating wine lists to compliment the food and theme of the establishment. This is not an easy task, and requires years of experience in order to create a list that matches the cuisine/strategy of the establishment, sells well, and is appreciated by customers.

Negotiation Skills & Financial Acumen: Though previously mentioned in the retail management section, anyone who buys wine must maintain a focus on margins and final profitability for their establishment. Buying a wine they love, but that customers will not purchase, does not serve anyone well. Therefore, wine buyers need to develop excellent negotiation skills to get the best price, and yet still maintain positive working relationships with wine distributors and winemakers. They then need to track the financial performance of the wine and make decisions on whether or not to carry it in the future.

Online Wine Retail Sales Skills: A growing number of wine retail shops are going virtual and do not have a physical wine shop from which to sell wine. At the same time, many retail wine shops also sell a large portion of their wine via the Internet. A good example is Gary Vaynerchuk, who uses his Wine Library TV to bring customers into his shop or to buy online. Therefore it is becoming increasingly important to develop Internet sales skills such as doing online advertising, using blogs and digital video, linking into social networking sights, working with web designers to design the most effective e-commerce engine, and staying up-to-date with competitor moves in the online wine sales arena.

WINE RETAIL CAREER LADDERS

There are three common wine retail career ladders (illustrations follow). The bottom two levels of each ladder are nearly identical as they are entry-level part-time or full-time positions in on- and off-premise establishments. These are excellent starting points for anyone wanting to experience wine retail, because they usually don't call for a college degree and some may not require prior experience. However, almost all will demand that you have acquired three of the basic abilities which appear in the preceding list of skills: wine knowledge; food and wine pairing; and customer service. These can be attained through self-study and experience in other industries.

The off-premise wine career ladder shown illustrates the entry-level positions of part-time and full-time wine retail sales reps within wine shops, grocery stores, and multi-retailers. Moving further up the ladder to wine buyer, wine manager, or regional director (in larger chains) usually requires advanced education, experience, and proven competencies in the advanced skills set. Very large grocery chains, such as Safeway, and multi-retailers, such as Costco and Walmart, usually have a corporate wine VP/director role that requires a college degree with MBA and/or MW (Masters of Wine) preferred, plus at least five to seven years of wine experience.

Figure 1: Off Premise Wine Career Ladder

The on-premise wine career ladder for wine bars and casual restaurants illustrates the entry-level positions of part-time and full-time wait staff. In a small wine bar or restaurant, the owner may be the manager/director, or may hire someone else to manage and buy wine. In larger casual chain restaurants, such as Olive Garden, Red Lobster, TGI Fridays, Applebee's, and many chain steak houses, regional wine directors and a corporate wine VP/director position are often found. Again, these higher-level management and executive positions usually require advanced education, experience, and proven competencies in the advanced skills set.

Figure 2: On-Premise Wine Career Ladder

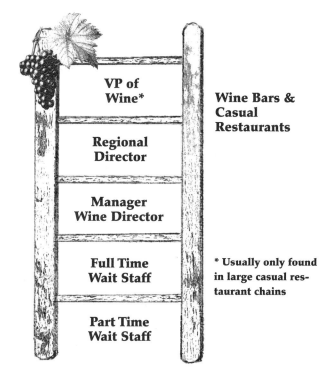

VP of Wine*

Regional Director

Manager Wine Director

Full Time Wait Staff

Part Time Wait Staff

Wine Bars & Casual Restaurants

* Usually only found in large casual restaurant chains

The on-premise wine career ladder for fine dining restaurants illustrates the same entry-level positions of part-time and full-time wait staff at the bottom, but changes quite significantly in the middle and top. Here, the positions of sommelier (referred to as wine steward in some restaurants) and Master Sommelier can be found. These are highly specialized and coveted positions that take years of training and experience to obtain. The most sophisticated four- and five-star restaurants usually prefer to hire someone who has at least passed the Level 2 exam with the Court of Master Sommeliers. Very prestigious establishments, such as The Breakers and Bellagio mentioned earlier, prefer to hire someone who has attained the MS (they actually have several MS's on their staff). The top position is the Director or Master Sommelier, who oversees the work of the other sommeliers and wait staff as well as interfaces with the chef. They are also highly involved in wine list development, which may require traveling to wineries and meeting with distributors to taste and purchase wine.

Figure 3: On-Premise Wine Career Ladder

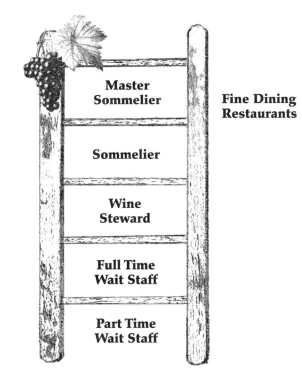

Master Sommelier

Sommelier

Wine Steward

Full Time Wait Staff

Part Time Wait Staff

Fine Dining Restaurants

HELPFUL PUBLICATIONS, WEBSITES AND EVENTS/ CONFERENCES

Following is a list of resources which wine retailers have identified as being useful for their careers and profession.

Helpful Journals

Most professionals in wine retail are avid readers of wine journals, which help them stay up-to-date with what is happening in the global wine industry. They also allow professionals to review ratings and stay current with vintages. Since many purchase allocated wines, they often buy on "futures," or buy wine in advance for a specific price, even though it will not be received for two to three years in the future. The wine journals do a good job rating and describing wine futures as well as current releases. Some of the retailers also advertise in the wine journals.

- *Decanter*
- *Harper's* (UK based wine and spirits journal)
- *Patterson's: The Tasting Panel Magazine*
- *Sante*
- *Wine & Spirits Magazine*
- *Wine Enthusiast*
- *Wine Spectator*

Useful Books to Learn About Retail Management & Entrepreneurism

- *Consumer-Centric Category Management: How to Increase Profits by Managing Categories based on Consumer Needs* by ACNielsen
- *Kick Start Your Dream Business: Getting It Started and Keeping You Going* by Romanus Wolter
- *Retail Success!* by George Whalin
- *So You Want To Own The Store : Secrets to Running a Successful Retail Operation* by Mort Brown and Thomas Tilling
- *Start Your Own Bar and Club* by Entrepreneur Press
- *What No One Ever Tells You About Starting Your Own Business: Real-Life Start-Up Advice from 101 Successful Entrepreneurs* by Jan Norman

- ***Winning*** by Jack Welch and Suzy Welch

Useful Books to Enhance Your Wine Knowledge & Tasting Skills

- ***The Commonsense Book of Wine: The Only Book that Demystifies Wine Without Destroying its Magic*** by Leon D. Adams
- ***How to Taste: A Guide to Enjoying Wine*** by Jancis Robinson
- ***Making Sense of Wine Tasting: Your Essential Guide to Enjoying Wine*** by Alan Young
- ***Tasting and Grading Wine*** by Clive S. Michelsen
- ***The Taste of Wine: The Art and Science of Wine Appreciation*** by Emile Peynaud
- ***The University Wine Course: A Wine Appreciation Text & Self Tutorial*** by Marian Baldy
- ***Windows on the World Complete Wine Course*** by Kevin Zraly
- ***Wine for Dummies*** by Ed McCarthy, Mary Ewing-Mulligan, and Piero Antinori
- ***The Wine Bible*** by Karen MacNeil
- ***The Wine Tasting Party Kit: Everything You Need to Host a Fun & Easy Wine Tasting Party at Home*** by St. Pierre and Karen Greenberg

Helpful Websites

- **eRobertParker.com:** Provides a link to the ***Wine Advocate,*** an online newsletter by influential wine critic Robert Parker **(http://www.erobertparker.com/)**
- **iSanté:** The online version of *Santé,* the magazine for restaurant and hospitality professionals. **(http://www.santemagazine.com/)**

- **Harpers.co.uk:** Resource for wine and spirits trade news in the UK, plus coverage of key European wine business. **(http://www.harpers.co.uk/)**
- *Wine & Spirits* online edition, with excellent resources for news in the wine industry. **(http://www.wineandspirits-magazine.com)**
- *Wine Enthusiast Magazine:* The online edition of the print publication. **(http://www.winemag.com/)**
- **Wine-Searcher:** A major online wine research database. **(http://www.wine-searcher.com/)**
- **WineSpectator.com:** The online version of *Wine Spectator,* one of the largest and most popular wine enthusiast magazines. **(http://www.winespectator.com/)**

Wine Events/Conferences

Though you may not be able to gain admittance to all of these events and conferences, these are examples of the types of functions that wine buyers and other trade professionals attend, and it is useful to know about them. Often, when a wine trade tasting event is held in a major city, such as the Australian wine tour of the US, they also sponsor a public tasting as part of the event. Attendance at these events is beneficial for enhancing your wine tasting skills and knowledge.

- **Bordeaux En Primeur:** Annual tasting for wine buyers held in April in Bordeaux, France
- **London International Wine Fair:** Largest annual wine trade show in the UK. Held in Spring.
- **Unified Wine & Grape Symposium:** The largest wine conference in the US held each January in Sacramento, California.
- **Vin Expo:** Large international wine conference held annually in France

- **Vin-Italy:** Large international wine conference held annually in Italy
- **Wine trade tasting events:** Offered throughout the year in major US cities
- **Special wine auctions:** Based on buyer needs
- **Regional, national and international wine competitions**

TIPS ON GETTING STARTED/JOB HUNTING STRATEGIES

In order to prepare yourself for a career in wine retail, the best way to get started is to improve your wine knowledge and tasting skills. This is relatively easy to implement and is usually quite fun.

- Enroll in a wine class at your local community college.
- Start your own wine-tasting group.
- Grab a copy of one of the wine tasting books listed previously and read it!
- Consider taking some of the WSET courses. Check out their online website to find locations near you or complete the distance learning version. **(http://www.wset.co.uk/)**
- Brush up on your customer service and sales skills. Remember in selling wine you don't want to intimidate people or come off like a wine snob. Practice asking your friends about their wine preferences and then role play by recommending a wine to meet their needs. Get some feedback on how to enhance your technique.

Once you have some wine knowledge under your belt, you are ready to begin job hunting for an entry-level position. Keep in mind that these types of jobs usually do not pay much. Working part-time in a wine shop or the wine division of a grocery store, you will most likely receive an hourly wage and perhaps commission. In a wine bar or restaurant, tips may supplement your hourly wage. Therefore, you may need to keep your full-time job and work part-time during evenings and weekends until you get the experience needed to advance to full-time, salaried positions.

When applying for these types of positions, be honest and let the hiring manager know that you are trying to break into wine retail and are looking to gain experience. Working part-time in a local wine shop is a great way to start and usually provides the most diverse tasting opportunities, though the other types of entry-level jobs are also very useful and can be equally as fun.

If your goal is to become a sommelier, keep in mind that you will have to "put in the time" and continue your wine education in order to obtain one of the top paying positions. It is also highly recommended that you pursue one of the certifications listed previously.

If you want to own and manage your own wine bar someday, then obviously working in a well-run wine bar is the best way to learn the ropes. Likewise, if your goal is to be a wine buyer for a grocery store, wine shop, or other retail establishment (which can be quite a glamorous career, as winery owners and wine distributors line up to meet with you so you can taste their wine), then get a job where you can be near a professional wine buyer so you can watch and learn from an expert.

ADVICE FROM WINE RETAILERS

Following are excerpts of interviews with four wine retailers, each representing the different types of on- and off-premises discussed in this chapter. Their stories and advice are very useful in helping you to understand the various ways in which you can enter and work in the exciting field of wine retail

True Tales from the Wine Industry

CHUCK LEFEVRE, OWNER, ESQUIN'S WINE MERCHANTS SEATTLE, WASHINGTON

Born in San Jose, California, Chuck LeFevre successfully pursued several other careers before purchasing Esquin's Wine Merchants in Seattle, Washington in 1997. "I became interested in wine later in life," says Chuck. "It was actually when I was CEO at my previous company that some of my customers introduced me to wine. I got hooked and started to learn about wine, read Wine Spectator *religiously, and began shopping at Esquin's." A few years later, after selling his first business, Chuck had the opportunity to purchase Esquin's from the original owner, who was retiring. And that was how Chuck was able to turn his passion for wine into a full-time job and acquire the oldest and largest wine retail shop in Seattle.*

EDUCATION AND TRAINING

Chuck acknowledges that it was his previous business and retail management experience which helped him turn Esquin's into such a successful wine shop. "Attending college was important," says Chuck, "and I enjoyed majoring in history at UC Santa Barbara, but it was my first job after college where I worked in golf retail management that really helped to prepare me to run this business."

Chuck seems to be blessed with natural business acumen. His next career move was to Alaska, where for ten years he worked in a large commercial company, and moved quickly up into the executive ranks. From there, he relocated to Seattle, where he started and became CEO of his own successful company, NutraSource. "It was in this position that I first became interested in wine, and discovered Esquin's. It was established in 1969 and had a great reputation. I became acquainted with the owner, and when he said he wanted to retire and sell the business, I jumped at the chance."

So after several years of immersing himself in the world of wine as a hobby, Chuck was now able to combine his passion and business savvy into a new venture. "I could see a lot of opportunity with Esquins," says Chuck. Today, more than a decade after he took ownership, the company has grown from a modest mailing list of 2200 customers to more than 20,000, and produces the most widely-read wine publication in the state. They offer more than 4000 wines, host over 100 tasting events per year, have eighteen full- and part-time employees, and are known throughout the city for their exceptional customer service.

MOST IMPORTANT SKILLS FOR WINE RETAIL

When asked about the most important skills for wine retail, Chuck differentiates between wine sales and wine management: "Without a doubt, passion for wine is the most important attribute for someone selling wine in a retail shop. When I hire people that is what I look for first." Chuck says Esquin's has about nine full-time and nine part-time people and is a good starting place for someone looking to break into wine as a career. "If you know about a wine and can talk

234

to people in an engaging style without intimidating them, this is a great place to be."

He says that customer service is their most important tenant, and that it is critical that sales staff know how to build positive relationships with customers and to develop their own personal style of selling. "We sell wine face-to-face in the shop and at tasting events," says Chuck, "and via telephone and email to our mailing list. Each rep develops close relationships with a set of clients and stays in contact with them to meet their ongoing wine needs."

Having a good wine palate is also helpful. "You don't have to be an expert taster," says Chuck. "I don't think of myself that way, but it does help to know how to taste and describe wine. My staff and I taste 500-600 wines per month in trying to determine which ones to buy and stock. Then we have to write about these for our newsletter and website, and also talk to customers about them."

The wine management side of the job calls for even more expertise. "Without a doubt, you need retail management experience and a strong discipline to succeed in wine retail," says Chuck. "The margins are not that high and therefore you need to know how to manage your operation efficiently, to track inventory, sponsor promotions, and measure results." Chuck mentions that they have special software that allows them to run reports several times a day in order to determine which wines are moving and which are not. He has hired a full-time marketing person to run promotions and manage tasting events. As another aspect of customer service, they have also branched out into the wine storage business, and are investigating expanding into online sales.

MOST CHALLENGING ASPECT OF THE JOB

"Though wine is viewed as a glamorous product by many, you have to keep in mind that this is retail business, and therefore you have all of the challenges that any other retail industry faces," says Chuck. "Therefore, human resource issues are usually the biggest concern, as we have high staff turnover just like other retail businesses." Chuck mentions that because they are open seven-days-a-week, they need to have both full- and part-time staff, which means recruiting and training a new person anytime someone leaves. "The positive part is we are a great starting point for people who know and love wine, but the downside is that people move on to other opportunities."

Another issue is the importance of focusing on customer service and keeping the business profitable. "You can succeed in wine retail," says Chuck, "but it takes hard work and focus on operational efficiencies to make a decent profit. You also have to find something that sets your wine shop apart from the competition. We have decided that customer service is where we can compete against the grocery stores and Costco. We like to call ourselves the "Nordstrom's of Wine Retail."

BEST PART OF THE JOB

"The best part of the job" says Chuck, "is owning and running my own business. It is hard to describe the intense satisfaction of managing this wine shop. It is wonderful to be able to service [existing] customers and welcome new ones; to provide jobs for employees; and to make decisions that impact the positive future of the business. There is also

a great sense of freedom in running your own business, rather than working for someone else."

Chuck mentions that another positive aspect of the job is tasting so much wine and attending fun wine events and dinners. "In Washington, we are required to buy wine from distributors, so I don't have to travel much," says Chuck, "because the distributors bring the wine to us. Many of my employees really appreciate the opportunity to taste so many wines from around the world. It is really an extra perk of this job."

RENAY SANTERO, WINE MANAGER & BUYER, OLIVER'S GROCERY STORE, SONOMA COUNTY, CALIFORNIA

As a Sonoma County native, Renay grew up surrounded by vineyards and wineries, but it wasn't until fifteen years into her career in grocery management that she transitioned into wine. "When my boss asked me if I knew anything about wine," says Renay, "I had to say no—but I was more than willing to learn." Now twelve years later, Renay is considered to have one of the best wine palates in California and is continually sought after to be a wine judge for multiple competitions. She is highly respected as a top wine professional and buyer for the 2,100-plus bottle selection at all three locations of Oliver's in Sonoma County.

EDUCATION AND TRAINING

"I began working part-time in grocery retail at age fifteen," says Renay with a smile. "I really enjoyed interacting with customers." Indeed, Renay was so talented that she was recruited right out of high school to work for the Lucky grocery store chain in the San Francisco Bay Area. At Lucky, she moved rapidly up the management ladder and became an expert at grocery retail. Then after working there for more than fifteen years, she accepted an offer with Oliver's Market, an upscale gourmet grocer with a sophisticated wine, beer and spirits section.

"My grocery management experience has been extremely helpful in preparing me to be the wine manager and head wine buyer for Oliver's," reports Renay. "Knowing how to track inventory, manage margins, and negotiate for the best price, [all] while maintaining positive relationships with sellers, is just as critical in wine as it is with food."

In order to prepare herself to take over as wine manager, Renay hit the books and Internet to learn all she could about wine. "I was primarily self-taught," says Renay. "I tasted through every single wine we sell and took detailed notes. Then I compared my tasting notes with local experts and was pleasantly surprised to find that they matched." That's when Renay realized she was gifted with a sensitive wine palate. Over the years, her wine knowledge grew as she visited many of the local wineries and traveled to other regions. "Today, I usually visit at least one foreign wine region per year," reports Renay. "I also have become good friends with some of the key wine distributors and winemakers. They have helped me to continually enhance my wine knowledge."

In fact, Renay is so successful as a professional taster that she regularly judges at ten to fifteen major wine competitions per year, including the famous San Francisco Chronicle and Orange County competitions, often evaluating more than 100 wines per day.

Renay continues to hone her wine education and training skills by teaching her staff and using the Internet to do wine research. "I've developed a sixteen-week training program for my staff of eight people. We meet once a week in the evenings at my house to taste wines from different regions and learn about new winemaking techniques." Renay mentions that this helps her staff to communicate more effectively about wine to customers in the store.

MOST IMPORTANT SKILLS FOR WINE RETAIL

Renay lists five important skill areas to succeed in wine retail. "The first skill that comes to mind," says Renay, "is the ability to negotiate with sellers. I meet twice a week with wineries who want to sell their wine directly, as well as the wine distributors. I like to give small, new wineries a chance, and that is part of the reason we have such a unique wine selection at Oliver's." Renay stocks many of the regular brands too, but she likes to highlight new and upcoming stars. She is so popular that the waiting time to get an appointment with her is usually around two months. She is known as a tough, but fair, negotiator. "Sometimes an extra dime per bottle can make all the difference to your margins," laughs Renay.

"Negotiation leads to the second important skill, which is interpersonal communications," reports Renay. "Even though I have to be a tough negotiator at times, I still try to respect the other person and maintain a good relationship." She men-

tions that this is equally important in dealing with her staff, customers, and other store employees. "Our customers are the most important asset we have. In the beginning, I was the one on the floor hand-selling wine to each and every customer. Now that we've grown, my staff is doing most of the selling, but I still make sure I interact with customers at least once a week in each store location.

"Wine knowledge and tasting ability are a given," says Renay. "You do need to develop this competency in order to succeed as a wine retailer." It is for this reason that Renay spends so much time insuring that her staff stays up-to-date on wine. "Staying current about what is happening in the wine world is a critical piece of this," says Renay. "For example, 2005 Bordeaux. If you didn't read the press early enough and put in your order, you would be left out in the cold on obtaining one of the greatest vintages ever."

Business savvy and wine retail skills are the other two areas which Renay lists as very important. "I have been given very clear revenue and profitability goals," reports Renay, "so I have huge spreadsheets to track how well each wine is selling. If I see an issue, we consider promotions, new types of POS (point of sale) materials, or purchase additional advertising." Renay mentions that she also must stay up-to-date on promotions in competitor stores, and also spends much time getting feedback from customers.

MOST CHALLENGING ASPECT OF THE JOB

"I know that other people have told me they would like to have my job, because I get to taste great wines and make buying decisions," says Renay. "I think what they don't real-

ize is that I usually put in at least sixty hours per week, and that there is a lot of paperwork that is required. Probably the most tedious part of my job is all of the spreadsheet work and inventory analysis to track how well a wine is selling."

Renay mentions that deadlines are also an issue for her. "I'm usually up against a lot of deadlines," says Renay, "such as advertising deadlines, and there is pressure to respond to requests from multiple parties."

BEST PART OF THE JOB

"I really enjoy developing and motivating my staff," says Renay. "They are great employees, and I like seeing them shine and do well with our customers." Renay herself also enjoys customer interaction. "I started our Friday evening wine and cheese tasting at the Cotati location," says Renay, "and I try to be there every time so I can talk with our customers and see how they enjoyed the last wine we sold them.

"Another great part of my job is meeting with the suppliers," says Renay, smiling. "I've become good friends with many distributors and winemakers and I really like seeing them, tasting their new wines, and creating a win-win partnership."

JACK THORNTON, OWNER, NOAH'S: A WINE BAR, MCMINNVILLE, OREGON

Jack Thornton grew up as part of a farming family in Quincy, Washington with dreams of becoming a teacher and eventually owning his own business. He achieved the first goal when he headed to Western Oregon University and obtained his B.A. in Elementary Education. Then one afternoon in the mid 1980's, he went wine-tasting in Oregon wine country with his girlfriend and fell in love with Pinot Noir. Today, he has achieved the second goal by translating his love for wine into Oregon's oldest wine bar, Noah's, located in McMinnville, in the heart of Oregon's world-famous wine region, the Willamette Valley.

EDUCATION AND TRAINING

Jack admits that his wine knowledge was developed over the past twenty years in tasting Oregon wines and Pinot Noirs from around the world. "I'm just fascinated by the Pinot Noir grape," says Jack. "It is the focus of my wine bar and what I specialize in. I do stock and serve other types of wine, but Pinot Noir is my true passion."

Jack's degree in education has also been quite helpful, as it fits in perfectly with his informal role as a wine educator and as part of his customer service culture. "My philosophy is to make wine accessible to everyone," says Jack. "There-

fore, I like to give people the opportunity to stop by Noah's and taste some wine. I ask them some questions about their preferences, and if they seem to be interested, I tell them more about the wine they are tasting and suggest a few others. This seems to help people relax and keeps them coming back again." Jack says that 40% of his clientele are locals, many of whom are repeat customers.

Jack mentions that he has sharpened his wine knowledge by visiting many wineries, attending wine festivals, reading wine books, and staying current through top wine journals. His wine bar management skills came via experience. "When I first opened the wine bar," says Jack, "I had a hard time making it financially. It wasn't until I really focused on a specific style—Oregon wines and Pinot Noir, which are my passion—that I started to turn a profit. In the beginning, I was trying to be all things to all people. That doesn't work. You need to focus and find your niche as a wine bar."

Jack has been operating Noah's since 1994. The wine bar is open five evenings a week, serving eight to twelve wines by the glass and showcasing a bottle selection of over 200 wines. Three entrées are available each evening, and special music events are held each month. Despite the demanding nature of his business, Jack still teaches part-time as a substitute teacher. "I like to stay connected to the community. Besides, many of the locals are my best customers!"

MOST IMPORTANT SKILLS FOR OPERATING A WINE BAR

"Since Noah's was one of the first wine bars in the nation," says Jack, "I learned many of the most important skills the hard way—by experience. Therefore, I would have to boil it

243

down to three important areas. The first is to stay involved as an owner on a daily basis. At first, I tried to outsource the work to others, but it wasn't as effective. The wine bar reflects the spirit of the owner, so the owner needs to be closely involved."

Jack mentions that the second most important skill has to do with negotiation. "Margins are tight in wine retail," reports Jack, "and you have to be careful not to get carried away and buy every case you like. It is important to negotiate a good deal which is fair for all parties—my wine bar, the wineries, and the distributors. We help each other; we each provide a service; and we all succeed."

The third most critical skill area is customer service. "You really need to treat people special so they will come back," says Jack. "I try to create a feeling that we are the 'living room of Oregon wine country.' I want people to be able to come in, relax, have a glass of wine, eat if they want, and have a casual conversation if they are so disposed. I chat with people and try to put them together seamlessly." Jack's method seems to work, because many of his best customers tell him that they "met so and so" when they came to his wine bar, and that is the "good wine and good company" aspect of his bar that keeps them coming back.

MOST CHALLENGING ASPECT OF THE JOB

Jack admits that the most challenging part of the job is the financials. "I really love wine and running this wine bar," says Jack, "but you always have to remember it is a business. It is profitable now, but you always have to keep your eye on the bottom line. As a buyer, you have to control your inventory and track what is selling and what is not. If there is an issue you have to take action."

Jack mentions that he uses promotions as needed and regularly advertises in the Yamhill Visitor's Guide. He also changes his wine by the glass offering based on the season. "In hot weather, I usually don't serve so many huge reds," says Jack, "because the customers are looking for something lighter and more refreshing. However, there are wines that always sell well by the glass, such as well-known brands of Oregon Pinot Noir and Argyle sparkling."

BEST PART OF THE JOB

"The best part of the job" says Jack, "is meeting interesting people. I really enjoy interacting with my customers and helping them to meet others in the wine bar. We have had some of the most fascinating people come in here. It is continually intriguing."

Jack admits that he also likes teaching people about the wines if they show an interest. "I really enjoy giving people an opportunity to discover a new wine," he says. "Our wines range from $8 to $20 by the glass, and if someone orders a more expensive wine, I always give them a little bit more and ask what they think of it. Many of our customers already know a lot about wine, so I don't lecture, but if they seem to be interested, I enjoy telling them about all the special attributes about the wine and the winery."

VIRGINIA PHILIP, MASTER SOMMELIER, THE BREAKERS, PALM BEACH, FLORIDA

Virginia Philip, a native of Connecticut, became entranced with wine when she took a wine class at Johnson & Wales in Rhode Island while pursuing a degree. "I just became fascinated with the subject of wine," says Virginia, "so when I graduated with my degree I took a part-time job as clerk of a wine shop in Aspen, Colorado." This small role led to increasingly more sophisticated posts in the world of wine retail, until Virginia achieved one of the most coveted appointments in the wine industry—Wine Director and head sommelier at the world reknown Breakers resort in Palm Beach, Florida.

EDUCATION AND TRAINING

Virginia's B.A. in Restaurant & Hotel Management provides an excellent foundation for her work at The Breakers, but she didn't stop with just one degree. "I decided to pursue the Master Sommelier (MS) Diploma with the Court of Master Sommelier in 1999," reports Virginia. "It was a challenging process and took almost five years to complete, but it has helped me in my job. The strict and critical service component and extensive wine knowledge that is required are very useful when I train my own staff." Virginia designed and teaches an annual sixteen-week wine course to employees of The Breakers.

Virginia acknowledges that her prior work experience was also instrumental in helping her to obtain her current position. "After the wine shop in Aspen, I moved to the Little Nell Resort, which is a five-star/five-diamond property, where I had the opportunity to be trained by some of the best managers in the industry." It was here that Virginia began honing her wine service skills. "After four years in Colorado, I moved to San Antonio, Texas where I worked for Ruth Chris as wine director and manager. Then, I became a wine buyer for A&S Holdings. That is where I gained many of my wine purchasing and negotiation skills."

All of her education and work experience has paid off. "I've been at The Breakers for more than seven years now," says Virginia, "and it is difficult to imagine a more fulfilling job." Not only does she oversee a staff of five other sommeliers, but Virginia is responsible for a multi-million dollar wine collection of more than 28,000 bottles, containing one of the largest collections of Domaine de la Romanee-Conti in the country. "The Breakers actually has nine restaurants and approximately 2,300 employees," says Virginia, "so I am continually updating wine lists, creating new food and wine pairings, working with the chefs and managing staff." Virginia and her team meet with wine distributors twice a week to taste wine. She also travels about three times per year to France, Spain, South America and other wine regions to visit wineries and purchase wine.

But Virginia is not resting on her laurels. She is continuing her wine education by pursuing the Masters of Wine (MW) degree. "It is important to stay up-to-date in the wine industry," advises Virginia. "The MW emphasis on viticulture and winemaking helps round out what I learned in the MS program. Even if I do not pass, it is the learning experience that makes it all worthwhile."

MOST IMPORTANT SKILLS FOR A SOMMELIER

"Putting in your time, [and] having patience and dedication, are among the most important attributes for obtaining a job as a sommelier," reports Virginia. "There are a limited number of sommelier positions at premium restaurants, so when we do have an opening, we receive stacks of applications." Virginia mentions that all of the sommeliers at The Breakers have a college education and at least five years experience in wine and food service.

"It is also vital for a sommelier to possess the ability to connect with guests and deliver a unique and memorable experience for them," says Virginia. "This requires excellent interpersonal skills, the ability to read the customer and not speak above or below their level of wine knowledge." Wine and food pairing expertise is obviously another key skill set, and a strong prerequisite for even being considered for the job. "It is expected that all of our sommeliers are familiar with the different sauces and ingredients the chefs are using, and should easily be able to recommend several wine matches to meet the needs of the customer."

Retail management expertise is another essential competency. "Negotiation and relationship-building skills are very important when dealing with wine distributors and wineries," says Virginia. "In addition, we are held accountable for revenue and profitability goals. I analyze the wine financials daily and mentor my staff on tracking their inventory and margins."

MOST CHALLENGING ASPECT OF THE JOB

For Virginia, the most challenging aspect is finding and keeping rare, allocated wines: "Obviously, it is wonderful to be able to obtain these types of wines for The Breakers, but once they sell, we need to replenish. Therefore, I spend much of my time buying wine at auctions, as well as futures." Virginia mentions that in order to succeed at this, it is important to build and maintain solid personal relationships with wineries and sellers around the world.

BEST PART OF THE JOB

"The best part of the job" says Virginia "is that it is always different—it's a profession that continually evolves. Since our resort operation is quite large, I am continually updating wine lists, meeting with chefs to create new wine and food pairings, and traveling to different wine regions." She mentions that the wine industry remains fascinating because there is always a new vintage to taste, or a new winery opening up in a different part of the globe.

Indeed, a love of learning and new challenges seems to be part of Virginia's make-up. In addition to being one of only seventeen women in the world to achieve the MS title, she is currently pursuing the MW and recently won the title of Best Sommelier in America.

Wine Writers & Educators

I don't get it. Ask him to start over.

Chapter 9

Many people will tell you that it was attending a wine appreciation class that first introduced them to the world of wine. This led them to search for books, articles, and websites about wine to feed their need for more information on wine reviews, wine destinations, or matching wine with food. Wine writers and educators are extremely important people in the world of wine. They are responsible for reaching thousands of consumers on a daily basis and help to shape perceptions, buying habits, and develop life-long passions for wine. Without them, the wine industry would suffer.

So how do you obtain a job as a wine writer or educator, and what are the different settings for these types of positions? This chapter begins with definitions for wine writers and educators, and then describes the various venues for these types of jobs, ranging from wine journals to newspaper writing for wine writers and teaching wine shop seminars to university classes for wine educators. Next is more detailed information regarding required skills, experience, and education for wine writers and educators, as well as tips on how to get started, helpful resources and job hunting strategies. It ends with interview excerpts from two wine writers and two wine educators who provide helpful advice on the challenges and rewards of these fascinating careers in wine.

JOB DESCRIPTION FOR WINE WRITERS AND EDUCATORS

One of the most famous and prolific wine writers in the world is Jancis Robinson. She has written many books, newspaper columns, articles, and blogs on wine, and also manages her own subscription based website. Though a professed wine writer, she also serves as wine educator by providing self-study materials for thousands of wine students around the world. More importantly, she writes and edits the *Oxford Wine Dictionary* and includes these two very helpful descriptions of wine writer and wine education (3rd edition, 2006):

> **Wine Writer:** Term to include all those who communicate through the various media on the subject of wine. Some of them style themselves wine critics (notably the consumerist Robert Parker) while such literary stylists as Hugh Johnson and Gerald Asher are undoubtedly wine writers….And myriad wine websites have provided some wine writers with an international reputation far quicker than is usually possible with the printed word. (p. 778)

> **Wine Education:** Education plays an important part in the production, sale, and enjoyment of a product as complex and, in many countries, as foreign as wine. Detailed knowledge of wine involves an appreciation of history, geography (inevitably including a host of foreign names), science, and technology, quite apart from the development of practical tasting skills. (p. 252)

Therefore wine educators engage in wine education for consumers, retailers, distributors, and other interested parties.

JOB FORMATS AND SETTINGS

There are many part-time or freelance jobs as wine writers and educators. Unfortunately, most of the part-time jobs do not pay that well. For example, often beginning wine writers only receive $100 to $200 per article, and starting wine educators may only receive $150 per hour to teach a wine class. However, these positions are a good place to start. From there you can apply for full-time positions. Top wine writers can get paid as much as $1 per word for an article, and well-known wine educators can command $2500 to $4000 a day for specialized wine training events. Fortunately, there are many different venues or settings to work as a wine writer or educator. Table 1 below lists the majority of these settings.

Table 1: Job Formats and Settings for Wine Writers & Educators

Wine Writers	Wine Educators
Part-time or full-time positions writing for the following types of publications: **Wine Newspaper Columnist** - Wine Writer—general - Food & Wine Writer - Wine Critic Examples: *New York Times, San Francisco Chronicle, Wall Street Journal, Miami Herald, Napa Registrar* **Wine Journal/Magazines** - Feature wine writer - Business wine writer - Food & Travel wine writer - Wine Critic - Technical wine writing - Academic wine writing Examples: *Wine Spectator, Wine Business Monthly, Practical Winery & Vineyard, Sunset Magazine, Winemaker Magazine* **Wine Newsletters/Blogs** - Feature wine writer - Business wine writer - Food & Travel wine writer - Wine Critic - Technical wine writing Examples: Robert Parker's Wine Advocate, Pinotblogger **Wine Books** - All types of wine subjects **Wine Writer for a Winery** - See Chapter 5 "Wine Marketing, Sales & Public Relations for a Winery"	Part-time or full-time positions teaching in the following settings or establishments: **Wine Educator for a Wine Shop** Conduct wine tasting seminars for customers; usually as part of other duties as a wine retailer **Wine Educator for a Distributor** Providing wine education classes to distributor reps and clients. In large distribution houses, can begin as entry-level trainer and move up career ladder to Director of Wine Education. **Wine Educator for a Winery** Conduct wine education seminars and tours for employees and customers. In large wineries, can begin as entry-level trainer and move up career ladder to Director/VP of Wine Education. **Wine Educator in Junior College/University** Teach wine education classes to students. Many junior colleges offer as part of continuing education. Large universities will offer wine classes to support a degree in wine. **Wine Educator in a Wine School** Teach WSET, Society of Wine Educators or other curriculum in private wine school. Examples include Copia in Napa and the Culinary Institute in New York. **Consulting Wine Educator** Teach wine seminars in different venues such as restaurants, hotels, cruise ships, private companies, teambuilding activities, etc.

SKILL, EXPERIENCE AND EDUCATION REQUIREMENTS FOR WINE WRITERS

In speaking with editors of wine-oriented publications, there are three primary skill sets they look for:

1) Excellent writing skills: You must have the basics of good writing skills including grammar, spelling, and an ability to write in a fashion or format that matches the style of the publication. For example, if writing for a wine and travel journal, the author must be able to match the journalistic style of the publication. If writing for an academic journal, the writer must be able to use APA format or other requirements called forth in the author's guidelines.

2) Solid wine knowledge: It is expected that wine writers have a good foundation in wine with much tasting and wine travel experience. Without this their readers may not take them as seriously. Therefore, they must know different grape varietals, wine-making styles, and other relevant information to support the needs and interest of the target audience of the publication.

3) Distinctive style and/or unique angle: Successful writers are similar to successful artists in that they are able to develop a unique signature style of writing that is different from others. For example, they may describe wine in a humorous way or compare it to human attributes, such as "this wine is like Marilyn Monroe: full and voluptuous." This unique voice allows readers to recognize their work. This is especially important for writers who are critiquing wine. If writing for a specific type of wine journal, such as a business magazine, they will need to find an angle and style of writing that grabs the interest of those working in the industry.

Required Experience

In terms of experience, most publishers prefer to select authors who have prior publishing experience. This could be from another writing field, or even self-published articles on wine blogs or other formats. Occasionally, a wine publication will accept an article from an unpublished author—that is, if they believe it fits the needs of their readers and is written in a style that matches the publication. See Tips on Getting Started section.

Required Education

In terms of education, the majority of wine writers have a Bachelor's degree from a four-year college in journalism, english, psychology, or a related field. However, this is usually not a requirement for freelance writing positions. Full-time writing jobs with major wine journals, however, usually require at least a B.A. or B.S. degree.

THE WINE WRITING CAREER LADDER

Figure 1 illustrates the basic career ladder for wine writers. Many people begin as freelance or part-time writers, and admit that they need to have another job to make ends meet. A lucky few are eventually able to obtain full-time positions with major wine publications such as *Wine Spectator* and *Wine Enthusiast,* or as a full-time wine columnist for a national newspaper. One way to gain some experience is to begin as a volunteer writer by creating short articles and submitting them to wine journals for no pay. This way you can build up your portfolio of articles and have a list of publications to show. Some writers have also started their own wine blogs which is a good way to get your name in front of Internet wine readers and hopefully build a following.

Figure 1: Wine Writer Career Ladder

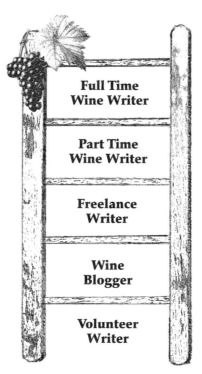

Full Time
Wine Writer

Part Time
Wine Writer

Freelance
Writer

Wine
Blogger

Volunteer
Writer

TIPS ON GETTING STARTED/
JOB HUNTING STRATEGIES FOR WINE WRITING

Following is a list of tips to help you get started in your wine writing career:

- **Read:** Make sure to read books, articles, columns, and blogs from successful wine writers in order to understand the types of concepts, data, and writing styles that are being published.
- **Write:** Take every opportunity to write about wine in order to fine tune your own individual writing style and "voice."
- **Ask for Feedback:** Show your wine writing pieces to others to gain feedback on what is interesting and what can be improved.

Remember that the best writers never get defensive about their writing. View feedback as a gift and try to incorporate ideas you believe will help you to be more successful in the future.

- **Informational Interviews:** Schedule informational interviews with successful wine writers. Ask how they got started and what advice they may have for you. Also do this with editors of wine journals to gain a clearer understanding of the types of submissions they prefer.

- **Submit Your Work for Publication:** Make sure to submit your articles to your favorite wine publications, but first, make sure you read their writer's guidelines and submit work that will match the needs of their readers. If you are rejected, don't take it personally. All writers experience refusals. Don't give up. Consider revising the article and submit elsewhere. Also contemplate submitting as a volunteer writer without pay.

- **Start Your Own Wine Blog:** Review other successful wine blogs, then find an area of the wine world that you are passionate about and start your own blog.

- **Approach Newspapers That Don't Have a Wine Column:** Volunteer to write a weekly column for them.

- **Join One of the Wine Writer Associations:** See section on helpful websites and consider joining one of the wine writer associations.

- **Obtain a Wine Credential:** Many of the most famous wine writers have obtained advance certification in wine, such as the WSET diploma or a Masters of Wine (MW). Though these are both rigorous and time-consuming educational programs, obtaining some type of certification may be helpful in rounding out your wine writer's biography. See Advanced Certifications and Programs for Wine Writers and Educators.

SKILL, EXPERIENCE AND EDUCATION REQUIREMENTS FOR WINE EDUCATORS

There are many different avenues to obtain a position as a wine educator, and some people admit they accidently fell into the job because of their passion for wine. This, indeed, is one of the three primary skills necessary to succeed as a wine educator:

1) **Passion & Knowledge of Wine:** It is vital to have a passion for wine in order to be a successful wine educator. This is because you will be sharing this enthusiasm with your audience when you are teaching. Without an internal sense of excitement about wine, you will not have much repeat business. Related to this is the obvious need to have a background in wine—at least in a few specific areas. Some wine educators specialize in French wines; others focus on the viticulture side of the business; while still others enjoy teaching introductory wine appreciation classes to people who are new to wine. Ideally you will eventually have a solid background in all areas of wine, but to get started you may only need to know a few areas. For example, many people start as wine educators in wine shops where they do short one-hour seminars for customers on the wines in the shop.

2) **Teaching Skills:** The best wine educators have a formal background in education and training skills, or have learned it from others. This means they don't spend the whole time "talking at" people, but establish an interactive and relaxed environment where people can learn and ask questions. The best learning involves two-way communication, and with wine this often includes wine tasting. Experienced educators realize they need to design their courses so that critical information is provided

in the beginning before the audience gets too deeply into the tasting experience. Questions and comments should be encouraged, and tasting ground rules established early.

3) Flexible to Needs of Learners: One of the challenges of teaching wine is that you will always have people with different levels of experience in your audience. Some may be able to lecture to you on the various yeast strains and enzymes used in winemaking, whereas other will not know the difference between Chardonnay and Sauvignon Blanc. Therefore, it is important to be flexible and respectful of the needs of all learners. Never talk down to anyone or lecture too long on a topic that may be very obscure to them. In a way, wine educators are like sales people. They need to begin with the consumer in mind and ask discovery questions to understand the background of their audience. This can be accomplished in a variety of ways, such as fun icebreakers in the beginning of a session. Then the training material can be geared to meet the needs of the group. Finally, a successful educator will maintain the self-esteem of all members of the audience, which usually means complimenting beginners and encouraging experts to share their experience in a positive way.

Required Experience

In terms of prior work experience, it depends on the venue in which you perform as a wine educator. If you are conducting short seminars for customers in a wine shop, the store will expect you to have wine knowledge and sales experience, but may not require that you have taught wine in the past. Likewise, if you begin by working in a winery tasting room and interact well with customers, many small wineries may give you a chance to conduct short wine training sessions at the winery. However, if you want to teach at a community college, university, or private wine school you will be required to show on your resume that you have experience teaching wine elsewhere. This usually applies when doing wine education for a distributor as well.

Required Education

In terms of education, the same model applies. Wine shops and smaller wineries may not have specific educational requirements for you to teach wine seminars to their customers—just as long as you have the required skill set (passion, wine knowledge, teaching skills, and flexible to audience needs). With community colleges and universities, however, you will be required to have a minimum of a Bachelor's degree and most require at least a Master's degree. If you are teaching full-time at a university, you will likely be required to have a Ph.D. Private wine schools and distributors generally expect a minimum of a Bachelor's as well as some type of wine certification (WSET, SWE, MW, MS, CWE, etc.). See Advanced Certifications and Programs for Wine Writers and Educators.

THE WINE EDUCATION CAREER LADDER

The career ladder for wine education may appear to be shorter, but as it includes a variety of venues ranging from teaching in wine shops and wineries to universities and wine schools, there are actually more career opportunities and salary ranges. As mentioned earlier, many people accidently fall into wine education because they are good at wine sales and enjoy talking with people. In this way, they may begin doing wine education part-time in a tasting room or retail shop and then move into a full-time position if the establishment is large enough. Certain wineries, such as Robert Mondavi in Napa, have a staff of full-time wine educators as well as a director of wine education.

Full- and part-time jobs are also available within community colleges, universities and wine schools. Larger establishments may also have a Director of Education. For example, Copia in Napa has several full-time and part-time wine educators, as well as a Senior VP of Wine Education.

Figure 2: Wine Educator Ladder

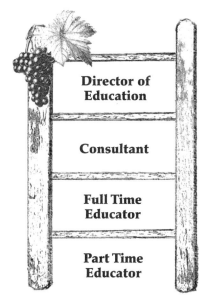

The larger wine distributors expect their distribution sales reps to conduct wine seminars for restaurants and retailers, and provide training assistance to help them do so. For example, Southern Wine & Spirits, the largest wine distributor in the US, has several full-time Directors of Wine Education who provide education for both their employees and customers.

Finally, there are other wine experts who have moved into the consulting side of wine education and offer their services to private companies, cruise ships, airlines, hotels, and other associations who hire them to conduct fun wine education seminars for their employees and customers. Wine tasting and blending seminars, as well as a day helping in the vineyard and cellar, have become a new type of team building for some corporations.

TIPS ON GETTING STARTED/JOB HUNTING STRATEGIES FOR WINE EDUCATION

Following is a list of tips to help you get started in your wine education career:

- **Attend Wine Seminars:** If you haven't already done so, it is important to attend as many wine training classes, seminars, or educational events as you can so you can see the wide range of different wine teaching venues and topics.
- **Read:** In addition to reading wine books, read some teaching and training books so you understand how to write learning objectives, design courses, and learn the basics of presentation and facilitation skills.
- **Brush up Your Presentation Skills:** If you don't enjoy presenting in front of people, then wine education is probably not for you. It is important to brush up your presentation skills. You can do this by taking classes in how to present, lead a training session, facilitate, and/or by joining organizations such as Toastmasters.
- **Volunteer To Gain Experience:** Volunteer to conduct a wine tasting for your friends or company so that you can see if you like it. Ask for feedback and make sure to pass out an evaluation form at the end of the course so you can read what people like and areas for improvement. All good trainers and educators always provide evaluation forms so they can continually improve.

- **Informational Interviews:** Schedule meetings with current wine educators so you can learn more about how they obtained their position and ask for advice.
- **Responsible Drinking:** Learn about responsible drinking etiquette, because you will have to teach and monitor this in your sessions. Always encourage people to drink wine in moderation.
- **Join a Wine Education Association:** See helpful websites below and consider joining one of the wine education associations.
- **Obtain a Wine Credential:** Many of the top wine educators and consultants have obtained advance certification in wine. Refer to the list below.

ADVANCED CERTIFICATIONS AND PROGRAMS FOR WINE EDUCATORS & WRITERS

- **CWP:** Certified Wine Professional Level 1 and Advanced Level 2. Offered by the Culinary Institute in Napa. Course work and exams completed in Napa. (http://www.ciaprochef.com/winestudies)
- **MS:** Master Sommelier. Offered by the Court of Master Sommeliers. Four levels of certification, each including coursework and exam: Introductory, Certified, Advanced, and Master. Offered in major cities. Over the twenty-year history of the program, there are only 124 MS's in the world. **(http://www.mastersommeliers.org)**
- **MW:** Masters of Wine. Very rigorous two- to five-year program offered by the Institute of Masters of Wine in London. Prerequisites include five years wine industry experience, with comple-

tion of WSET Diploma preferred. Self-study, online, and course work required before sitting the four day exam. Currently there are only 277 MWs in the world who have been credentialed in the last sixty years. **(www.mastersofwine.org)**

- **SWE:** Society of Wine Educators. Offers three certifications, including exams: Certified Specialist of Wine (CSW), Certified Wine Educator (CWE) and Master Wine Educator (MWE). Online self-study available, plus optional courses at various locations. **(http://www.societyofwineeducators.org)**

- **WSET:** Wine & Spirits Education Trust. Provide several wine certifications ranging from a one-day Level 1 Foundation Certificate to much more lengthy certifications at the Intermediate, Advanced, and Diploma levels. Requires completion of examinations. Available in most major cities around the world. **(http://www.wset.co.uk/)**

HELPFUL CONFERENCES, BOOKS, AND WEBSITES FOR WINE WRITERS & EDUCATORS

Following is a list of useful resources to help you learn more about becoming a wine writer or educator:

Wine Writing & Education Conferences/Seminars/Associations

- **Association of Wine Educators:** Based out of the UK, but is available in many countries. They hold wine seminars and events for members and customers. **(http://www.wineeducators.com/)**

- **Circle of Wine Writers:** An association of professionals engaged in writing about wine and spirits. Based in England, but with members from around the globe. **(http://www.winewriters.org/)**

- **International Food, Wine, & Travel Writers Association:** Holds an annual conference and meetings at various locations. **(http://www.ifwtwa.org/mediatrips/index.lasso)**

- **Society of Wine Education Conference:** Three to four day conference for wine educators including multiple tastings. Held each summer in various locations. **(http://www.societyofwineeducators.org).**
- **Unified Wine Symposium:** Largest wine conference in the US Held each January in Sacramento, California. Includes multiple wine-related topics as well as tastings.
- **Wine Writer's Network:** A non-profit networking group of wine journalists and writers with global membership. **(http://www.winewritersnetwork.org/)**

Books on Wine Writing & Education

- *How to Write Articles That Sell* by L. Perry Wilbur and Jon Samsel
- *Instant Trainer* by C. Leslie Charles
- *Making Sense of Wine Tasting: Your Guide to Enjoying Wine* by Alan Young
- *Putting Your Passion Into Print: Get Your Book Published Successfully!* by Arielle Eckstut and David Sterry
- *The Oxford Companion to Wine, 3rd Edition* by Jancis Robinson
- *Tasting & Grading Wine* by Clive Michelsen
- *Turning Training into Learning: How to Design and Deliver Programs that Get Results* by Sheila W. Furjanic and Laurie A. Trotman
- *The University Wine Course: A Wine Appreciation Text & Self Tutorial* by Marian Baldy
- *Windows on the World Complete Wine Course: 2007 Edition* by Kevin Zraly
- *Wine: The 8,000 Year-Old Story of the Wine Trade* by Thomas Pellechia
- *Wine For Dummies* by Ed McCarthy and Mary Ewing-Mulligan

ADVICE FROM WINE WRITERS AND EDUCATORS

Following are excerpts of interviews with wine writers and educators. The first two are well-known wine writers who have published books, articles and wine ratings. The second two are wine educators, one who works in a university setting and the second who works in a private wine school and center.

True Tales from the Wine Industry

JAMES LAUBE, SENIOR EDITOR, WINE SPECTATOR, NAPA, CA

As one of the most powerful wine critics in the world, James Laube always knew he wanted to be a writer, but his first writing job was about sports rather than wine. "There is a linkage between sports and wine," says Jim. "With sports, there is always a new season, just as with wine there is always a new vintage." So it was when Jim moved to Napa Valley in 1978 to be a reporter with the Vallejo Times Herald *in its Napa news bureau that he became immersed in the world of wine. When he was offered a job with* Wine Spectator *a few years later he jumped at the chance, and his articles, ratings, books and blogs are read by millions of people around the world.*

EDUCATION AND TRAINING

"I started writing part-time for a newspaper when I was sixteen," says Jim, *"so when it came time to go to college I decided to major in history instead of journalism because I thought I wanted to write biographies."* For a while Jim also entertained the idea of being a college professor, completing his Master's and applying for a Ph.D. program, but the challenge and drama of journalism lured him back to writing.

"I relished the fast-pace of being a reporter and having to write five stories in one day," says Jim. *"So, I took a job with a newspaper in Colorado Springs for a year, and then moved back to California where I got the job with the* Vallejo Times Herald *in Napa. It was great experience because I had to report on everything in Napa from agriculture to bank robberies."* And that was how Jim started to get involved with the wine industry. *"It was a fabulous opportunity,"* reminisces Jim, *"I got to spend a lot of time with some of the early great winemakers, such as Andre Tchelistcheff, Robert Mondavi, and Chuck Wagner. They provided me with much advice, support, and mentoring."*

In fact, it was Robert Mondavi who encouraged Jim to write critically about wine. *"He told me,"* says Jim, *"that the wine industry needed more writers to tell the story of wine and to evaluate it. He said that some of the winemakers may not like it, but the industry needed writers who could critique wine. He said I would be fulfilling a purpose."*

To develop his wine palate, Jim tasted with some of the great wine judges such as Hugh Johnson and Michael Broadbent, as well as many talented winemakers in Napa Valley. When he started with Wine Spectator *in 1980 he had even more chances to taste great wines. "From 1983 to 1990, we*

met as a team once a week to evaluate wines from around the world. It was an incredible tasting opportunity."

In 1983, Jim was also promoted to senior editor, and eventually began to focus more on California wines. Jim is now considered to be the preeminent expert on California wines and has published four books on the subject: California's Great Cabernets, California's Great Chardonnays, *and two editions of* Wine Spectator's California Wine 1995 *and* 1999, *for which he won the prestigious James Beard Award for the best wine book of the year with the first edition.*

MOST IMPORTANT SKILLS FOR A WINE WRITER

According to Jim, there are four major requirements to become a wine writer. "Obviously, the first is to have excellent writing skills," says Jim. "A background in journalism or prior experience writing is important. Second is wine knowledge and education. It is important to read extensively and travel, if possible, in order to understand the global wine industry and meet winemakers from around the world.

"The third skill area, which I think is the most fun, is to develop your palate and wine tasting skills. You need to attend wine tasting workshops, take classes, and start your own tasting group in order to gain exposure to as many wines as possible. Most importantly you need to take careful notes and develop your tasting memory. Memory is very critical for wine evaluation."

The fourth area which Jim recommends is the attribute of passion. "You need to have a passion for wine in order to be a successful wine writer," states Jim. "If you're not interested in wine, then this is not the right field for you because everyone else in the wine industry is in it because of the excitement and creativity they experience from being around wine."

Jim mentions that there are also five major categories of wine writing: 1) feature writing with profiles of wineries and people; 2) wine tasting reports; 3) wine opinion pieces, such as columns and blogs, 4) food and travel articles that feature wine, and 5) wine business writing.

MOST CHALLENGING ASPECT OF THE JOB

From afar, the job of a wine critic may appear to be appealing, but Jim identifies three major challenges which anyone considering entering the field should consider. The first has to do with the backlash that may come from writing critical reviews, and the second has to do with misconceptions people have about advertising and writers 'being on the take.'

"Obviously, as a wine critic, you are going to have some winemakers who are not happy if you give their wine a lower score than they think it deserves. However, since I taste all wines blind, I have no idea of whose wine I'm evaluating. Do I get pleasure out of giving a low score? No. But sometimes people want to shoot the messenger, and as a wine critic, I am the messenger."

Jim also admits that there are some misconceptions that wineries who advertise in Wine Spectator *get preferential treatment. "That is absolutely not true," says Jim. "In fact, one of our biggest advertisers hasn't received a rating above ninety in the last ten years. We evaluate blind and are very objective in the process."*

The issue of business ethics is extremely important to Jim. "Some people assume that wine writers get to fly around the world tasting great food and wine and have the wineries pay for it," states Jim. Wine Spectator *has clear company rules that require writers to pay for their own expences.*

BEST PART OF THE JOB

"There are many aspects of this job that I enjoy," says Jim. "There is great satisfaction in meeting a reader who is excited about an article and is using the information to help them make more informed and confident decisions." Jim mentions that they receive hundreds of positive letters and emails each month in the Wine Spectator *offices, and that when the Top Wine 100 ratings were published on the web they had over 1 million views.*

Jim also enjoys working with the people around him, and meeting others in the wine industry. "There is so much passion and enthusiasm in this industry," he says. "People are here because they want to be, and they are very gracious in sharing their wines. There is so much beauty in the landscape and creativity in the winemaking process."

"Finally," says Jim, "I have the opportunity to taste the truly great wines of the world and write about them." He ends by describing the satisfaction he receives from writing his daily blog and creating short digital video blogs (vlogs). "I feel like I'm getting even closer to my readers with this new online format," says Jim.

LESLIE SBROCCO, WINE WRITER & COMMUNICATOR, SONOMA COUNTY, CA

Not only is Leslie Sbrocco an award-winning wine writer, but she is considered to be one of the most talented and entertaining wine communicators in the world. To her credit, she has conducted a series of television shows, keynote speeches, and countless wine seminars. "I just fell in love with wine when I moved to northern California," explains Leslie, who was born in Denver and grew up in Chicago. "My father, a commercial airline pilot, also deserves some of the credit," says Leslie. "He had a small wine collection at home and we were able to fly to Europe for free, so I was introduced to the world of food and wine at an early age." Since then, Leslie has managed to match her love of wine to her professional talents as a writer and producer, and is considered to be one of the most successful female wine writers in America.

EDUCATION AND TRAINING

"I actually majored in political science in college," admits Leslie, who graduated from Washington University in St. Louis, MO. "Originally, I thought I wanted to be a lawyer, and moved to San Francisco with plans to start law school. However, I soon realized that was not for me and began working in theater. My friends would take me to Napa and Sonoma on the weekends, and before I knew it I was entranced by wine.

By that time, I had started my own production company, and so I began looking for ways to combine my professional job with my passion for wine."

Leslie's first break came when she was asked to produce a small film for a winery. This grew into similar opportunities, until eventually her wine films and photos reached the attention of Microsoft, who asked her to launch the wine portion of their San Francisco Sidewalk project. "Before I knew it, I was producing a whole wine website on the Internet, complete with wine reviews and photos," says Leslie. The site was so successful that Leslie was approached by other companies, and eventually landed the prestigious post of general manager/co-founder of WineToday.com, the wine site of The New York Times.

Leslie has published hundreds of articles and thousands of wine reviews for a variety of publications, including: Epicurious.com, WineReview Online, The San Francisco Chronicle, Coastal Living, Woman's Day, Good Housekeeping, Glamour, Santé and O, the Oprah magazine. Her first book, Wine for Women: A Guide to Buying, Pairing and Sharing Wine, won the famous Georges Duboeuf Best Wine Book of the Year award, and her second book, The Simple & Savvy Wine Guide, has received very positive reviews by both critics and consumers.

MOST IMPORTANT SKILLS FOR A WINE WRITER

"I actually think one of the most important skills for a wine writer is to be a good networker," suggests Leslie. "It is important to meet people in the wine industry and follow-up with them. So many people don't take the time to follow-up, and that is critically important to getting a good story."

When it comes to writing skills and wine knowledge, Leslie believes in a combination of formal education, self-study and hands-on experience. "I've always enjoyed writing," reports Leslie, "and I was able to hone my writing skills in college. Developing my wine knowledge was primarily through reading many books and meetings so many fascinating winemakers and other wine professionals on my travels to the many wine regions of the world."

In order to improve wine tasting skills, Leslie recommends participating in many wine tasting venues. "Pure wine tasting and a good memory are the only ways to become an expert in wine tasting," advises Leslie. "I take lots of notes and taste hundreds of wines. Over time you can develop this skill."

MOST CHALLENGING ASPECT OF THE JOB

"One of the most challenging parts of my job is the flipside of one of the best parts of my job, and that is getting paid to eat and drink for a living. Though the food, wine and travel are fabulous, one of my biggest challenges is to stay fit and active."

Another issue Leslie faces is how to continue building her business to the next level. "As a wine writer and communicator, I am always looking for fresh ideas and angles. It is important to stay creative and be aware of customer trends and needs."

Finally, as a working mother and wife, Leslie has to balance her intense travel schedule and heavy work load with raising two children and being part of the community. "It is sometimes difficult," admits Leslie, "because I get asked to do so many things and it is difficult to say no, because they all sound so fun."

273

BEST PART OF THE JOB

"I absolutely love my job," enthuses Leslie. "Everyday people ask me how they can get a job like mine. I basically get paid to travel, eat and drink—and then write and talk about it! What could be better?"

Leslie says she really enjoys engaging with people at her seminars and book signings. "I love to communicate about wine," says Leslie. "Over the years, I've developed my own personal voice about wine. I like making it easy to understand and put a humorous twist on it. It's such a high when someone in the audience 'gets it,' and I can see the light go on in their eyes and the smile on their face. It feels really good to help people understand more about this magical drink."

RAY JOHNSON, WINE EDUCATOR, SANTA ROSA JUNIOR COLLEGE & UC BERKELEY EXTENSION, CA

Ray grew up in Pittsburgh, Pennsylvania, far from the sunny vineyards of California (where he lives today). But it was in Pittsburg that Ray developed his lifelong love of wine. "My original motivation to learn about wine was actually driven by practical reasons," says Ray. "I was in college and realized that knowing about wine would make me look more sophisticated to the women I was dating, and I needed to earn some extra money. So I got a job at a restaurant in Pittsburg and memorized all eighty wines on their wine list. Then my junior year, I went to France for the summer and that only increased my interest in wine." From there he was hooked, and the rest of Ray's career has been devoted to wine with a very impressive resume of wine jobs leading to his current position as a wine educator at both UC Berkeley and Santa Rosa Junior College.

EDUCATION AND TRAINING

"Actually, I believe that both my wine experience and college education have helped me to obtain the position I have today," says Ray. "I received my Bachelor's in Philosophy and studied French in college, both of which are useful in the wine industry. After college, I worked for three years in a very high-end French restaurant in Pittsburg, and was able to travel with the owner several times to France to visit wine estates and purchase wine." From there, Ray moved to California where he worked for Christian Brothers in Napa Valley, first as a tour guide and then as a sales rep. He did so well in wine sales that he was recruited by Safeway to be a wine buyer for five years in several of their stores in the South Bay of San Francisco. This eventually led to a job offer from Draegers—a gourmet wine and food store in Menlo Park.

"It was at Draeger's," remembers Ray, "that I first had the opportunity to do wine education. Several of us taught evening wine classes at UC Berkeley Extension and also conducted seminars for store customers. I found that I really enjoyed sharing my knowledge with others and helping to introduce people to the joy of wine." From there, Ray moved to Sonoma County where he received an opportunity to teach in the wine department at Santa Rosa Junior College *and still teach part-time with Berkeley Extension. He recently finished his Master's in Wine Business from the University of Adelaide in South Australia.*

"Right now I'm teaching classes on French, Italian, Californian, Australian and New Zealand wines," says Ray. He also just published a book entitled The Good Life Guide to Enjoying Wine *and receives many consulting jobs to conduct wine appreciation seminars in corporations.*

MOST IMPORTANT SKILLS FOR A WINE EDUCATOR

"Obviously you need a background in wine," says Ray, "but I think the most important thing is to have good teaching skills so that the students can relax and enjoy themselves. Wine can be very intimidating and so I try to create a classroom environment in which everyone feels comfortable and can have fun. My mission in life is to make learning about wine fun.

"The first thing I do in my classes is to encourage people to describe what they are seeing, smelling and tasting," explains Ray. "Then, no matter what they say, I validate them. This helps build confidence and they participate more. Then others get involved and soon we are all having fun learning about wine."

Another important skill for a wine educator, according to Ray, is a global perspective. "It is important as an educator to have tasted broadly and look at the wine industry in a global context. This is why I participate in wine judgings, continue to travel every year to difference wine regions, and provide all of my tasting notes on my website. I think this makes me a better educator and I can share this with my students."

MOST CHALLENGING ASPECT OF THE JOB

"The most challenging part of being a wine educator is the schedule," states Ray. "Most colleges schedule wine classes in the evenings because the students are primarily working adults. Therefore, I teach every weeknight from Monday to Friday. Sometimes I wish I could teach during the day." Ray also mentions that the prep and clean-up for wine classes is more complicated than a regular college course. "You have to order all of the wines in advance, make sure they are stored and served at the right temperature. It's not a big issue, but it is a unique aspect of being a wine educator."

Finally, Ray adds that he sometimes misses the welcome he received at wineries and trade shows as a wine retailer, which isn't as obvious as a wine educator. "I find it curious," says Ray, "that even though I am introducing hundreds of students to many new wine brands every year that I'm not courted in the same fashion as I was when I was a wine buyer."

BEST PART OF THE JOB

"The most satisfying part of the job" says Ray, "is helping people to become more comfortable with wine. I have people at all levels in my classes, from beginners to advanced, but it is when a student tells me that they were able to order a wine off a wine list in restaurant that they really enjoyed that I have the most satisfaction. It is very rewarding to be able to empower others to learn about wine and be excited about their new knowledge. The students then become more confident and grow into great advocates of the pleasure of wine. The primary thrill of being a wine educator is that you really can make a positive difference in people's lives."

LILY PETERSON, WINE EDUCATOR, COPIA, NAPA, CA

Lily grew up in North Carolina with plans to become a psychologist or lawyer, but when she offered to help her father launch a gourmet food and wine store in Wilmington she became entranced with wine. "I found myself tasting, buying, and selling wine for the store and grew more and more fascinated with all of the varieties from around the world," says Lily. "Then I started doing tasting seminars for customers and found I loved the wine educator role." Today Lily has taught hundreds of wine classes across the US and serves as full-time wine educator with COPIA—the American Center for Food, Wine and the Arts in Napa, California.

EDUCATION AND TRAINING

"My bachelor's degree is in psychology and english, which does help with teaching," says Lily, "but I have to credit the WSET (Wine and Spirits Education Trust) program with giving me a solid background in wine, as well as much reading on my part, two long trips to Europe, and all of my wine retail experience." Lily completed the intermediate and advanced Levels of the WSET and is currently studying for the Diploma.

It was after working for three years in the Wilmington grocery/wine market, which she co-owned with her father, that Lily decided she wanted to further her wine education.

278

As a result, she spent a summer traveling around France, Italy, and Spain before moving to New York City and getting a job selling wine at Best Cellars. "It was an incredible experience working for Best Cellars in New York," reports Lily, "and Josh Wesson, the owner, was an excellent wine mentor. He and the rest of the management team encouraged me to start the WSET courses." While at Best Cellars Lily was a wine educator for in-store customers, as well as conducting training sessions for private events.

After three years with Best Cellars, Lily decided it was time to expand her horizons, so she enrolled in a three month independent wine study course in Florence, Italy where she immersed herself in Italian wines—her specialty. Upon returning to the US, Lily decided to move to California and applied for a wine educator job at Copia. Now Lily teaches Wine Tasting 101, Wine & Food Pairing, Wine 102, and WSET Intermediate classes at Copia.

MOST IMPORTANT SKILLS FOR A WINE EDUCATOR

"I think the most important skill for a wine educator is to be approachable," says Lily. "Wine can be so intimidating, and therefore it is absolutely critical to convey your message in a way that is inviting and encourages people to respond. I tell my students that the exciting thing about wine is that you are always learning. This is because there are so many wines, and with new brands being launched every week there is no way any one person can ever learn all of them. This makes learning about wine always fresh and intriguing."

Lily admits that her psychology background has been helpful in understanding her students and making sure to begin at their level. "I always try to customize my session based on where the student is," says Lily. "I'm hoping they will become as excited about wine as I am.

"So in the end," advises Lily, "wine knowledge and teaching skills are very important, but it's making sure that you are approachable that really counts. Wine is so subjective, and we all taste different things. It is important to validate everyone."

MOST CHALLENGING ASPECT OF THE JOB

"The most challenging part of being a wine educator is staying up to date with all of the changes in the wine industry and new wines coming out," states Lily. "I always read the major wine journals, such as Wine Spectator, Decanter, Jancis Robinson's Purple Pages, and Wine & Spirits Magazine. I also really like Karen McNeil's Wine Bible. It is a classic.

"Another challenge," continues Lily, "is the long hours. Some days I teach four classes, and I work weekends as well. It is lucky the work is so fun because it makes the hours pass more quickly. Also, sometimes I'm not sure of the results. My goal is to really help students learn, and I think most of them do, but since many of our public classes are so short—around forty-five minutes in length—I don't necessarily see the students again and I'm not always sure of the educational impact."

BEST PART OF THE JOB

"Everyday, I have someone tell me, 'You are so lucky to do this. How did you get this job?' I have to agree with them. It is a wonderful and very fulfilling job being a wine educator, especially when you realize you are helping someone to develop an interest in wine.

"Another great aspect of this job is meeting all of the people in the wine industry. I am surrounded by talented winemakers; we are always doing tastings; and I am continually learning. People in the wine industry are very kind and I've been fortunate enough to have some great mentors. One example is Peter Marks, who is an MW. He has been responsible for wine education at Copia and now at Icon Estates.

"Even though I didn't plan to go into wine in college—and instead almost accidentally fell into this industry—I find that it is the right place for me. I plan to continue to grow as a wine educator and wine enthusiast for the rest of my life."

Winery Administration

Just one minor message while you were out—
Phil Loxera was seen in the vineyards this morning.

Chapter 10

W hile wineries can be quite different from other businesses, there are a few ways in which they're very much like other companies. Those similarities show up in the administrative careers available in wine. "Administrative" primarily refers to careers in **finance, human resources (HR),** and **information technology (IT).**

The first thing to know about administrative careers in wine is that the job functions in these fields are perhaps the most similar to roles in other industries.

The second thing to keep in mind is how winery size impacts the availability and breadth of roles in these functions. In small wineries, you're likely to find office or administrative managers who manage accounting, HR, and occasionally IT functions for the winery. They may have several other hats as well! It's pretty unusual to find pure roles in any of these functions at a smaller winery. Small wineries may also choose to use outside contractors when needed for HR and IT services. What's key to landing one of these roles? Having strong financial and organizational skills; past experience working in small-business environments; and convincing the owner or owners that you have the skills and initiative to efficiently manage these functions (often freeing them to do other things).

In medium-sized wineries, you will likely find true accounting roles, and possibly a finance manager or VP as part of the winery's leadership team. You may have HR and IT functions as well; they are likely to be small (one to three people) and often report to the head of finance. Human resources will be focused on payroll, benefits administration, hiring, and employee relations. Information technology will be focused on providing network administration, managing whatever enterprise software (if any) the winery uses, and overseeing direct-to-consumer technologies like websites, club databases, and cash register systems.

Only at large wine companies are you likely to find true finance, HR and IT functions of more than ten people. You will find that even at the large wine companies, these functions have fewer roles and have fewer organization levels than their counterparts in other industries. Most will have a very simple organizational structure, with individual contributor roles reporting to managers, who in turn report to a vice president or equivalent position who heads up that department.

The third thing to know is that wine is generally not a great place to get an entry-level role in any of these functions. Because the functions tend to be leaner and flatter, wine companies often look for individuals with a minimum of three-to five-years previous experience in the same or related role that they are hiring for, though exceptions happen. Your best bets as a recent college graduate are as a junior accountant; an HR coordinator or recruiter; or as a help-desk technician. Remember, however, that wine is typically not a training ground for recent college graduates in any of these administrative fields.

The final thing to know is that flatter organizational structures have a direct impact on your ability to advance your career in the wine business. Is it possible to move up in administrative professions in wine? Absolutely! What's required to advance your career once you've made it into wine? Three primary things:

1) A generalist or broad skill-set: Because administrative functions in wine are lean and mean, managers, directors and VPs are expected to have a broad understanding of their area. This means specialists who want to remain in these roles will have difficulty finding organizations that have more than one or two levels of roles in their sub-discipline.

2) Willingness to move laterally: This is a direct result of point number one. To grow your wine career in administrative functions, be prepared to make two moves laterally, or even one laterally and one back, before making that final move forward into your desired role. You should also expect to come into wine at the same position (or even one that's a step lower) than the level you currently hold outside of the wine industry. This is driven by the small number of roles available in wine, and the need to come in and learn the industry before advancing. Be patient! Such moves tend to pay off very well in the medium- to long-term.

3) Flexibility, Adaptability and Initiative: The individuals who struggle to make the transition from other industries into wine tend to have a few things in common. They expect very clearly defined roles and responsibilities. They expect a lot of resources and have fairly rigid ideas about what they are, and are not, willing to do. They expect the organization to manage their career and their development in a very structured, directive way.

None of these things are characteristic of wine companies of any size. Individuals who succeed in making the jump to wine—and end up thriving in the business—tend to have an entrepreneurial, can-do, hands-on attitude. They are quite interested in going above and beyond their current abilities and role. Their next move isn't a role that exists currently—it's one they create through their results, drive, and relationship-building skills.

Let's be clear—none of this means a move into wine will add ten years onto your career plan! While it's important to understand how careers work in wine, remember that advancement in wine can come very quickly. This is one of the other benefits of working in a flat, less-structured industry.

Because careers in administrative professions will be more similar to equivalent roles outside of wine, this chapter focuses less on specific job duties, and more on what individuals in those professions need to know about how their function looks in wine.

FINANCE

Finance is a core function in any business. Winery finance has the same core responsibilities for accounting, treasury, tax, reporting, and audit as in other industries. The highest percentage of finance headcount tends to be concentrated in the core areas of accounting and finance. Treasury, tax and reporting are usually staffed with a small number of highly-skilled experts. Sometimes those functions will be combined, or added to the plate of someone in an accounting or finance role. Finance functions vary in size. For perspective, fifty people, spanning all sub-disciplines, is a very large finance function in the wine business.

Finance is currently a hot career field. The supply of talented and capable finance professionals is smaller than the demand, particularly in Northern California. That's one of two pieces of good news for finance professionals looking to get into wine. (It's always nice to be in demand!)

The other piece of good news is that there really aren't any barriers for finance professionals to make the move into wine, other than finding the opportunities available, and being poised to take advantage of them. Most finance professionals in wine have significant experience in other industries.

"It still seems like a very small, very new industry," says Chris Crowe, VP Finance/Central Coast Controller for Jackson Family Wines. On the differences between finance in wine versus other industries, Chris cites a couple of other key differences. "Monstrous changes" at someplace like Procter & Gamble (his last non-wine employer) felt less impactful than they do in big wine companies. He likens being at those non-wine companies to being on a big ship, where the waves scarcely make an impact.

At large wine companies, he relates, it feels more like being in a sailboat: the changes rock your boat in a much more substantial way.

In addition, "Some of the things I grew to expect—for example, having this huge IT group that could generate great new things for the business, making information more readily available—don't seem to be as typical in the wine companies I've been in, which makes your job a challenge. Information is not always there when you need it. You're finding that you have to develop a lot more things daily [than you would at other large companies]." Chris adds, "Other support groups seem to be stretched a lot thinner in wine than at other big companies."

UNIQUE EDUCATION AND EXPERIENCE REQUIREMENTS

- None to enter the industry, just the core technical skills for your field.
- Wine experience is a plus, not a requirement.
- Once you've entered the industry, you'll need to learn the differences in tax regulations and requirements for alcoholic beverages upon entering the wine industry.
- If you enter cost accounting and work on anything to do with winemaking and winery operations, you will also learn how you account for a product that, quite literally, evaporates over time in the barrel!

FINANCE CAREER LADDER IN WINE

The finance career ladder is essentially the same, if flatter, than what you will find in other industries. See Figure 1 for a common ladder and some typical finance titles in wine.

Figure 1: The Finance Career Ladder

Sr. Leadership Roles
- VP Finance/Controller
- Finance Director
- Director of Accounting

Supervisory Roles
- Accounting Manager
- AP Supervisor
- Finance Manager
- Tax Manager

Individual Contributor/ Specialist Roles
- Accountant, Sr./ Accountant
- Finance Analyst/ Sr. Analyst
- Treasury Analyst
- Tax Analyst
- Accounts Payable/ Accounts Receivable

HUMAN RESOURCES

A former VP of HR in the wine business is fond of saying, "HR is HR, no matter where you go." Individuals looking to start their wine HR career will find that observation to be very true.

Human resources, like finance, has the same core disciplines across industries. You'll have a payroll function. You'll have HR generalists or business partners. You'll have specialists compensation and benefits (often one person managing both, occasionally a group of two to three people). You'll have an HRIS system of some kind, and someone responsible for it (either a dedicated role or an added duty for someone in compensation or payroll). Regarding HRIS systems, either it will be a separate function overseen by an individual, or it will be rolled into the duties of a payroll clerk or benefits/compensation specialist.

Generalists typically manage their own recruitment: internal, dedicated staffing functions are a rare and newly emerging phenomenon in wine. As HR continues to grow in the industry, the number of these roles will likely increase. For those interested in staffing, another possibility is seeking a role with one of the number of temporary staffing and contingency recruitment agencies who wholly or partially specialize in wine industry staffing.

Training and development roles are a similarly newer phenomenon in wine. Like staffing positions, TD jobs are rare. The opportunities for these kinds of roles will also continue to grow, but at a slower rate.

There are a few differences between HR in wine and in other industries. First, wine is an agricultural business (many candidates overlook this simple, yet important, fact). So what does that mean? It means HR is very concerned with issues like seasonal hiring of staff for harvest and crush, and the releasing of that same staff at the end of the season. It means HR professionals may have to juggle multiple wage and hour requirements—one set for agricultural employees, and one set for winery and office staff. It can also mean having an agricultural business, a bottling business, a direct-to-consumer business, and a national sales business all under one roof.

Second, HR also needs to be at the forefront of understanding the demographic and legal shifts in the workforce. For HR practitioners in the Western US, that means being keenly aware of the needs of our large (and growing!) Latino/a workforce and adopting HR practices that address those needs. The demands of the industry include highly physical manual labor, an aging workforce, and an increasingly competitive labor market remain challenges for the industry.

Third, HR in wine is not well-established as a professional function. It has made great strides in the past ten to fifteen years, and is rapidly coming up to speed with the practices and talent of other industries. You will likely experience quite a lot of basic process deficiency, and a significant lack of automation and systems support. As the industry as a whole works to close these gaps in their businesses, HR professionals often find themselves at the back of the line for dollars and time to build infrastructure. That said, the picture continues to improve.

Finally, HR in wine tends to be very lean. For perspective, a winery's HR workforce of thirty people would be quite large by industry standards. You can expect to wear multiple hats, even in the largest wine companies, which will keep you quite busy. You may very well need to travel several hours in different directions from your primary office to visit vineyards, wineries and hospitality locations associated with your company.

UNIQUE EDUCATION AND EXPERIENCE REQUIREMENTS

- Understanding of agricultural HR law and practices, if you're going to work at all on the winemaking or operations side of the business.
- Understanding of immigration policy and law, and cultural issues associated with a highly Latino/a workforce.
- As with many hospitality, agricultural and operational businesses, strong understanding of wage and hour law, and non-exempt employee policies and practices.

HR CAREER LADDER IN WINE

Human resources careers offer the potential for advancement within wine. That advancement will most likely come through the generalist career ladder. That's not a huge distinction between HR in and out of the wine business. The thing to understand is that the specialist functions, like compensation, staffing, benefits, and training/OD (organization development), aren't as well-established in wine. Consequently, there tend to be only a few roles in these subsets of HR in any given organization.

If you're in a medium-sized winery, you will likely need to look after the entire operation. You should expect to lean heavily on outsource partners for benefits, payroll, HRIS, and training, and to be quite busy yourself.

In the largest wine companies, HR departments can range anywhere from ten to thirty people. If you're interested in advancing, you can anticipate rotating through at least a couple of generalist assignments, though most organizations will offer you a chance to rotate through a specialist assignment. With increasing offshore ownership in the wine business, it's also possible to join a global organization and look for expat experience down the road. Following is a typical career ladder for HR in Wine.

Figure 2: Human Resources Career Ladder

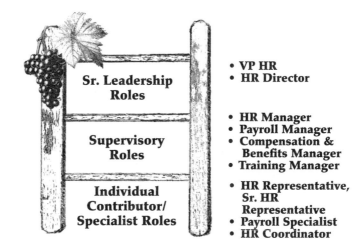

- **VP HR**
- **HR Director**

- **HR Manager**
- **Payroll Manager**
- **Compensation & Benefits Manager**
- **Training Manager**

- **HR Representative, Sr. HR Representative**
- **Payroll Specialist**
- **HR Coordinator**

INFORMATION TECHNOLOGY

The wine profession that's perhaps the most similar to its respective position in other industries is IT.

Information technology roles look essentially the same in wine as they are elsewhere. IT professionals will tend to focus in one of three areas; technical specialty, project management, and people management.

IT departments, like finance and HR departments, tend to be lean in wine. A forty-person IT department is quite large by industry standards. That department will be sub-divided into technical support roles focused on enterprise architecture; application tools supporting sales, winemaking, operations, supply chain, and the general user community; some user-support functions; and project management roles. Management structures are quite lean, often with only two to three layers in the organization.

IT in wine tends not to be the place to get access to the newest, hottest technologies. IT in wine will provide a fast-paced, close-to-the business environment. Most wineries are significantly under-leveraged in their technology infrastructure—something that many of them are trying to address as they face additional pressures from industry growth and consolidation.

UNIQUE EDUCATION AND EXPERIENCE REQUIREMENTS

- None to get into the industry.
- Core technical skills for the job in question.
- Working for smaller companies, you will need to get a pretty good idea of what the company's needs are and how the company works, as you will be in a generalist role.

- You will need to understand the technology aspects of direct wine selling, especially small- to medium-sized wineries, their website, their cash register system, how to get their transactions into QuickBooks or equivalent.

Following is a typical career ladder for IT in wine.

Figure 3: Information Technology Career Ladder

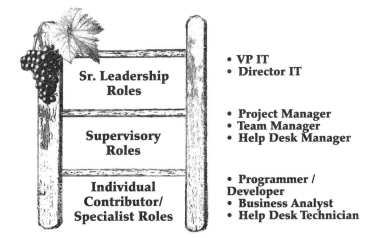

HELPFUL CONFERENCES, PUBLICATIONS & WEBSITES

Following is a list of helpful books, websites, and conferences to assist you in finding and/or preparing for finance, IT, or HR jobs in the wine industry.

Finance

- Jobs are posted on sites such as **winejobs.com, craigslist. org,** as well as in print mediums such as the ***Santa Rosa Press Democrat*** and ***Napa Register.*** Robert Half also does job placements for finance in wine.

- There is no large finance networking association or forum. If you're interested in industry networking, you will likely be attending meetings of other functions (e.g., **Unified Wine & Grape Symposium, ASEV,** or local vintners association groups).
- Chris Crowe, VP of finance for Jackson Family Wines reads *The Wine Advocate and Wine Spectator.* He also reads **winebusiness.com** on a daily basis.

Human Resources

- Jobs are posted on **winejobs.com, craigslist.org, shrm.org** and **nchra.org.**
- **The Northern California Human Resources Association (NCHRA)** offers at least one wine industry focused conference each year, which is a good opportunity to network and learn more about the industry.
- Diane Holst, VP of Human Resources, Sales& Marketing for Constellation Wines U.S reads *Just-Drinks, Wine Business Monthly,* and *Wine Spectator.* She subscribes to industry update blogs which source materials from places like *Advertising Age* and *MediaPost.* She also surfs **winejobs.com** to see what other organizations are looking for.

Information Technology

- Jobs are posted on **winejobs.com, craigslist.org,** and **dice.com.**
- John Collins, VP of Business Process & Information Technology for Foster's Wine Estates Americas reads *Consumer Goods Technology* and *Wine Business Monthly.*
- There is an IT-focused symposium called the **Wine Industry Technology Symposium (WITS)** that is held every July. John has observed jobseekers there using the symposium as an op-

portunity to find out about the industry and to start networking. **Unified Wine & Grape Symposium** is another great industry forum that takes place every January that is a great opportunity for jobseekers to network and get up to speed on the industry.

TIPS ON GETTING STARTED/JOB HUNTING STRATEGIES FOR ADMINISTRATION POSITIONS

Here are some suggestions to help you start your winery administration job search.

- **Network, Network, Network:** Networking is a key for finding any wine job. It can be extremely useful in winery administration careers. With more and more individuals shifting into wine from other industries, you should be able to find alumni from your alma mater, prior coworkers, and friends of friends who hold roles in winery administration professions. This network will be invaluable for finding out how your profession looks in wine—and for getting your foot in the door.
- **Do Your Industry Homework:** While out of industry experience is sought after for many winery administrative professions, doing your homework on wine is still a must. One of the biggest turn-offs in an interview is someone who hasn't bothered to research the company, or who demonstrates no understanding of the industry. See the preceding recommendations on industry publications to read.
- **Be Ready To Get Your Hands Dirty:** While wine is a lot of fun, it's also hard work! In particular, understand that you may not have the resources (dollars, staff, systems infrastructure) that you're accustomed to, and may find yourself wearing a number of different hats. You may also have to take personal

responsibility for more administrative tasks that you're accustomed to.

- **Adjust Your Expectations:** With smaller, flatter organizations, don't expect to automatically make a lateral move into wine. It's possible, particularly in winery administration professions, but not guaranteed. Be ready to come in at a lower level, and to work your way up from there. Be realistic about this plan as well. You will be asked about it in your interviews, and you'll need to be convincing about your willingness to pay your industry dues.

ADVICE FROM ADMINISTRATIVE PROFESSIONALS

Following are three interviews with administrative professionals. Hopefully they will be useful to you, as each of the individuals made the move from a first career into wine.

True Tales from the Wine Industry

CHRIS CROWE, VP FINANCE, CENTRAL COAST CONTROLLER, JACKSON FAMILY WINES

Chris Crowe is a prime example of someone who made the jump from fast-moving consumer goods into wine. He spent six years with Proctor & Gamble in Cincinnati, OH, then moved into the wine industry with Foster's Wine Estates in Napa, CA. After a couple of years with Foster's, he had a brief stint with Constellation Wines in St. Helena, CA. He is currently with Jackson Family Wines, located in the Central Coast of California.

When asked how he got into wine, Chris replied, "Why wouldn't I look into a job in the wine industry? It has great companies, great places to live, and you get to work with wine [and] be around wine all the time!"

EDUCATION AND TRAINING

Chris is very clear on what it takes to succeed in finance in the wine business. First, you "have to have a very strong financial/accounting background, [and] have the basis for good finance understanding." This includes going to college for finance or a similar business concentration, as Chris did.

Second is gathering the right kinds of experience, often in corporate environments. Through the different companies he has worked for, Chris has been able to gain "varying, increasing levels of finance responsibility," along with training at Procter & Gamble in finance. His experience ranges from supporting sales to manufacturing plants to working within wineries. He also has experience with the various sub-functions within finance.

MOST IMPORTANT SKILLS FOR FINANCE PROFESSIONALS IN WINE

"First and foremost," Chris says, "is to develop a strong sense of financial understanding across the business." It's vitally important to be able to "take all of the everyday activities and turn them into an overall picture for the given winery.

Being able to understand the everyday transactions, how they relate to the overall budget, being able to understand from beginning to end how that process works.

"The second most important is adaptability: willingness for change and growth. The wine industry is a constantly changing environment. What you may be doing one day will completely change two weeks later. Change seems much more prevalent [in wine] than it was in the earlier part of my career. My first criteria [in assessing candidates] is, 'Are you adaptable? Are you flexible?' Someone who can handle the change and be flexible."

For Chris, the third most important skill is "being willing to learn new things outside your realm of everyday responsibility. You can't strictly be a finance and accounting person. You have to be involved in every aspect of the business." Chris strongly advises against being narrowly focused on your specific role in finance if you're interested in progressing. "You won't get anywhere that way," he states clearly. "The finance background is only going to get you so far."

Additionally, if you want to progress to senior levels, Chris says, "You won't be effective unless you understand what other people are doing and how it affects you. Someone who is tethered to their desk, someone who is sitting in front of their desk and building spreadsheets twelve hours a day—that doesn't breed success. If you want to be successful, you need to get out into the business and need to understand what the winemakers do, what the vineyard people do, what the logistics people do—understand what each group does, how they help you get your job done, and how you can help them be successful."

Finally, for individuals looking to get into the business, Chris says, "I always like to see folks who have a lot of systems background and a lot of production or sales finance experience. Those folks are usually a little more lateral. You have to think across multiple levels of the business [in those roles]. Those are the folks who are most successful, who I would look to first as best fits for wine industry jobs."

MOST CHALLENGING ASPECT OF THE JOB

"Balancing all of the change that goes on. The amount of work never seems to slow: there's always something new, something changing, something different to do, and it never slows down.

"Being able to priority-set. It seems to be more difficult [in wine] than I've experienced in the past because things are ever-evolving. You think you know where you're going this week, you have things all planned out, then you have a new deliverable that you have two days to complete. You're constantly in a state of flux, and it never seems to rest. It's a constant challenge that you learn to live with after a while.

"As you move deeper into your career, you're a bigger resource for other people. Your time is always needed by others."

BEST PART OF THE JOB

"Helping to provide some of the change. It's exciting to see the work that you do get turned into something, be it a new plant or product, putting in a solar project to help a winery go green. Being a key asset in building the business plan for

that, being able to see all the different things that happen besides the numbers that go on the page—it's kind of exciting to see those things develop. You're the key resource for making sure all the financials work. You get to provide some exciting input into building the overall winery.

"It's a fantastic industry to be a part of. If it's something you're seriously considering doing, don't take no for an answer. One of the things I've found is that there are some unbelievable opportunities and some great people to be around. You get up in the morning and you're actually excited and interested in what you're going to do today. And that's kind of a hard thing in today's times—to find in a job—but you can find it here.

"You can live and breathe your work every day. You can sit down at the table and know you provided a big benefit into the wonderful bottle of wine you're about to drink."

ADVICE FOR PEOPLE LOOKING TO START THEIR FINANCE CAREER IN WINE

CHRIS' DO'S:

- *"The biggest 'do' is when you're gearing up for interviews. You really have to show your ability to be lateral across different functions, as I mentioned before. What I have found is that hiring managers [in wine] are most impressed by that lateral experience, having worked in a plant, worked with sales, worked on a customer team, worked in profit forecasting."*

- *"Show that you are adaptable. Show that you are really interested in everything, willing to do everything. The majority of the people I've talked to, that's the first thing they go to."*
- *"Show your energy, your passion [for wine]. Winemakers are passionate about [the industry], the vineyard managers are passionate about their grapes. They want that from their admin types."*

CHRIS' DON'TS:

- *"Emphasize the school that you went to too much. Most of us have been to good schools. Your experience is the more important key to you getting the job."*
- *"Let your ego get in the way. You can walk out of a P&G, a Clorox, a Microsoft, you can assume [the winery] has to have you, you're doing them a favor by coming down to the wine industry. Don't look at it that way. Job structures are different, organizational chains of command are different. The rules are kind of different in this game. Check your ego at the door. You're coming to an environment that is probably quite different than the one you're leaving. It's a very artistic, very romantic industry. It's a whole different world."*

DIANE HOLST, VP HUMAN RESOURCES, SALES & MARKETING, CONSTELLATION WINES US

Diane Holst has been part of the wine business for nearly a decade. She started her career with The Walt Disney Company, where she spent ten years in HR. She then moved to The Clorox Company. After a little more than three years there, she moved to Beringer Wine Estates, which later became Foster's Wine Estates. She's been with Constellation for a little over a year.

When asked how she got into wine, Diane responded, "I followed a former colleague of mine who joined the wine business. Wine had always been a great passion. I didn't realize [at the time] that there would be corporate roles available, that there were major corporations in the wine industry." That is, until her colleague recruited her to Beringer.

When asked how HR is different in wine, Diane responded, "I don't know if I see that it is different—what I do, what we do—in the wine business. I think it's a whole lot more fun! I have a great deal of passion about what we do, which makes it easier to do what we do even in the most difficult of times or situations.

"Essentially, people are people, organizations are organizations. While we have winemakers and enologists that *are unique to our business—and that's fabulous—at the end of the day they're still people. So, from a human resources point of view, I don't really see that it's different, except for the extraordinary places we get to work, and the wines we get to consume."*

EDUCATION AND TRAINING

"For HR professionals, Diane says, "I don't think [candidates] need to come from the wine business. [That's my] personal point of view. I think it's important that they have a passion for the business, that they want to be here. I think that's important, and comes through in what we do.

"Then it's core technical skills. Are they a good problem solver? Do they have good employee relations expertise? What's their recruitment experience like? Because sourcing candidates is a lot of what we do, being able to zone in and find out what skill sets someone brings to the table and how that applies to our organization."

MOST IMPORTANT SKILLS FOR HR PROFESSIONALS IN WINE

"Good instincts, first and foremost. People instincts, fit instincts, organizational instincts. How do things work, what does it take to be successful. How to get the right people in place to make the organization successful.

"[Second is] insight into the business. Understanding the business in general. I look at my role—HR's role—as the oil that makes the engine work. It's our job to make sure the business achieves its results. It's hard to do that without understanding the business."

MOST CHALLENGING ASPECT OF THE JOB

"First, when it comes time to tell someone that they don't have a role going forward. Oftentimes that's a partnership conversation between the manager and HR. Being on the planning side of that and making those decisions is never easy.

"Second, dealing with trying to get all of the children in the sandbox to play nice with each other—whether in the wine business or anywhere else. Trying to help everyone understand each others' points of view."

BEST PART OF THE JOB

"Seeing great business results. Seeing organizations come together [in mergers and acquisitions] and [having] things really work. You make decisions oftentimes on the forefront of things or on the back-side of things, and it's that fingers-crossed, let's-hope-this-works-out attitude. It's really cool when it does!"

ADVICE FOR PEOPLE LOOKING TO START THEIR HR CAREER IN WINE

DIANE'S DO'S:

- *"Research the organizations in which they're coming to work. Understand the competitive set. Read up on what your organization is doing, what's current, where's it going, and what you're going to do to make that organization be a better place."*
- *"Research distributors, wine shops, [and] how the business works from a larger perspective."*
- *"Think about where you want to be, and how this organization takes you to what that goal is."*

- *"It's important to network—to talk to a number of different people in the business. Realize what a tiny industry it is. Don't burn bridges. Because [the industry] is so small, it's great to be competitive—but always be respectful."*

DIANE'S DON'TS:

- *"Don't just think that this is your favorite winery and that's why you want to come to work here."*
- *"Sometimes people from the outside are so enticed by the romance of the industry they forget there's a reason why we call it work. It is a job, you do have to contribute. There are core capabilities we need to bring to the table. Be prepared for what you're getting into."*

JOHN COLLINS, VP, BUSINESS PROCESS & INFORMATION TECHNOLOGY, FOSTER'S WINE ESTATES AMERICAS

John Collins heads up one of the larger information technology functions in the wine business. With nearly a decade in the industry, he's seen firsthand the rapid growth and consolidation of the industry and how that change has impacted IT.

About his experience, John says, "I came to then-Beringer Vineyards managing the IT function. I had an IT manage-

ment background—I managed the consulting practice at IBM, which meant I did a lot of people management, sales, a lot of project management. Prior to that, I'd worked for a software company in the newspaper industry. I have a high-tech background."

EDUCATION AND TRAINING

John says, "I didn't think it was particularly hard [to get into wine]. I knew someone who was involved with Beringer going public—they knew of the opportunity, I sent in my resume, came in and interviewed, [and] got hired.

"I was the tenth member of the IT department, which is now roughly forty people. In almost nine years, I've been involved in hiring almost fifty people. In most roles I didn't care one bit whether the candidate had wine industry background.

"To be an IT professional, there's lots of different paths. Nowadays, of course, universities provide pretty specific degrees in information technology, and not just in one flavor. You can be highly technical, you can be managerial, you can be more project-focused. It would be good to think about what you want to get into and start addressing it as early as when you're in school. When I went to school, there were computer science programs—they were designing everyone to be a programmer. As early as university level, start to zone in on what you want and start to manage your career that way. Go find roles that are pretty interesting to you.

"You do have to make up your mind. If you're really technology-curious, and you really enjoy problem-solving, then you probably want to be pretty technical. It used to be that if you were going to be real technical, you would be *bottom-rung [in terms of career ladder, managing people and salary]. Now you can make as much money, as long as you pick reasonably hot technologies, which tends to be fun and interesting so I don't know why you wouldn't. But you have to pick.*

"There are more technical roles than non-technical ones in wine. There are very few winery IT management roles."

MOST IMPORTANT SKILLS FOR IT PROFESSIONALS IN WINE

"For my role, the most important skills are to understand our business priorities, the desires of management (which I have two sets: the people in Australia and the people here), and being able to process that into allocation of our IT resources. So, setting our IT priorities, and then managing people and process."

For other roles, John says, *"Be interested in wine. Being a wine drinker is not required—we have several people who don't drink at all.*

"Be geographically located [near a wine industry center]. You probably want to live somewhere where there are wineries.

"If you're being flexible, I can't see it being that difficult getting into the industry. It's more about finding a job that matches your background and skill-set. Your skills have to match the opening that the company has. You either have the skills or you don't. It's about the role."

MOST CHALLENGING ASPECT OF THE JOB

"Our size. Our size presents challenges because we're big enough to need to do things correctly, but small enough to

not quite be able to always afford to, so you have to make choices about where you're going to step up and staff and resource things, and where you're going to be light. That's a big challenge.

"Keeping up with the needs in the user community. Keeping up with them in some areas, and pushing them in others—that's a challenge."

BEST PART OF THE JOB

"It's a fast-paced, fun, [and] interesting organization and industry. People are very passionate. It's fun to be involved. The subject matter is something I enjoy. I like the people, [I] care about the people."

ADVICE FOR PEOPLE LOOKING TO START THEIR IT CAREER IN WINE

JOHN'S DO'S:
- *"Show enthusiasm for wine."*
- *"Be prepared to make some sacrifices to get into the industry. It's not compensated like, for example, South San Jose would be."*
- *"Consider looking at the Washington or Oregon wine industries if you're looking for a better work-life balance. You might actually be able to afford a home in Washington or Oregon on a wine industry salary!"* That's not a rap on salary levels (which John says are competitive for the areas), it's simply that "homes in Santa Rosa [and other northern California areas] are really, really expensive."
- Be specific about the kind of opportunity you're looking for. John says, "Believe it or not, not all propel-

308

ler-heads are the same! If you're using non-technical folks to network, make sure they convey what kind of IT person you are, and what kind of role you're looking for."

JOHN'S DON'TS

- *"Make yourself sound like an alcoholic, though, or a wine snob. [What's] more interesting is someone who says, 'Yeah I tried home winemaking!' and shows interest in the process."*
- *Think you have to be a wine drinker. "We have plenty of people we've hired who don't drink at all—which is kind of common in high-tech—or people who only drink beer. We usually convert the latter over time [to drinking wine]."*
- *"Expect that because you're super-enthusiastic about wine that that's going to get you into the industry. It's a great separator for two otherwise completely equal candidates—in that case, I'm totally going for the really enthusiastic one."*

Working for a Winery Supplier

Dad, the wine's been put into used barrels, just like you ordered.
I got a great deal on them from Exxon.

Chapter 11

An excellent way to enter the wine industry is to obtain a job with one of the thousands of suppliers to the industry. These can be quite exciting jobs, ranging from providing corks, bottles, and barrels to wineries to designing and selling sophisticated winery or point-of-sale (POS) software systems. One of the nice aspects of working for a supplier is that they are often more open to hiring people from other industries who have the skills, experience, and education they require, but who may lack the wine knowledge. For example, if you have worked in accounting, human resources, or information technology for another industry, such as insurance, biotech, or consumer goods, your skill set can easily transfer to those same departments in a wine industry supplier. In addition, suppliers usually have many entry-level sales positions in order to market and sell their products or services to wineries. Therefore, if you have some sales experience, this is another good entry-point to the wine industry.

One of the nice benefits about working for a wine industry supplier is the opportunity to travel to wine regions and represent your products as part of wine trade shows. In addition, you will have the chance to taste wines from around the world, and learn about the wines of your client accounts. Obviously through this close proximity to wineries, you will learn more about the industry and develop a good network of contacts. Many people who start working with a wine supplier enjoy it so much that they stay with that company. Others may later choose to transition to working in another part of the wine industry value chain, such as for a vineyard operation, a winery, a distributor, or wine retail.

This chapter provides an overview of the major types of suppliers to the wine industry, beginning with a review of the wine industry value chain. It then provides some resources to consider, job hunting strategies, and concludes with interviews of two experts working in the winery supplier world.

MAJOR CATEGORIES OF WINE INDUSTRY SUPPLIERS

There are three major supply categories for the wine industry, and logically, they match the three major categories of the wine industry supply chain as illustrated in Figure 1. These categories are: 1) viticulture supplies to assist with grape growing; 2) winemaking or enology supplies to assist with winemaking; and 3) marketing and sales supplies to assist with getting wine to distributors, retailers and the end-consumer. There is a fourth category of general business supplies not illustrated. These are the supplies that any business needs to operate, such as computers, paper, pens, pencils, etc. These are not listed in this chapter because they are the same for any industry. Suppliers listed are specific to the wine industry or have created customized products for wine.

Figure 1: Major Supply Categories for the Wine Industry

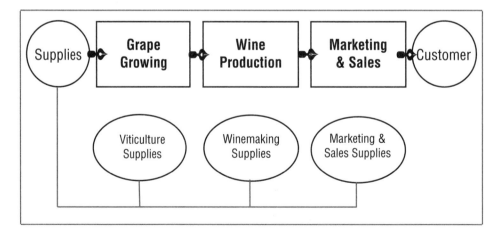

SUPPLIERS FOR VITICULTURE

A company that supplies products or services to help in the production of wine grapes fits in this category. They may include any of the following:

Vineyard Development/Consultants: Provide services to prepare the land for vineyard development. Also includes consultants who can perform studies, conduct soil analyses, design the vineyard spacing and layout, and assist in obtaining the necessary permits to install a vineyard. Firms can also provide equipment to clear trees, rocks, disc soil, and add any necessary nutrients or soil treatment.

Vineyard Set-Up/Maintenance Supplies: These types of firms sell all of the supplies necessary to set up a new vineyard and/or maintain an existing one. Primary supplies include trellis and irrigation systems, fencing to keep out deer, frost protection equipment such as heaters, blowers, or sprinkler systems, bird guards, gopher traps, and other set-up/maintenance supplies. Additional supplies include pruning shears, picking bins, gloves, protective clothing, refractometers, etc.

Grapevine Nurseries/Grafters: Provide green vines, bench graft vines or budwood in order to plant or graft over a vineyard. Can grow vines to meet specific rootstock, varietal, and clone needs of the vineyard owner. Grafters provide a specialized service of grafting over vines from one varietal to another.

Vineyard Applications: These types of businesses provide the various applications needed in a vineyard. These include organically farmed vineyards using sulfur and other approved organic applications; biodynamic vineyard preps; and traditional applications of pesticides, herbicides, fungicides and fertilizers.

Vineyard IT Equipment: Companies that provide sophisticated computer equipment to monitor vineyards, including weather monitoring equipment, soil sensors, GPS (global positioning systems) for vineyards, and computer software.

Vineyard Equipment/Tractor Manufacturers: Companies which provide some or all of the vineyard equipment necessary to manage and harvest the grapes. This includes tractors, sprayers, harvesters, automatic pruners, and all of the associated parts.

Vineyard Labor Contractors: These groups train and provide full or part-time labor for vineyard operations, especially during harvest and pruning times.

Vineyard Consultants: Offer services to improve quality/safety in vineyards and solve problems, as well as to assist with vineyard development and set-up.

SUPPLIERS FOR WINEMAKING

The list of supplies which support winemaking operations could cover many pages. However, following is an abbreviated inventory of the major supplies needed to make wine:

Crusher/Destemmer/Presses: As the picked grapes enter the winery, the first stop is either the destemmer, crusher, and/or press depending on the type of grapes and winemaking technique being used. This is very important and usually rather expensive equipment along with supporting parts.

Tanks/Fermentation Vessels: Stainless steel tanks and other types of vessels in which to ferment and age wine are one of the major costs in a winery. The larger the winery, the more tanks are needed. Most modern wineries use tanks made of stainless steel which are temperature controlled. However, tanks can also be made of cement, wood, and special types of plastic. Companies that design and produce these are located all over the world. Support parts such as temperature monitors, self-cleaning mechanisms, and connecting pipes are also produced by these types of wine equipment suppliers.

Yeasts/Additives: Though some winemakers use the naturally occurring yeast that lives on the grapes and in some old cellars, many purchase yeast to ferment their wine. In addition to this, there are many other additives that winemakers can use in order to produce the specific wine style they desire. These include enzymes, bacteria (such as malolactic), tannins, acid, sugar, SO2, and other legal additives.

Barrels/Oak Additives: Barrels are another expensive supply needed to produce high-quality wines. Some customized barrel producers charge over $2000 for a fine French oak barrel. Barrels are primarily used to age wine and impart more complex flavors to the final product. They can be made from different kinds of wood, but French, American, Hungarian, and Slovenian oak are the most common types. Less expensive options to flavor wines include oak chips, oak staves, and oak powder. Toasting the oak at different char levels also impacts flavor and pricing.

Cellar Equipment/Gases: There are many other types of cellar equipment that need to be purchased to make wine. A few of these include filtration devices, pumps, hoses, and fittings—not to mention cleaning and sanitation equipment. Many wineries use gases such as nitrogen, CO2, and argon to protect wine. Likewise, temperature control and humidity equipment must be installed, as well as air quality detection and filtration. There are many other parts and supplies that are too numerous to mention here.

Lab Equipment: Most wineries will purchase at least basic lab equipment to measure acid and pH, but others will actually outfit a room in their winery with a complete wine laboratory to perform all of the necessary analyses required for winemaking and regulatory requirements.

Laboratory Analysis Services: Smaller wineries will often outsource lab work to an outside service because it is more cost-effective for them than purchasing all of the equipment and supplies.

Record Keeping (Paper, Software and Barcodes): In most countries, winemakers are required by law to keep track of all ingredients added to wine, especially SO2 levels. Therefore, some wineries will purchase software to track every addition or action taken with a particular batch of wine, including pumpovers, rackings, temperature monitoring, measurements, etc. Others will use paper and pencil to track all of their actions. Some have added bar-coding at every step, starting in the vineyard to track lots.

Bottles/Alternative Packaging: Obviously wine bottles are a very important supply to the wine industry, and can be manufactured and purchased at a variety or price points, depending on how specialized the bottle needs to be. Of course, there are many alternative packaging options now including bag-in-box, tetra-pak, PET plastic bottles, aluminum cans, and more to be developed in the future.

Corks/Alternative Closures/Foils: Working for a cork supplier can also be an interesting occupation. Corks have been used to protect wine for centuries and are still highly desired by many top winemakers. At the same time, there are new alternative closures such as screw-cap and glass stoppers. Foils which cover the closure are another supply often used by wineries to protect the cork and also assist with aesthetic appeal and branding.

Bottling Lines/Mobile Services: Larger wineries will usually purchase a bottling line, but smaller ones may use the services of a mobile bottling line that arrives at their winery on the back of a truck. Alternatively, they may ship their wine to another location to be bottled.

Wine Warehousing/Storage: Once the wine is bottled, it must be boxed and stored in temperature controlled warehouses. It is usually shrink-wrapped and shipped in pallets with bar-coding. All of this equipment is also needed. Smaller wineries will often outsource to a warehousing and storage company. Many distributors also offer these services.

Winemaking Consultants: Many start-up wineries will make use of the services of a consulting winemaker. At the same time, established wineries will often call in an outside expert to help with a particular problem or just to provide some objective wine making advice.

Grape/Bulk Wine Suppliers: If a winery has excess grapes or wine they will often sell it in bulk to wine brokerage houses that will resell it for them. Likewise, if they find themselves in a shortage situation, they may also purchase grapes or bulk wine from these types of suppliers.

SUPPLIERS FOR MARKETING & SELLING WINE

Working for a supplier who focuses on providing products and services to the wine industry to help them market and sell wine is also a rewarding career choice. Following is a list of the most common suppliers in this category.

Wine Label Designers: There are some graphic design firms that specialize in wine label design. Most of them also provide design assistance with other marketing support materials.

Wine Marketing Support Material Designers: The wine label is very important in attracting customers, as are other POS (point of sale) materials. Examples include box designs that can be used for an end of aisle or floor display, posters, bottle tags, shelf-talkers, recipe cards and other promotion materials. In addition, most wineries like to provide winemaker spec sheets, waiter cards, press kits, and trade show set-ups as part of their marketing and sales materials. These types of suppliers can design and product all of these materials.

Wine Marketing Research Firms: These types of firms provide research services including conducting focus groups and customer surveys, as well as making recommendations on how to move forward with a new or existing brand.

Web Design & Online Wine Marketing/Sales Firms: These are suppliers which design winery and wine retail websites. They may also offer other online services such as creating and sending newsletters, email, event announcements, advertising, and wine club management. Some are beginning to offer services with Wine 2.0 applications such as social networking linkages and viral marketing.

Wine Sales Registers & Inventory Tracking Systems: Companies which design, manufacture and service cash registers for tasting rooms, wine shops, restaurants, and other retailers which are customized for wine sales. Many have software that is linked to wine inventory and can automatically place new orders, as well as provide useful sales and margin reports. Another form is a depletion report which links distributor depletions to wineries, so everyone can track where and how well the wine is selling, and make necessary adjustments to inventory.

Transportation Services: These are firms that ship wine. They can include ground services such as refrigerated trucks and train compartments, to ships which transport wine containers or bulk wine. In rare instances, wine is shipped by air. In all cases, special storage, handling, and temperature control is required to insure wine quality. Most sophisticated suppliers also offer computerized software tracking systems to track wine shipments and improve just-in-time inventory control.

Direct Shipping & Compliance Firms: Companies which ship to consumers for wineries and handle all regulatory compliance issues, including obtaining permits and administering taxes and reporting requirements. Used by many small wineries to manage their wine club shipments.

Wine Marketing/Sales Consultants: Firms that advice and assist wineries with the marketing and sales strategy and execution. They provide a range of services. Some also serve as brokers who work in partnership with distributors to sell wine (see Chapter 7 "Wine Marketing and Sales with Distributors and Importers").

HELPFUL RESOURCES

Following is a list of helpful books, websites, and conferences to assist you in finding and/or preparing for a job with a wine supplier.

- ***Harper's Wine and Spirit Directory:*** Directory which is useful for international trade and UK/Ireland suppliers.
- ***Understanding Wine Technology*** by David Bird: Covers winemaking supplies.
- **Unified Wine & Grape Symposium:** Held each January in Sacramento, California. Largest trade show of US wine industry suppliers. Great place to network with suppliers.
- ***The Wines & Vines Wine Industry Directory & Buyer's Guide:*** Directory which can be **purchased at http://www. winesandvines.com/directoryonline.**
- ***Wine: A Global Business*** edited by Liz Thach & Tim Matz: Covers all aspects of the wine industry, including a special chapter on the wine supply chain.
- ***Wine Business Monthly:*** Journal which covers the wine industry and often features special issues on wine industry supplies, services, and equipment.

JOB HUNTING TIPS TO WORK FOR A SUPPLIER

If you want to work for a supplier to the wine industry, the job hunting strategy is not that different from other industries. Consider some of the following steps:

- Review the supplier categories in this chapter and select two to three types of suppliers in which you are interested.
- Hop online or obtain a copy of one of the wine supplier directories listed earlier and find several companies in which you are interested.

- Go to their website and research them. Check to see if they have any jobs posted.
- Review your skill set including your experience and education to see how well it matches the needs of the supplier.
- Begin networking, using your contacts to see if you know anyone who works at those firms. If not, begin attending wine conferences and talking with people. Going to the **Unified Wine & Grape Symposium** in Sacramento, California is a great way to meet and talk directly with suppliers.
- Brush up your resume and customize it to meet the needs of the companies you are targeting. Consider sending it directly to the company, or use networking and contacts.
- Search online wine job sites to see if any jobs are posted. Send in your resume. Also consider contacting a wine industry placement firm such as **Benchmark** or **Newlin & Associates.**
- Follow-up with email or phone call one week after sending your resume. Continue to follow-up—especially if it is a sales position—so they can see that you demonstrate perseverance.
- While you are job hunting, take the time to learn more about the wine industry. Read wine books, journals, and blogs; attend seminars and classes; and join a wine tasting group.
- Don't give-up. Keep trying, and eventually you will obtain a great job with a supplier to the wine industry.

ADVICE FROM EXPERTS

Following are excerpts of interviews with two experts working on the supplier side of the wine industry. They both provide very useful advice and perspective on skills and experience needed to succeed in this exciting part of the wine industry.

True Tales from the Wine Industry

MEL KNOX, CEO & OWNER, KNOX BARREL BROKER, SAN FRANCISCO, CALIFORNIA

Mel Knox grew up in Olympia, Washington with no intention of going into the wine industry. "My parents wanted me to be a lawyer," says Mel, "so I studied Psychology in college with plans to go onto law school." On the way, Mel got sidetracked into being a delivery truck driver for a wine shop. "The next thing I knew I was a full-fledged wine nut," reports Mel.

That passion has translated into more than thirty years of successfully running a wine barrel brokerage based out of San Francisco. Renown for selling some of the best quality French and Hungarian barrels in the US, Mel Knox has helped to shape some of the top wine brands in the industry through his role as a wine industry supplier.

EDUCATION AND TRAINING

"I left Washington State to attend college in California," says Mel. "I got a B.A. in Psychology at Stanford, which, I suppose, has been helpful in the sales part of being a barrel broker. The key to successful selling in the wine industry is building long-term relationships with people.

"Most of my wine education and training though," says Mel, "was really through experience." After college Mel was thinking about attending law school when he obtained the

delivery truck driver job. "Two of my college friends were working at a store for which I was delivering wine. It was Rolly Somer, which today is K&L Wine Merchants. They really got me interested in wine, and soon I was tasting with them and learning about Bordeaux, Sauternes, Barolo, and California Cabs." From there, Mel obtained a position as wine buyer at the Wine & Cheese Center in San Francisco, and ran the tasting bar and wine education classes for the next seven years.

"Through this job, I met a tremendous number of wine-makers, tasted wines from all over the world, and learned a lot," says Mel. One of the people he met was Becky Wasserman, an American living in France, who started a barrel brokerage. "Becky became a legend in the industry," says Mel. "She was one of the first American experts on Burgundy and mentored some now famous people, such as Kermit Lynch. One day, she asked me to help her sell barrels when she had the flu. I was able to sell all of the wine barrels within a week, and she asked me to join her in the business."

Eventually, Becky sold the barrel broker business to Mel, and the rest is history. Today, he works closely with winemakers to craft customized French and Hungarian oak barrels of all sizes, with the coopers of François Frères and Taransaud Tonnellerie. His business is doing well and has grown large enough for him to hire four other employees. He still enjoys traveling frequently to Europe.

MOST IMPORTANT SKILLS FOR SUPPLY-SIDE PROFESSIONALS

"In the wine industry supply side of the business, the most important skills are professional selling and relationship

building," says Mel. "The wine industry is all about relationships—all over the world. I consider the people I work
with—the families in France—to be part of my family. The
winemakers I work with are very important to me, and I
make sure to really understand their needs and vision for
their wine."

Another important skills area, according to Mel, is wine
industry knowledge. "You have to know the industry and
understand how oak impacts wine. This means you also have
to know about winemaking and some of the chemistry. I
actually think it is helpful to work in a winery for a while so
you can gain some experience. This helps when you interact
with winemakers."

Mel describes some of the variables that go into barrel
making, including the type of wood, forests they are derived
from, the toasting levels, way the barrel is crafted, air drying
of the wood, size of the barrel, and type of wine that will
eventually reside in the barrel. "There are many nuances to
this," says Mel. "Both the winemaker and cooper are artists,
and they are aware of the impact of oak on the final product
and its price."

MOST CHALLENGING ASPECT OF THE JOB

"I have to admit that I still don't like doing the paperwork
or working with computer files," smiles Mel. "For many
years, I sold all the barrels and kept records all by myself.
Now, fortunately, I have a staff that doesn't keep records in
a cardboard box like I used to do.

"Another thing to keep in mind," cautions Mel, "is the
fact that the wine industry doesn't always pay that well.
People who want to transfer from other industries to wine

are often amazed at the lower salaries they will be required to take. However, there are many other dividends working with wine," says Mel, "such as great people and a wonderful lifestyle."

BEST PART OF THE JOB

"The people I meet in the wine industry are the best part of the job," says Mel. "Wine business people are good people. They want to work in the industry; are fun, interesting, and intelligent. Working with them is like working with friends, and we often get to travel to the great wine regions of the world together. Just this last weekend I was in the Willamette Valley of Oregon tasting 1961 Chateau Palmer and 1985 La Tache. It's definitely a nice lifestyle."

PHIL DURRETT, NORTH AMERICAN SALES DIRECTOR, ACI CORK, CA

Phil Durrett admits that growing up in a restaurant family in Southern California helped to introduce him to the world of wine. "My father, brother, and uncle were all in the restaurant industry," says Phil. "Hamburger stands, casual restaurants, and fine dining—you name it, we tried it." And through that food connection, Phil came to understand wine. "One of my earliest memories is visiting the Italian Swiss Colony Winery in Sonoma County with my parents when I was a kid," smiles

Phil. "We frequently visited wineries to taste and buy wine for our stores."

Phil's love for wine has taken him on a whirlwind ride through the wine industry where he has held jobs in winery sales, wine recruiting, and wine supplies. Now he holds the prestigious position of North American Sales Director for ACI Cork, the second largest cork manufacturer in the world.

EDUCATION AND TRAINING

"Actually, my parents didn't really want me to pursue a career in food and wine," admits Phil. "So they encouraged me to attend University of Santa Clara, just south of San Francisco, and study history and law. After law school, I was a general practice attorney in the North Bay for ten years before finally getting back into food and wine."

Phil's legal experience and resulting interpersonal skills were highly useful in establishing his career in wine. He began by starting several Good Earth franchise restaurants, followed by owning a fine dining restaurant where he managed to achieve a Wine Spectator's Award of Excellence for one of his wine lists. From there, he obtained a job in sales with Sysco, one of the largest food supplier companies in America. "Both jobs were great," says Phil, "and they both helped to hone my sales and management skills. Sysco's sales training program, one of the best in the nation, was especially helpful and I was able to become one of the top twenty salespeople in the Bay Area."

But wine was still calling to Phil, so he finally accepted a job as a wine sales rep with a small winery in Sonoma County. "It was a great experience," said Phil, "but I had to take a pay cut to work in the wine industry. After a while, I *had to move on in order to increase my salary." Therefore, Phil moved into the more lucrative field of executive recruiting for the wine industry, and eventually rose to his current position at ACI Cork. As a global wine company operating in more than twenty-seven countries and with 800 employees, ACI Cork is well respected in the industry and pays more competitive salaries.*

MOST IMPORTANT SKILLS FOR THE JOB

"Developing my sales skills was the most important thing I did in order to be successful in the wine supplier side of the business," states Phil. "As a supplier to the wine industry, you have to know how to build relationships and do professional selling.

"Another important skill set when working for an international company," continues Phil, "is intercultural awareness. Since ACI Cork is based in Portugal, I've had to learn about the culture there, as well as understand the global diversity issues at our other seventeen facilities around the world. For example, doing things quickly is very important in the US, but not always as important in other countries.

"Wine industry technical knowledge is also critical," explains Phil. "Though sales skills are the most important in the wine supply-side of the business, we also prefer to hire people who know how wine is made and the research around closures. As a salesperson, I talk with enologists, winemakers, and winery purchasing managers, and it is important that I understand their specific wine quality and image issues. We also sell screwcaps and provide customized coating and brand stamps for our corks, so it is important to be familiar with the technical side of the business."

A final skill set that Phil mentions is sales management and business development. "Since I am both a manager and a salesperson," says Phil, "I have to make sure that all of the paperwork, reports, follow-up, and other administrative issues are handled. In addition, I am continually scanning the environment for new business opportunities. We like to focus on customer service in the hopes that satisfied customers will recommend new customers."

MOST CHALLENGING ASPECT OF THE JOB

"I would have to say that the downside is the paperwork and administrative side," smiles Phil. "It is not enjoyable having to do collection follow-up with clients or filling out all of the reports. I prefer to be out talking with people at the wineries.

"Salaries are another issue in the wine industry," informs Phil. "Having worked in other industries and having served as an executive recruiter trying to hire people into wine, I have to admit that the salaries are a bit lower. The upside is the chance to taste a lot of great wine and work with very nice people."

BEST PART OF THE JOB

"I really enjoy the people I meet in the wine industry," Phil states. "They are very passionate about what they do, and this creates a very unique and wonderful culture. It is enjoyable to taste new wines, eat great food, and have interesting conversations with people about the many wine regions to which they have traveled.

"Another part of my job that I enjoy," says Phil, "is the excitement of new products and new projects. The closure side of the business is very innovative with new discoveries and new products being launched every year. I enjoy the challenge of staying up-to-date and introducing my clients to new types of corks, screwcaps, and other closures to match their wine bottle needs."

Creating Your
Action Plan

*I dunno, maybe joining a wine club that meets at 7 a.m.
on Monday mornings wasn't such a good idea after all.*

Chapter 12

hew! Are you tired of wine yet? In all probability, the answer is no—and that's a good thing! Wine is, as you have heard, an amazing business that offers a great number of exciting, rewarding, and interesting career options.

So, you ask, what do I do with all this knowledge? How do I get a job in wine?

This final chapter will provide you with advice on how to build your plan for making your move into wine. You'll also find an "Action Plan Worksheet" in the appendix to this book. It's a useful tool to help chart your course of action and keep track of your progress. There are six key steps to your plan. They are:

- Make Your Go/No Go Decision
- Narrow Your Focus
- Do Your Homework
- Networking Plan, Stat!
- Get On The Ground
- Be Patient

MAKE YOUR GO/NO GO DECISION

The first thing you need to do is decide if wine is indeed the industry for you. The preceding chapters have provided you with a number of factors that you will need to consider. To summarize, they are:

Location: Do you want to live in one of the areas which offers a wine career? Is the cost of living something you are willing to accept? Does the area offer the lifestyle you would like to lead?

Industry Realities: Are you willing to be very hands-on? Are you willing to do without some of the infrastructure, tools and resources you may be accustomed to in other industries? Does consolidation and change excite you or cause concern? Depending on your career choice, are you willing to work long hours during harvest, or work nights/weekends/holidays?

Some Education Required: For some careers, you may need to gather some wine knowledge, specific skills, and/or an undergraduate or advanced degree. Are you willing to invest the time, effort and dollars required to get your credentials?

Take A Step Back: Are you willing to consider taking a step (or two) backwards in your career to make a transition into wine?

Pay Considerations: Are you willing to accept the same or possibly a decrease in pay by moving into wine?

Wine Passion: Are you really passionate about wine? Is it something you want to live and breathe as both work and play?

The wine industry is an outstanding place to work. It's not easy, relaxed, nor the romantic industry you imagine from the outside or during a vacation in wine country. Yet the benefits, for those truly interested and passionate about wine, greatly outweigh the tradeoffs.

NARROW YOUR FOCUS

While it's tempting to say to yourself (and others), "I'm open, I just want to get my foot in the door," it is important to narrow your focus to a very specific target for your search. Individuals who succeed in getting into wine have one thing in common—focus (and a little luck). Following is a list of decisions you will need to make prior to initiating the rest of your plan.

Choose Your Career Field: For many, this may be easy—it could be the career you are already in. For potential career-changers, this may be more difficult. Unless you're targeting a very entry-level position, or volunteering to work harvest, you will need very specific focus to do the kinds of homework you need to do. You will also need to be clear about this in order for your networking contacts to help you (more on that later).

Pick Your Desired Location: When it comes to cost of living, where you live is critical. If you choose a place you like, and a place with a growing or thriving wine industry, you will be happier and have a pool of potential employers around you. Generally loving what you do and loving where you live is not a sustainable combination. An additional benefit is that if you at some point need to change employers, you won't have to move!

Choose Your Winery Size: As we've discussed in previous chapters, there are significant differences in the nature of jobs, the number of jobs, the work environment, the pay, and opportunities for growth depending on whether you choose to work in a small, medium, or large winery. There is no best size, only the size that is right for you. Focusing on one or two of these size wineries will help you. The strategies needed to secure a job in each are different.

Target Wineries You Are Passionate About: If you like wine, have visited wine country, and read industry press, chances are you have some favorite wineries. If they fit within your already narrowed focus, target them! As several of our interviewees have mentioned, a passion for wine, while never the only thing that matters, is always a plus. Passion for a specific winery and their products is even better when you're looking to work there.

Be Honest With Yourself About Pay And Title Requirements: There is no shame in admitting that you have to make car and, mortgage payments, or have minimum requirements to maintain your lifestyle. Similarly, there is no shame in admitting what titles or job duties you're not willing to do. This is a critical thing to determine before you start networking and interviewing in wine. With no industry experience to speak of, it is usually a very unrealistic expectation to require the same or higher rate of staring pay. In fact, many who are willing to step back may not realize how big a stride they're in for. Be honest with yourself about what sacrifices (if any) you are willing to make to get into the industry.

List Out Your Priorities and Rank Them: Though this is a long, detailed process, it is also a vital step. Fortunately, some of the work has been done for you as it relates to the wine industry. When it gets down to evaluating particular wineries and people you may end up working for, only you can decide what will and will not work for you. Knowing what your priorities are helps in all sorts of ways. Two critical ones are 1) giving you specific things to find out in your research, networking, and (if you're successful) in your interviews with the winery, and 2) helping to decide whether to accept an offer or not.

DO YOUR HOMEWORK

The importance of a narrowed focus may now become clear. If you have selected some clear targets, you can now start researching the wine region, local wineries, industry resources, networking possibilities, and jobs that may be of interest to you.

Now that you have finished this book, review the chapter or chapters that apply to your career field. It is especially important to review Chapter 2 "Overview of the Wine Industry," and its recommendations on general industry resources. Set aside some time to review websites. Get yourself copies of some of the key publications for the industry and your field and start reading them. Call industry, regional, or professional associations relevant to your focus, tell them you are looking to make a move into wine, and ask them about resources and advice.

These days, there's no excuse to go into any sort of encounter unprepared, be it a networking conversation, a trade show or industry symposium, an informational interview, or a true job interview. Being unprepared is a separator between those who are serious about getting a job, and those making a half-hearted effort. The internet makes it very easy to find out about wineries, sometimes individuals, and often about professional associations.

Whether online or in the newspaper, look at job postings. Review them to see what is the same and what has changed. Find out what is important in your career field.

If available, start reading the wine column in your local newspaper.

One of the pleasures of doing your homework in wine is also popping some corks! Drink wines from your target region and wineries. Talk to wine buyers at your local retailer about the wines and the wineries that produce them. Start a tasting journal and keep notes about the wines you try. Include notes on what you see, smell and taste in the glass.

DEVELOP A NETWORKING PLAN

Networking was touched on in Chapter 1 and will be explored in greater detail here. In a small industry, where it seems everyone knows everyone else, networking is, at minimum, a huge potential source of information, insights, and leads. In many cases, you simply will not succeed in breaking into the business if you don't network effectively.

The good news is that wine people are friendly! The hard work is usually in figuring out how to access the right people. Once you've done that, it is a matter of using your interpersonal skills, getting out there, making a few calls, and attending some events.

Throughout the book, you have come across tips and advice on industry and professional associations dedicated to wine. The interviewees in previous chapters have provided their own stories and tips on how to network successfully. With your narrowed focus, you should have some specific organizations and wineries in mind that will give you a target for your first calls.

It is always a good idea to leverage your existing network. Find out who in your web of family and friends knows someone who knows someone who works in wine. Call them, and ask to buy them lunch or meet for coffee, and start gathering information about the industry. Talk to a neighborhood wine merchant or restaurateur that you are friendly with, and tell them you're interested in getting into wine.

Most major cities have multiple groups dedicated to wine appreciation. Check a few out. Join one or two that feel right to you and match your interests. If you take any classes offered by colleges or retailers, make sure to talk to the instructors.

If you belong to a wine club, visit the winery, and talk to the wine club representative or manager.

Once your list of potential contacts is compiled, develop a list of questions for them. Have a clear goal in mind of what you want to gain from your conversations with them. This is no time to be shy: be up-front with your contacts about what you are trying to accomplish and ask for their advice. If possible, try to get them to provide you with at least one more contact for you to network with.

Touching on an earlier point, you must give your networking contacts something to work with. Being too open or blasé will not work here. Your networking contacts are busy, hardworking people, and while they may be very willing to spend some of their time assisting you, it is too much to ask them to make your choices for you. The more focused you are, the more you help your contacts to open doors and provide leads!

Once someone's been gracious enough to spend time with you, send them a hand-written thank you note to show your appreciation. Keep their names and contact details handy and on file. If you do secure a job, send the appropriate contact another note letting them know where you have landed, and thank them again for their time and advice (a simple email is acceptable).

In any industry, a network is a precious commodity. For wine, it is often a separator between those who succeed and those who do not.

In these days of PDAs, cell phones, and the Internet, many folks find their way into jobs with minimal—and occasionally no—person-to-person contact. This is not a model for success in starting your wine career.

First, it is not the most effective way to network. Though some of your networking may be done via phone calls and emails, in-person meetings are often the most valuable method. When is the last time you recommended someone without having ever met them in-person? Would you ever recommend someone to a family member or friend without having first met them? For the vast majority of us, the answer is no. The same is true for networking contacts. If you want your contacts to pass you on to their contacts, provide leads, or even recommend you for jobs, be smart and invest the on-the-ground time talking to them.

Second, being local to your target wineries has huge advantages. All things being equal, if there are two qualified candidates, one local, one out-of-state, whom do you think will get the phone call asking them to come in for an interview?

Many times wineries do not have the dollars or inclination to pay relocation costs. In addition, even if you don't expect paid relocation (and mention that prominently in your cover letter). Wineries, like any employer, are looking to get roles filled as quickly as possible. The perception, if not the reality, is that it will take longer for an out-of-state candidate to get started in a role.

However, do not think that an out-of-state address or area code goes unnoticed. True, being local is best, yet there are options for nonlocal job seekers. State clearly in cover letters and emails that you will be visiting the area and spending some time specifically to network and seek job opportunities. Provide the dates, and say you would welcome getting together in-person.

Finally, being local shows active interest and investment in starting your wine career. It is easy to send off an email to someone, but it bodes well if you make the effort to take a vacation in or relocate to a prospective region on your own accord.

This is clearly a commitment at some level, which includes time, money, and a potential relocation of you and your family. However, this can be another divider between the casual job seeker and an individual serious about moving into wine.

BE PATIENT

Our society is hard-wired these days for instant gratification. Send in your resume tonight, and get an email tomorrow morning asking for a phone screen or an interview. Want to find another job? Call your preferred recruiter, and have three leads by the end of the week. Need that book or CD tomorrow? Order it online this morning and choose one-day shipping.

For most of us, starting our wine careers will not be quite that efficient.

Networking is a process. It is an essential element of starting—and maintaining—your wine career. Remember to take the time and have the patience to slowly build a great network.

Remember that wine is a small industry. It is possible your ideal job is not yet available today. It may, however, be available in three, four or six months from now.

Often the hardest part of getting into wine is actually getting into wine! Landing that first opportunity can be a lengthy process. Candidates may correspond regularly with wineries for over a year as they seek getting into the business, and many are successful. The good news is that, once you officially enter the industry, if you are successful and maintain a great network, then you are well on your way to a life-long career in the business.

Be persistent. If this is something you want, do not get discouraged if your first efforts are not initially successful. Patience and persistence will eventually see you in the wine business.

Above all else, the most important thing to do throughout your wine career is to educate yourself. There is always something to learn about in this business, from a new varietal wine, to a region you haven't experienced, to a winery that is doing something new and interesting. There will always be another change in technology, or another new winery on the scene. This process will never end. Hopefully, that's good news! One of the benefits of the industry is that it continues to provide you with new things to learn and experience. And there is no reason to not start that process immediately.

We'll conclude by raising a glass, and wishing you the best of luck in launching your wine career.

Cheers!

Appendix: Your Action Plan Worksheet

(Go to www.eWineBooks.com to download free copies of this worksheet)

Before you transition into wine, it is important to think about the trajectory you would like your career to follow. Below is a worksheet to help you get started. As you plan your future in wine, ask yourself these key questions from Chapter 12:

- What's your actual level of interest in wine? Is wine something you want to "live and breath?
- Is wine something you want to live and breathe at both work and play?
- How far are you willing to relocate?
- Are you able to foot the bill for relocation costs?
- Does your target wine region offer the lifestyle you would like to lead?
- What cost-of-living range are you comfortable with?
- If you are considering commuting, how far are you willing to travel?
- How much wine knowledge and education do you already have?
- If necessary, are you willing to invest time, effort and money to strengthen your credentials?
- What are your pay and title requirements?
- Will you accept a reduction in pay to what you receive now?
- Are you willing to take a brief step backwards in your career to move forward into wine?
- Are you willing to be hands-on and work with fewer resources than you are used to?

- If needed or required, are you willing to work long hours or evenings and weekends?

Once you've answered these questions, the next step is to map out where in the wine industry you would like to find yourself. Determining the following will help you narrow your focus:

- My desired career field in wine is: _____
  _____
  _____
  _____

- The wine country regions I would like to work in are:
  _____
  _____
  _____

- The size of winery would I prefer to work for is:_____
  _____

- The wineries I am passionate about are: _____
  _____
  _____
  _____

Now that you have narrowed your focus, it is time to evaluate your target wineries. This will help you in choosing the wineries you want to work for. First, list your work priorities and rank them below. Having a set of priorities will be a useful tool as you begin researching and networking in the industry. Then, with list in hand, visit or research your target wineries to see how they measure up.

Work Priorities	_Rank_
_____	_____
_____	_____
_____	_____
_____	_____
_____	_____
_____	_____
_____	_____

The final step in your action plan is to do your homework and make connections with industry insiders. Utilize the two checklists below as you pursue your career in wine.

EDUCATIONAL RESOURCES CHECKLIST

- Review chapters of this book that were beneficial and important to you.
- Obtain copies of key industry publications relevant to your career field.
- Read the wine column in your local newspaper.

343

- Browse websites to familiarize yourself with current issues and wine industry events.
- Browse websites to familiarize yourself with current issues and wine industry events.
- Subscribe to the newsletters of your target wineries.
- Scan job postings to see what is important to employers.
- Contact industry, regional, and professional associations and inquire about resources.
- Drink from wines in your target regions and keep a tasting journal.

NETWORKING CHECKLIST

- Review pertinent interviews in this book. They provide tested examples of successful marketing.
- Develop a contact list of HR personnel or the key contacts at your targeted wineries or retailer.
- Leverage your existing network of family and friends for additional industry contacts.
- Check out local and online groups dedicated to wine appreciation.
- Talk to your wine club representative or manager.
- Mention to a neighborhood wine merchant or restaurateur that you're interested in getting into wine.
- Draft a list of focused questions to ask your contacts.
- Meet with your contacts, and let them know what specifically interests you in wine.
- Be up front and ask your contacts for advice.
- Send your contacts a thank you note after meeting with them.

NETWORKING CONTACTS

Name_____**Affiliation**_____

Home Address:

Street_____

City/State_____ZIP_____

Home Phone_____

Personal email address_____

Business Address:

Street_____

City/State_____ZIP_____

Phone_____Fax_____

Business email address_____

Notes:_____

_____

_____

_____

_____

Name_____**Affiliation**_____

Home Address:

Street_____

City/State_____ZIP_____

Home Phone_____

Personal email address_____

Business Address:

Street_____

City/State_____ZIP_____

Phone_____Fax_____

Business email address_____

Notes:_____

_____

_____

_____

_____

NETWORKING CONTACTS *(CONTINUED)*

Name_____**Affiliation**_____

Home Address:

Street_____

City/State_____ZIP_____

Home Phone_____

Personal email address_____

Business Address:

Street_____

City/State_____ZIP_____

Phone_____Fax_____

Business email address_____

Notes:_____

_____

_____

_____

_____

Name_____**Affiliation**_____

Home Address:

Street_____

City/State_____ZIP_____

Home Phone_____

Personal email address_____

Business Address:

Street_____

City/State_____ZIP_____

Phone_____Fax_____

Business email address_____

Notes:_____

_____

_____

_____

_____

INDEX

Wine Book Publisher of the Year
Gourmand World Book Awards, 2004

The Wine Appreciation Guild has been an educational pioneer in our fascinating community.

—Robert Mondavi

Your opinion matters to us...

You may not think it, but customer input is important to the ultimate quality of any revised work or second edition. We invite and appreciate any comments you may have. And by registering your WAG book you are enrolled to receive prepublication discounts, special offers, or alerts to various wine events, only available to registered members.

As your first bonus for registering you will receive, free of charge, our bestselling, interactive GLOBAL ENCYCLOPEDIA OF WINE, on CD- ROM (a $29.95 value). This CD is compatible with PCs and Macs running Mac Classic. It has:

- Wine regions
- The process: from grapes to glass
- Enjoying wine: rituals and tasting
- Wine Guide, a fascinating database for choosing different wines
- Cellar Log Book, that will allow you to document your own wine collection.

You can register your book by phone: (800) 231-9463; Fax: (650) 866-3513; E-Mail: Info@WineAppreciation.com; or snail mail the form on the following page.

REGISTRATION CARD

for How to Launch Your Wine Career

Name_____Date_____

Professional Affiliation_____

Address_____

_____

City_____State_____Zip_____

E-Mail_____

How did you discover this book?_____

Did a career counselor suggest this book? Y N

His or her school/organizational affiliation_____

Where did you acquire this book?_____

Was it a good read? (circle)   Poor 1 2 3   Excellent
Was it useful to your career planning? (circle)   Poor 1 2 3   Excellent

Suggestions_____

_____

Comments_____

_____

_____

You can register your book by phone: (800) 231-9463; Fax: (650) 866-3513;
Email: Info@WineAppreciation.com; or snail mail.

THE WINE APPRECIATION GUILD
360 Swift Avenue
South San Francisco, CA 94080

www.wineappreciation.com

Fold Here ▲

Tape Closed Here ▼